MW01613062

MRS. MALINDA'S™

Southern Style

COOKING

Compiled by
Jeremiah Johnson

Unless otherwise indicated, all Scripture quotations are taken from the *King James Version* (KJV) of the Holy Bible.

Spirit Publishers

dba: Springhill Books of Tennessee, Inc.
6554 Winchester Road, #144
Memphis, TN 38115
Website: *www.springhillbooksonline.com*
E-mail: springhillbooks@bellsouth.net

Copyright © 2005 by Jeremiah C. Johnson
All rights reserved,
including the right of reproduction
in whole or in part, in any form.

Mrs. Malinda's Southern Style Cooking
ISBN: 0-9773720-0-6
Manufactured in the United States of America

Printed on acid free paper

This book is not intended to provide any health or nutritional advice or take the place of medical advice and treatment from your personal physician.
Readers are advised to consult their own doctors or other qualified health professional Regarding the treatment of their medical problems. Neither the publisher nor the author takes any responsibility for any possible consequences from any treatment, action or application of medicine, supplement, herb or preparation to any person reading or following the information in this book. If readers are taking prescription medications, they should consult with their physicians and not take themselves off medicines to start supplementation without the proper supervision of a physician.

ACKNOWLEDGMENTS

This work is a synergistic product of many great minds of whom Iam forever grateful.
I am particularly grateful to my sister Balinda, whose inspiration, faith and wisdom
has caused this project to manifest from a simple vision, into a reality.

To my dear mother, know to many as "*Mrs. Malinda*," whose life has touched many,
and impacted us all. Because of your great legacy, we have the opportunity to
touch generations to come. To us, you will always be *Momma*.

To our siblings and other relatives, this is an honor for Balinda and I to release a
Cookbook that reflects the spirit and passion of Momma. We trust that you will also
find it as enjoyable as we have compiling it.

To my wonderful wife Pamela, and our children; Jeffrey, Jerrod, Barsheba,
Wesley, Jeremy and Sean. Thank you for your support, love and encouragement.
I know each of you will enjoy this.

To the team of contributing writers and friends who have submitted their recipes
for our use. It has been a pleasure and a privilege for us. We are anticipating your
involvement in many projects to come. Thank you for your contribution to this work
and the spirit of *Mrs. Malinda*.

And finally, to the source of and supplier of all potential, the only wise God eternal.
Be glory and honor, dominion and power...Forever!

TABLE OF CONTENTS

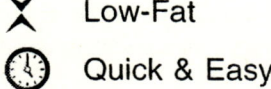 Low-Fat    Heart Healthy

Quick & Easy

Mrs. Malinda's
Cooking Baking and Household Hints and Remedies

Use 2 tablespoons of **flour** and ¼ cup water as a thickening agent. Dry **Instant Mashed Potatoes** work great to thicken, gravies, soups, vegetables, etc. also.

Use old **newspaper** to cover dark clothing when ironing them. This will keep them from shining or burning.

Soak clothes in **buttermilk** to remove rust stains.

Clean with **vinegar** and water: great for windows, mirrors, plastic, counter tops, stoves, refrigerators, etc.

Put **cloves** in cavity or jaw for toothaches.

Rinse mouth with **peroxide** and water for toothaches.

Soak swollen feet in **vinegar** or **salt water**.

Make hot tea of **garlic cloves** or **sages leaves** for pressure headaches. Sweeten to taste. Lemon juice optional.

Tonic for aches in joints and inflammation: 2 Tbsp Pasteurized **Apple Cider vinegar & Blackstrap Molasses**, 8 oz of water.

Diluted **Pine sol** in spray bottle: great disinfectant, bug killer.

Diluted **dishwashing liquid**: great bug spray, spray plants.

Cut flowers, honeysuckle, roses, etc put in vase or jar on dining room table.

Use your dishes, set your table and eat out of them while you are living.

Buy your washing powder, bleach, toilet paper, salt, pepper and other seasoning for the entire winter months.

Plant a row of butter beans and peas along your backyard fence. Plant okra, garlic and greens in your yard. Easy picking & fixing.

Always cook a little extra for unexpected guest. Or this makes great leftovers or meals for freezer.

Start on Wednesday getting ready for church on Sunday. Study your Sunday School Lesson and wash and iron your clothes. Carry your own children to church.

Bake your desserts for the weekend on Friday.

Always say the Blessing before you eat.

A large pot of hot waters simmering on the stove will help circulate the heat in winter. Cut it off before bed.

Cook for your own Children. Make your children sit down and read.

Never Cloak for your family and friends.

Don't shack. You need to marry.

Give God some of your time.

That road you are on it short, you had better get off of it

EDITORS NOTE; FOLLOW YOUR DOCTORS ADVICE FIRST. PRAY AND TRY REMEDIES AT YOUR OWN RISK.

Cakes, Pies, Ice Cream, Candy & Cookies

Candy Testing

Candy	Degrees	Stage	Cold Water Test
	230-234	Thread	Syrup spins 2-inch thread when dropped from spoon
Fudge, Fondant	234-240	Soft Ball	Candy will roll into soft ball but quickly flattens when removed from water.
Divinity, Caramels	244-248	Firm Ball	Candy will roll into a firm ball (but not hard ball) which will not lose its shape upon removal from water.
Taffy	250-266	Hard Ball	Syrup forms hard ball, although it is pliable.
Butterscotch	270-290	Light Crack	Candy will form threads in water which will soften when removed from water.
Peanut Brittle	300-310	Hard Crack	Candy will form hard, brittle threads in water which will not soften when removed from water
Caramelized Sugar	310-321	Caramelized	Sugar first melts, then becomes a golden brown and forms a hard, brittle ball in cold water

Substitutions

1 c. whole milk
1/2 c. evaporated milk and 1/2 c. water
1/2 c. condensed milk and 1/2 c. water
(reduce sugar in recipe) 4 T. powdered
milk and 1 c. water • 4 T. nonfat dry
milk plus 2 t. shortening and 1 c. water
1 c. sour milk
1 c. sweet milk and 1 T. lemon juice or
vinegar • 1 c. sweet milk mixed with 1
T. lemon juice or 1 T. vinegar or 1 3/4 t.
cream of tartar
1 c. sweet milk
1 c. sour milk or buttermilk plus 1/2 t.
baking soda
**1 c. sour, heavy cream
(for sour milk recipe)**
1/3 c. butter and 2/3 c. milk
**1 c. sour, thin cream
(for sour milk recipe)**
3 T. butter and 3/4 c. milk
**1 c. butter or margarine
(for shortening)**
4/5 c. bacon fat (clarified), increase liquid
in recipe 1/4 c. • 2/3 c. chicken fat (clarified),
increase liquid in recipe 1/4 c. • 7/8 c.
cottonseed, corn, nut oil (solid or liquid)
• 7/8 c. lard and salt • 1/2 c. suet and salt
(increase liquid in recipe 1/4 c.)
1 1-oz. square unsweetened chocolate
3 T. cocoa plus 1/2 T. shortening

1 T. cornstarch (for thickening)
2 T. flour (approx.)
1 T. flour (for thickening)
1/2 to 2/3 T. cornstarch or 1 T. minute
tapioca or 1 whole egg, 2 egg whites
or 2 egg yolks
1 c. sifted cake flour
1 c. minus 2 T. sifted all-purpose flour
1 c. sifted all-purpose flour
1 c. plus 2 T. sifted cake flour
1 whole egg
2 egg yolks, plus 1 T. water (in
cookies, etc.) or 2 egg yolks (in
custards, etc.)
1 c. molasses • 1 c. honey
1 c. honey
3/4 c. sugar plus 1/4 c. liquid
1 c. granulated sugar
1 1/3 c. brown sugar or 1 1/2 c.
powdered sugar
1 t. baking powder
1/4 t. baking soda plus 1/2 t. cream
of tartar
1 lb. cornmeal • 3 cups
1 lb. cornstarch • 3 cups
1 lemon rind • 1 Tbsp. grated
3-4 med. oranges • 1 cup
1 orange rind • 2 Tbsp. grated
23 soda crackers • 1 cup crumbs
15 graham crackers • 1 cup crumbs

Cakes, Pies, Ice Cream, Candy & Cookies

CUPCAKE CONES

Mrs. Malinda's Recipe Collection

1 cake mix (any brand or flavor, plus any ingredients needed to prepare cake mix as directed on pkg.)

24 ice cream cones (cake cup)
1 can frosting
1 jar maraschino cherries

Preheat oven to 350°. Prepare cake mix as directed on package. Spoon into ice cream cones about ¾ full. Bake according to package directions (approximately 20 to 30 minutes). Let cool completely. Frost with frosting. Top with 1 cherry. Preparation time: approximately 1 hour. Serves 24.

NOTE: Great to send for "school birthday" snacks.

AFRICAN AMERICAN RED VELVET CAKE

Mrs. Malinda's Recipe Collection

2 ¼ c. sifted cake flour
2 tsp. cocoa powder
1 tsp. baking soda
1 tsp. baking powder
1 tsp. salt
1 ½ c. sugar

½ c. (1 stick) unsalted butter,
  softened
2 large eggs
1 c. buttermilk
2 oz. red food coloring
1 tsp. distilled white vinegar
1 tsp. vanilla

Frosting:

1 (8 oz.) pkg. softened cream
  cheese
½ c. softened unsalted butter
  or margarine

1 (1 lb.) box icing sugar
1 tsp. vanilla extract
1 c. chopped pecans

Preheat the oven to 350°. Grease and flour 2 (9-inch) round cake pans. Sift the flour, cocoa, baking soda, baking powder and salt together. In a separate large bowl, cream the sugar with the butter, then beat in eggs, one at a time. Add the dry ingredients to mixture, alternating with the buttermilk. Beat in red food coloring and vinegar, then add vanilla. Spread batter in pans. Bake for 20 minutes or longer until toothpck inserted in center comes out clean. Remove recipe African American Red Velvet Cake from pans and cool on rack.

To prepare the frosting for recipe African American Red Velvet Cake, cream the cream cheese and butter. Beat in the icing sugar until fluffy. Beat in the vanilla. Stir in the pecans. Fill and frost the cake.

* * * * *

APPLE CAKE IN JAR

Mrs. Malinda's Recipe Collection

2/3 c. shortening	2 tsp. baking soda
2 2/3 c. white sugar	3 c. all-purpose flour
4 eggs	2/3 c. water
1 tsp. ground cinnamon	3 c. grated apples
1/2 tsp. ground nutmeg	2/3 c. raisins
1 1/2 tsp. salt	2/3 c. chopped walnuts

You will need 8 pint size wide-mouth canning jars.

Preheat oven to 325°F (165°C). Lightly grease the insides of 8 straight-sided wide-mouth pint canning jars. Sift together flour, baking soda, salt, nutmeg and cinnamon. Set aside.

Cream shortening and sugar until fluffy. Add eggs and beat in well. Add flour alternately with water and mix until smooth. Fold in apples, raisins and nuts. Fill jars 1/2 full of batter, being careful to keep the rims clean. Wipe off any batter that gets on the rims. Bake at 325°F (165°C) for 45 minutes.

Meanwhile, sterilize the lids and rings in boiling water. As soon as cake is done, remove from oven one at a time, wipe rims of jars and put on lid and ring. Jars will seal as cakes cool. Place the jars on the counter and listen for them to "ping" as they seal. If you miss the "ping," wait until they are completely cool and press on the top of the lid. If it doesn't move at all, it's sealed. Food in jars should be eaten or kept in the refrigerator for up to a week.

* * * * *

Weeping may endure for a night..
But joy cometh in the morning.

BANANA PUDDING CAKE

Mrs. Malinda's Recipe Collection

1 (18.25 oz.) pkg. yellow cake mix
1 (3.5 oz.) pkg. instant banana pudding mix
4 eggs
1 c. water
¼ c. vegetable oil
¾ c. mashed bananas
2 c. confectioners sugar
2 Tbsp. milk
1 dash vanilla extract
½ c. chopped walnuts (optional)

Preheat oven to 350°F (175°C). Grease and flour a 10-inch Bundt pan.

In a large bowl, stir together cake mix and pudding mix. Make a well in the center and pour in eggs, water, oil and mashed bananas. Beat on low speed until blended. Scrape bowl and beat 4 minutes on medium speed. Pour batter into prepared pan. Bake in a pre-heated oven for 50 to 55 minutes or until cake tests done. Let cool in pan for 10 minutes, then turn out onto a wire rack and cool completely.

To Make Glaze: In a small bowl, combine confectioners sugar, milk and vanilla. Whisk until smooth and of drizzling consistency. When cake is cooled, drizzle icing over cake with a zigzag motion. Sprinkle chopped nuts over wet icing if desired.

* * * * *

If you are willing and obedient,
You shall eat the Good of the Land.

BIRTHDAY CAKE FOR JESUS

Mrs. Malinda's Recipe Collection

The cake should be round to represent the world. It should be chocolate to show the sins of the world. Romans 3:23, Genesis 6:5.

The icing should be white to show Jesus' purity, covering our sins. 1 John 1:7, Psalm 51:7.

An angel should adorn the cake as the bearer of the Good News. Luke 2:10-11.

Add a star as the bearer of glad tidings. Matthew 2:9b-10.

Twelve red candles show Jesus' blood covering us all the time, twelve months of the year. Matthew 9:12, 28:20.

Evergreens should surround the cake to represent everlasting life. Isaiah 9:6, John 3:36.

Light the candles to show that Jesus is the light of the world. John 8:12, Ephesians 5:8.

Sing "Happy Birthday" to Jesus, then blow out the candles.

This cake can become a wonderful tradition. You can read the scripture or simply read the Christmas story and explain the symbols. Your children can participate more and more as they grow each year.

* * * * *

Be blessed!

A PLUS CARROT CAKE

Pastor Balinda Moore
Memphis, TN

2 c. all-purpose flour
2 tsp. baking powder
1 tsp. baking soda
½ tsp. salt
1 tsp. ground cinnamon
½ tsp. ground nutmeg
½ tsp. allspice
4 eggs
2 c. white sugar
2 tsp. vanilla extract

1 ¼ c. vegetable oil
2 c. grated carrots or 2 jars
  junior baby food carrots
1 (20 oz.) can crushed
  pineapple, drained
½ c. sweetened flaked
  coconut
1 c. chopped walnuts
1 c. raisins

Preheat the oven to 350°F (175°C). Coat a 10 x 15 x 2-inch baking dish or 10-inch Bundt pan with cooking spray.

In a medium bowl, stir together the flour, baking powder, baking soda, salt, cinnamon and nutmeg. Set aside. In a separate larger bowl, mix together the eggs, sugar and vanilla by hand. Stir in the oil; the mixture should resemble pudding. Gradually stir in the dry ingredients, then fold in the carrots, pineapple, coconut, walnuts and raisins. Pour the batter into the prepared pan and spread evenly. Bake for 55 to 60 minutes in the preheated oven or until a small knife inserted into the cake comes out clean.

Note: Feel free to omit the coconut, walnuts or raisins as you taste buds suit you. However, getting rid of the pineapple will take away from the moisture of the cake.

＊ ＊ ＊ ＊ ＊

Name it and claim it.
Believe it and receive it.

MINI CHEESECAKES

Mrs. Malinda's Recipe Collection

2 (8 oz.) pkg. cream cheese,
   softened
¾ c. sugar
2 eggs

1 Tbsp. vanilla
1 can fruit pie filling
40 vanilla wafers

Cream together all ingredients except vanilla wafers and pie filling. Using foil midget baking cups with the paper liners removed, insert a vanilla wafer in each of 40 baking cups. Spoon creamed mixture in each about ¾ full. Bake on a cookie sheet at 350° for 20 minutes. Let cool. Top with fruit filling.

NOTE: Cherries and blueberries look festive alternating.

* * * * *

MALINDA AND ELNORA'S FLAG CAKE

Mrs. Malinda's Recipe Collection

2 pkg. white cake mix
1 (16 ½ oz.) can ready to
   spread vanilla frosting
2 c. heavy cream

⅓ c. confectioners sugar
2 tsp. vanilla
2 pt. strawberries (fresh)
1 ½ c. fresh blueberries

You will need (No. 33) five pointed star decorating tube.

Prepare separately white cake mixes according to directions. Bake in two 15 ½ x 10 ½-inch pans lined with wax paper. Cool and turn cakes out of pans. Spread 1 can frosting between layers and stack them together. Whip cream until stiff peaks form. Add ½ cup confectioners sugar and vanilla and spread on top and sides of cake. Measure and mark cake with toothpicks into 13 horizontal strips and a 5 ½-inch square in the upper left corner. Using pastry bag, pipe 6 strips of whipped cream across cake. Slice strawberries and arrange to make 7 stripes. Place blueberries in upper left corner. Using 5 pointed star, pipe 50 stars on blueberries with cream in alternating rows of 5 to 6. Refrigerate.

Use Million Dollar Pound Cake recipe in book or substitute Cake Mix.

PATRIOTIC FLAG CAKE

Mrs. Malinda's Recipe Collection

1 (9 x 13-inch) sheet cake
vanilla frosting

sliced strawberries
blueberries

Frost cake with vanilla frosting. Place sliced strawberries in rows to make the red and white stripes of the flag. Place 50 blueberries in upper left hand corner of cake to make the stars.

This also may be made using red jelly in 9 x 13-inch pan. Use small white marshmallows to make the stripes and blueberries to make the stars.

GERMAN FRUITCAKE

1 ½ sticks butter
2 c. brown sugar
4 eggs, separated
3 c. flour
1 tsp. cinnamon
½ tsp. nutmeg

½ tsp. cloves
½ c. buttermilk
1 tsp. soda
⅔ c. each 3 types preserves
1 c. chopped nuts
1 tsp. vanilla

Cream butter and sugar. Add egg yolks and blend well. Add soda to buttermilk. Sift dry ingredients. Add alternately with buttermilk to butter and sugar. Add preserves, nuts and vanilla. Fold in stiffly beaten egg whites. Pour into 10-inch tube pan. Bake at 350° for 1 ½ hours.

* * * * *

OLD FASHIONED MOLASSES MERINGUE CAKE

Mrs. Malinda's Recipe Collection

¾ c. boiling water
3 Tbsp. butter
1 c. molasses
2 eggs
¾ c. dry fine bread crumbs
¾ c. seedless raisins
1 c. unsifted whole-wheat flour

1 tsp. soda
¼ tsp. cream of tartar
¾ tsp. salt
1 tsp. ginger
4 Tbsp. sugar
⅛ tsp. nutmeg or mace

Pour the boiling water over the butter and stir in the molasses. Separate the eggs; beat the yolks until creamy and add to molasses mixture. Stir in the bread crumbs and raisins. Mix the whole-wheat flour, soda, salt and ginger in a bowl, then gradually stir into the molasses mixture. Stir until well blended and pour into greased and floured 8 x 8-inch pan. Bake at 350° for 45 minutes or until well done. Cool on rack. Do not unmold. Beat egg whites with the cream of tartar until stiff. Beat in the 4 tablespoons sugar, one tablespoon at a time. Pile on cake. Dust with nutmeg or mace.

To brown the meringue, place cake 5-inches from broiler for 3 to 5 minutes, leaving door open slightly. Keep can in pan. Cut in squares.

* * * * *

Oh how beautiful it is for brethren to dwell together in unity.

MOLASSES STACK CAKE

Mrs. Melinda's Recipe Collection

2 c. brown sugar
2 c. molasses
4 eggs
1 c. buttermilk
5 c. flour
1 tsp. soda
1 tsp. salt
2 tsp. cinnamon
1 tsp. cloves

1 tsp. ginger
1 tsp. allspice
2 tsp. nutmeg
4 tsp. baking powder
1 c. butter, softened
1 qt. apple butter
whipping cream
1 tsp. vanilla

Preheat oven to 350°. Combine brown sugar and butter until creamy. Add molasses and buttermilk. Mix well. Add eggs, one at a time. In separate bowl, sift together flour, soda, salt, cinnamon, cloves, ginger, allspice, nutmeg and baking powder. Beat into molasses mixture with several additions. Pour into 6 greased and floured cake layer pans. Bake at 350° for 25 to 30 minutes or until done. Cool layers. Combine apple butter, whipping cream and vanilla. Put between cake layers (3 per cake) and ice as usual. Makes 2 cakes.

* * * * *

Come on over here, the table is spread. The feast is going on.

PINEAPPLE UPSIDE-DOWN CAKE II

Mrs. Malinda's Recipe Collection

3 (8.25 oz./234 g) cans sliced
  pineapple in own juice (12
  slices)
¼ c./60 ml butter or margarine
⅓ c./80 ml light brown sugar
9 maraschino cherries
1 c./250 ml all-purpose flour
¾ c./180 ml sugar

1 ½ tsp./7.5 ml baking powder
¼ tsp./1.2 ml salt
¼ tsp./1.2 ml nutmeg
¼ c./60 ml vegetable
  shortening
½ c./125 ml vanilla
1 egg
sweetened whipped cream

Drain pineapple, reserving 2 tablespoons/30 ml of the juice. In very heavy ovenproof 10-inch/25-cm skillet, melt butter over medium heat. Add brown sugar, stirring until sugar is melted; remove from heat. Arrange 8 pineapple slices over sugar mixture overlapping slightly. Place one slice in center; fill centers with cherries. Halve the remaining slices and arrange round edge of skillet. In large mixing bowl, combine flour, sugar, baking powder, salt and nutmeg. Add shortening and milk; beat with electric mixer on high 2 minutes. Add vanilla, egg and reserved pineapple juice; beat 2 minutes longer. Pour over pineapple, spreading carefully. Bake at 350°F/180°C for 40 to 45 minutes or until cake tests done. Let stand on wire rack 5 minutes. Loosen edges of cake. Cover with serving platter and invert; remove pan. Serve warm with whipped cream. Makes 8 servings.

* * * * *

Up above my head, I hear music. I hear music in the air. There must be a God somewhere.

STRAWBERRY CAKE

Pamela Johnson
Carson, CA

Pillsbury Plus strawberry cake
  mix
1 c. Crisco oil
1 pkg. strawberry jello
1 c. strawberries

1 c. coconut
1 c. chopped nuts
4 eggs
1 c. milk

Icing:

1 box confectioners sugar
1 stick oleo
½ c. strawberries

½ c. nuts
½ c. coconut

Mix cake mix, oil, jello, strawberries, coconut, nuts, eggs and milk together in large mixing bowl. Bake 1 hour at 325° to 350°. Frost with icing.

* * * * *

This little light of mine.
I'm going to let it shine.

SLICE OF WATERMELON CAKE

Mrs. Malinda's Recipe Collection

1 c. all-purpose flour
¾ c. sugar
1 ½ tsp. baking powder
½ tsp. salt
½ c. milk

¼ c. shortening
1 tsp. vanilla
2 egg whites
frosting
chocolate chips or raisins

Preheat oven to 350°. Grease and lightly flour one 8 or 9-inch round cake pan. In a mixing bowl, stir together flour, sugar, baking powder and salt. Add milk, shortening and vanilla; beat on low until combined, then for 2 minutes on medium speed. Add egg whites and beat on medium speed for 2 minutes more. Pour into pan. Bake 25 to 30 minutes. Cool on wire rack completely. Cut in half crosswise. Tint 1 cup frosting red. Tint ½ cup frosting green and tint ½ cup frosting white using paste food coloring. Spread about ¼ cup frosting on large flat side of 1 cake half and top with other half, flat side down. Cut ¼-inch piece off curve (opposite cut) so cake will sit upright. Place on serving platter, small cut/curve side down. Frost "rind" area green, making a ½-inch band. Then frost a ½-inch band white. Frost remainder red. Apply chocolate chips or raisins for seeds. Serves 6 (or 4 if they are boys).

＊ ＊ ＊ ＊ ＊

I have never seen the righteous forsaken, nor his seed begging bread.

STRIPE-IT-RICH CAKE

Mrs. Malinda's Recipe Collection

1 (2 layer) pkg. cake mix or
  pudding included cake mix
  (any flavor)
1 c. confectioners sugar

4 c. cold milk
2 (4 serving) pkg. Jell-O brand
  instant pudding (any
  complimentary flavor)

Prepare cake mix as directed on package, baking in a 9 x 13-inch pan. Remove from oven. Poke holes at once down through the cake to the pan with the round handle of a wooden spoon (or poke holes with a plastic drinking straw, using a turning motion to make large holes). Holes should be 1-inch apart. Only after poking holes, combine pudding mix with sugar in a large bowl; gradually stir in milk. Beat at low speed of electric mixer for not more than 1 minute (do not overbeat). Quickly, before pudding thickens, pour about ½ of the thin pudding evenly over warm cake and into holes to make stripes. Allow remaining pudding to thicken slightly, then spoon over the top, swirling it to "frost" the cake. Chill at least 1 hour. Store cake in the refrigerator.

* * * * *

SWEET POTATO CAKE

Pastor and Mrs. Chris Green
Rialto, CA

1 ½ c. cooking oil
4 eggs, separated
2 ½ c. sifted cake flour
½ tsp. ground cinnamon
1 ½ c. grated raw sweet
  potato
1 tsp. vanilla

2 c. sugar
4 Tbsp. hot water
3 tsp. baking powder
1 tsp. ground nutmeg
1 c. chopped nuts
½ tsp. salt

Combine oil and sugar; beat until smooth. Add egg yolks; beat well. Add hot water; beat well. Add dry ingredients, which have been sifted together. Stir in potato, nuts and vanilla; beat well. Beat egg whites until stiff; fold into mixture. Bake in greased cake pans at 350° for about 25 to 30 minutes until done.

Frosting:

1 large can evaporated milk
1 stick margarine
1 tsp. vanilla

1 c. sugar
3 egg yolks
1 ⅓ c. coconut

Combine all ingredients, except coconut. Cook in double boiler about 12 minutes. Remove from heat; add coconut and spread on cake.

† WEDDING CAKE AND CAKE † DECORATING FROSTING

Mrs. Malinda's Recipe Collection

1 ¼ c. Crisco
½ c. water
¼ tsp. vanilla
¼ tsp. orange flavoring

¼ tsp. lemon flavoring
dash of salt
2 boxes powdered sugar
food coloring (as needed)

Beat Crisco with mixer until fluffy. Add flavoring and salt. Alternate adding sugar and water just a little at a time until all ingredients are well mixed. Add coloring desired in small portions as needed and decorate.

VANILLA WAFER CAKE

Mrs. Malinda's Recipe Collection

1 c. butter
2 c. sugar
6 whole eggs
1 (12 oz.) box vanilla wafers, crushed

1 (7 oz.) can Angel Flake coconut
1 c. chopped pecans
¼ tsp. almond extract

Cream butter and sugar. Add well beaten eggs. Add crushed vanilla wafers. Add coconut, pecans and almond extract. Bake 1 ½ hours at 275° in stem pan.

Cream Cheese Icing:

1 (8 oz.) pkg. cream cheese
1 stick butter
1 box powdered sugar, sifted

1 tsp. vanilla
½ c. chopped pecans

Melt butter. Add cream cheese, powdered sugar, vanilla and nuts.

✝ LEMON CAKE FILLING OR TOPPING ✝

Mrs. Malinda's Recipe Collection
("Very Tart Taste")

1 c. sugar
1 stick butter or margarine

½ c. lemon juice (takes about 6 good size lemons)
6 egg yolks (do not use whites)

✝ LEMON GLAZE ✝

Mrs. Malinda's Recipe Collection

1 c. powdered sugar

juice of 1 lemon

Mix together. Pour over cake when cool.

FRESH BLACKBERRY CAKE

Late Mrs. Rosie B. Tucker
Memphis, TN

1 c. cooking oil
2 c. sugar
2 c. fresh blackberries
3 whole eggs
3 c. plain flour

1 tsp. soda
1 tsp. allspice
1 tsp. cinnamon
1 tsp. cloves

Combine cooking oil, sugar and blackberries; beat until sugar dissolves. Beat in eggs, then blend in the dry ingredients. Pour into 3 greased and floured cake pans or a 9 x 13-inch pan. Bake at 350° for about 40 minutes. Top with Caramel Icing.

Never Fail Caramel Icing:

2 ½ c. sugar
1 slightly beaten egg
1 stick margarine

¾ c. sweet milk
1 tsp. vanilla

Melt ½ cup sugar in iron skillet slowly until browned and runny. Mix egg, butter and remaining sugar and milk in saucepan; cook over heat until butter is melted. Turn heat to medium; add browned sugar. Cook until it forms a soft ball when dropped in water. Remove from heat. Cool slightly. Add vanilla beat until right consistency to spread. If too thick, add a little cream.

Note: Instead of using the egg in the icing, you can mix 1 tablespoon of flour with the sugar (which I do).

* * * * *

MOUNTAIN DEW CAKE

Mrs. Malinda's Recipe Collection

1 small box orange jello
1 box coconut cream pie
  filling
1 c. Crisco oil

1 box orange cake mix
4 eggs
10 oz. Mountain Dew

Mix all ingredients following directions on cake mix box. Bake in 3 layers.

Icing for Mountain Dew Cake:

1 (20 oz.) can crushed
  pineapple
1 (8 oz.) can crushed
  pineapple

5 Tbsp. flour
½ stick margarine
2 c. sugar
2 c. flaked coconut

Mix pineapple, sugar and flour in a saucepan; simmer over medium heat until thick. Stir in butter and coconut. Spread on cooled cake. Recipe will cover 3 layers.

* * * * *

STRAWBERRY CHEESECAKE

Rod and Debora Jackson
Memphis, TN

1/3 c. margarine
1/3 c. sugar
1 egg
1 1/4 c. flour (plain)
3 (8 oz.) pkg. cream cheese
3/4 c. sugar

2 Tbsp. flour
1 tsp. vanilla
3 eggs
2 Tbsp. milk
1 (10 oz.) jar strawberry jelly
2 c. whole strawberries

Cream margarine and 1/3 cup sugar until light and fluffy; blend in 1 egg. Add flour; mix well. Spread dough with spatula on bottom and 1 1/2-inches high around sides of a 9-inch spring-form pan. Bake at 450° for 5 minutes.

Combine softened cheese, sugar, flour and vanilla, mixing at medium speed on electric mixer until well blended. Add 3 eggs, one at a time, mixing well after each addition. Stir in milk. Pour into pastry lined pan. Bake at 450° for 10 minutes. Reduce heat to 250°; continue baking for 30 minutes. Loosen cake from rim of pan; cool before removing rim. Chill. Several hours before serving, melt jelly over low heat; cool slightly. Arrange strawberries on top of cake; spoon jelly over strawberries and chill.

* * * * *

He's still able and available.

PUMPKIN POUND CAKE

Mrs. Malinda's Recipe Collection

1 regular size can pumpkin
2 c. sugar
2 c. flour
4 eggs
1 c. salad oil
2 tsp. baking soda

1 tsp. baking powder
½ tsp. salt
1 tsp. nutmeg
2 tsp. cinnamon
1 tsp. vanilla

Combine sugar, oil and eggs; beat well. Sift all dry ingredients; add to oil mixture. Mix well. Stir in pumpkin and vanilla. Bake in tube pan at 350° for 1 ½ hours.

Cream Cheese Icing for Pumpkin Pound Cake:

1 stick softened margarine
1 box powdered sugar

1 (3 oz.) pkg. softened cream cheese

Blend well; spread on cake. Yield: 16 slices.

† CREAM CHEESE POUND CAKE †

Mrs. Malinda's Recipe Collection

3 sticks margarine
1 (8 oz.) pkg. cream cheese
3 c. sugar
dash of salt

1 ½ tsp. vanilla extract
½ tsp. butter flavoring
6 large eggs (unbeaten)
3 c. sifted plain or cake flour

Cream margarine, cream cheese and sugar until light and fluffy. Add salt, vanilla and butter flavoring; beat well. Add eggs, one at a time, beating well after each addition. Stir in flour. Spoon mixture into well-greased and floured 10-inch tube or Bundt pan. Bake 1 ½ hours at 325°. This makes a large, very moist cake.

MISSISSIPPI MUD CAKE

Mrs. Malinda's Recipe Collection

2 sticks butter or margarine
½ c. cocoa
2 c. sugar
4 eggs, slightly beaten
1 ½ c. all-purpose flour

pinch of salt
1 ½ c. chopped nuts
1 tsp. vanilla extract
miniature marshmallows

Melt butter and cocoa together. Remove from heat; stir in sugar and beaten eggs. Mix well. Add flour, salt, chopped nuts and vanilla; mix well. Spoon batter into a greased 13 x 9 x 2-inch pan. Bake at 350° for 35 to 45 minutes. Sprinkle marshmallows on top of warm cake; cover with Chocolate Frosting. Yield: 1 cake.

Chocolate Frosting:

1 (1 lb.) box powdered sugar
½ c. whole milk
⅓ c. cocoa

½ stick softened butter or margarine

Combine sugar, milk, cocoa and softened butter. Mix until smooth and spread on hot cake.

* * * * *

FRESH APPLE CAKE

Mrs. Malinda's Recipe Collection

Bake in a large loaf pan or a regular Bundt pan. Requires a large bowl or container to mix all ingredients. Bake in oven at 325° for 50 to 60 minutes, depending on whether you have a gas or an electric oven. Mix the following ingredients as listed:

2 c. sugar
1 c. oil
3 eggs (should be well beaten, then add at this point)
3 c. well diced fresh apples
3 c. plain sifted flour
½ tsp. salt

1 tsp. soda
2 tsp. cinnamon (if person does not like cinnamon, may be omitted)
2 Tbsp. vanilla
1 c. finely chopped pecans

Walnuts and a walnut flavoring may be used instead of the pecans and vanilla flavoring. Also can be baked several days ahead of time and allows the cake to become moist. A thin glaze could be used on this cake.

QUEEN ESTER'S DELIGHT CAKE

Mrs. Malinda's Recipe Collection

2 ½ c. or 20 oz. crushed pineapple with juice
1 can coconut

1 white cake mix (dry)
1 ½ c. chopped pecans
2 sticks chopped butter

Layer ingredients in order: pineapple, coconut, cake mix, pecans and butter in an 11 x 14-inch ungreased pan. Bake at 350° for 40 minutes.

* * * * *

There is a brighter day ahead.

RED VELVET CAKE

Sis. Sheryl Scott

1 stick butter, softened
1 ½ c. sugar
1 tsp. vanilla
2 eggs
1 tsp. red food paste
2 c. all-purpose flour
¼ c. cocoa powder
1 tsp. salt
1 c. buttermilk

1 ½ tsp. baking soda
1 Tbsp. vinegar
1 (8 oz.) pkg. cream cheese
½ c. butter, softened
4 c. confectioners sugar
1 tsp. vanilla extract
½ c. chopped pecans
(optional)

Preheat oven to 350°. Grease and flour two 9-inch round pans. In a large bowl, beat together butter, sugar and vanilla until creamy. Add the eggs and food paste; blend well. In another bowl, sift together the flour, salt and cocoa. Add this mixture to the batter alternately with the buttermilk; beat until well blended. Stir the baking soda into the vinegar; fold into the batter. Pour batter into pre-pared pans and bake for 30 to 35 minutes or until tooth-pick inserted in center comes out clean. Remove from the oven and allow to cool on a wire rack. After cake has cooled, mix together cream cheese, butter, confection-ers sugar and vanilla. Stir in the nuts, if using them, and frost the cake.

WORD OF GOD CAKE

Rivers of New Life Church
Memphis, TN

2 ½ c. 2 Samuel 13:8
5 tsp. Galatians 5:9
½ tsp. Mark 9:50
¾ tsp. 1 Kings 10:10
3 Tbsp. Proverbs 30:33

¾ c. Jeremiah 6:20
1 Isaiah 10:14
¾ c. 1 Corinthians 3:2
1 ½ c. Proverbs 23:11
½ c. 1 Samuel 30:12

Follow Numbers 11:8.

PERFECTION CONVECTION 7-UP CAKE

Mrs. Malinda's Recipe Collection

1 pkg. lemon cake mix
1 pkg. lemon instant pudding
  mix
1 c. oil
4 eggs
1 (10 oz.) can 7-Up

1 large can crushed pineapple
1 large can coconut
1 ½ c. sugar
3 egg yolks
1 Tbsp. cornstarch

Mix cake mix, pudding mix, oil, whole eggs and 7-Up together. Bake at 350° for 30 minutes. Put pineapple, sugar, egg yolks and cornstarch in the top of a double boiler and cook until thick. Add the coconut and spread over cooled cake.

* * * * *

According to your faith it shall be done unto you.

PECAN AND PEACH UPSIDE-DOWN CAKE

Sis. Sheryl Scott

1 ½ c. butter, divided
1 ⅓ c. all-purpose flour
5 eggs
1 ⅓ c. sugar
1 tsp. baking powder
¼ tsp. salt
1 c. light brown sugar

½ c. honey
½ tsp. almond extract
¼ tsp. vanilla extract
1 (29 oz.) can sliced peaches, drained
maraschino cherries
¾ c. chopped pecans

Combine 1 cup of butter with the flour until well mixed. Beat the eggs in one at a time. Continue beating while adding the sugar, baking powder, salt, vanilla and almond extract; beat until well combined. Set aside. Take ½ cup of butter and melt it in a 10-inch iron frying pan. Add in the brown sugar and the honey; mix well. Remove the pan from the heat and place the peaches in a pattern. Use the cherries for accent in between the peaches. Take the batter and pour over the fruit evenly. Leave room for the cake to rise without spilling over. Bake the cake for 30 minutes or more, if needed, in a 350° oven. When the cake is done, allow it to remain in the skillet until completely cooled, then invert the pan on a cake plate and store at room temperature.

* * * * *

DAMASCUS ROAD PINEAPPLE UPSIDE-DOWN CAKE

Mrs. Malinda's Recipe Collection

½ c. brown sugar, firmly
  packed
¼ c. butter, melted
6 canned pineapple slices,
  drained
6 maraschino cherries
2 eggs, separated

½ c. sugar
¾ c. all-purpose flour
½ tsp. baking powder
¼ tsp. salt
¼ c. pineapple juice
whipped cream

Preheat oven to 350°. In a small bowl, combine the brown sugar and butter; blend well. Spread it in the bottom of a 9-inch round cake pan. Arrange the pineapple slices and cherries over the brown sugar mixture; set aside.

In a small bowl, beat the egg yolks until thick and lemon-colored. Gradually add sugar; beat well. Lightly spoon flour into measuring cup; level off. Add the flour, baking powder, salt and pineapple juice to egg yolk mixture; mix well.

In another bowl, beat the egg whites until soft peaks form; fold into batter. Pour the batter into prepared pan, covering pineapple slices and cherries. Bake at 350° for 30 to 35 minutes or until toothpick inserted comes out clean. Cool upright for 2 minutes in pan; invert and serve with whipped cream.

* * * * *

STRAWBERRY HILL CAKE

Rod and Debora Jackson
Memphis, TN

1 pkg. strawberry gelatin
1 c. boiling water
2 small pkg. frozen strawberries
dash of salt
30 graham crackers
½ c. melted butter or
  margarine

½ c. chopped pecans
3 eggs
1 c. sugar
1 (6 oz.) pkg. cream cheese
1 pt. sour cream

Dissolve gelatin in boling water; add strawberries and dash of salt. Crush graham crackers; add butter and pecans and press into a 9 x 9 x 2-inch pan. Beat eggs, sugar, cream cheese and another dash of salt. Blend well and pour over crumb crust. Bake at 325° for 35 to 45 minutes, until it sets like a custard. Remove from oven. Spread sour cream over custard. Return to oven for 15 minutes. Remove from oven. Cool completely. Pour gelatin mixture over top. Chill in the refrigerator overnight. Cut into squares when ready to serve.

* * * * *

Love thy neighbor as thyself.

NEW YORK-STYLE CHEESECAKE

Mrs. Malinda's Recipe Collection

½ c. butter toffee bits
2 c. gingersnap cookie crumbs
4 Tbsp. butter (unsalted), melted
1 (16 oz.) cream cheese, softened
1 c. sugar

3 large eggs (room temperature)
1 ½ c. sour cream
1 Tbsp. vanilla extract
½ c. butter toffee bits
½ c. caramel sauce (jarred or homemade)

Preheat the oven to 300°. Butter the spring-form pan. In a large bowl, combine ½ cup butter toffee bits with the crumbs and stir in the butter until thoroughly combined. Press the crust over the bottom and up the sides of the prepared pan, then chill the pan in the refrigerator while preparing the filling.

Put the cream cheese and sugar in a large bowl and beat until smooth, using the electric mixer on medium speed. Add the eggs, one at a time, beating for 20 seconds after each addition. Add the sour cream and vanilla and beat until smooth. Scrape down the bowl. Pour the filling into the prepared crust and smooth the top. Fill a 2-quart baking pan halfway with hot water and place on the bottom rack in the oven. Bake the cake on the middle rack for 1 ¼ hours. Turn off the oven and leave the cake in for 30 minutes with the door closed. Remove the cake to a wire rack and cool to room temperature, about 1 hour. Cover cake with foil and refrigerate for 4 hours or overnight.

* * * * *

Do unto others as you would have them do unto you.

MILLION DOLLAR POUND CAKE I

Mrs. Malinda's Recipe Collection

3 c. sugar
7 eggs (room temperature)
¾ c. half and half
1 tsp. vanilla extract

1 lb. butter, softened
4 c. all-purpose flour or cake flour
1 tsp. almond extract

48

Combine sugar and butter until light and fluffy. Add eggs, one at a time, beating well after each addition. Add flour to creamed mixture alternately with milk, beating well after each addition. Stir in extracts. Pour batter into a well-greased and floured 10-inch tube pan. Bake at 300° for 1 hour and 40 minutes or until cake tests done. Yields 1 (10-inch) cake.

CHOCOLATE CHEESECAKE

Venus Roberts
LA, CA

1 pkg. Duncan Hines Moist Deluxe fudge marble cake mix, divided
2 (8 oz.) pkg. cream cheese, softened
8 oz. milk chocolate, melted

3 eggs
⅔ c. whipping cream
¼ c. plus 1 Tbsp. butter or margarine, melted
whipped cream and fresh strawberries (for garnish)

Preheat oven to 350°. Grease and flour a 13 x 9 x 2-inch dish.

Filling: For filling, combine cocoa packet, ¼ cup dry cake mix, cream cheese and melted chocolate in large bowl. Beat at high speed with an electric mixer for 2 minutes. Add eggs and whipped cream. Beat 1 minute at high speed.

Crust: For crust, stir remaining dry cake mix and melted butter in a medium bowl. The mixture will be crumbly. Sprinkle mixture into bottom of pan. Pour filling over crust mixture. Bake for 30 to 35 minutes. Cool in pan. Refrigerate until chilled. Garnish each serving with whipped topping and strawberries. Serves 12.

PECAN CARAMEL CHOCOLATE CHIP CHEESECAKE

Sister Shirley Bickham
Lancaster, CA

Crust:

½ c. butter, melted

1 ½ c. graham cracker crumbs

Filling:

3 (8 oz.) pkg. cream cheese
1 c. sour cream
1 Tbsp. vanilla extract
1 c. sugar

3 large eggs
1 c. semi-sweet chocolate
chips

Caramel Topping:

1 jar caramel

Heat oven to 350°. Mix melted butter and crumbs. Press in bottom and 2-inches up sides of a 9-inch spring-form pan. Bake crust 10 minutes.

TO PREPARE FILLING: Beat mixture after each filling ingredient addition. Stir in chocolate chips. Pour into spring-form pan. Sprinkle pecan pieces on top. Bake 40 minutes.

Turn oven off and leave cheesecake in the oven for 1 hour to set. Remove from oven and allow to cool. Chill in the refrigerator until firm. With the handle of wooden spoon, make holes randomly in cheesecake. Pour caramel topping over cheesecake. Make sure to fill holes. Return to the refrigerator until caramel sets.

* * * * *

You must be born again.

TRIPLE DECKER CHOCOLATE CAKE

Mel Mills
Memphis, TN

1 (2 layer) vanilla or white cake mix	4 eggs, separated
½ c. toasted ground almonds	1 c. granulated sugar
	1 c. sliced almonds

50

Prepare cake mix adding ground almonds and 4 egg yolks; reserve egg whites. Divide mixture between 3 (9-inch) greased and floured cake pans. In a bowl, whisk egg whites until foamy; continue whisking gradually adding sugar until stiff peaks form. Gently fold sliced almonds into whisked egg whites. Spread mixture evenly over cake batter in pans. Bake as directed. Cool for 20 minutes; remove from pans. Cool completely before putting filling between layers.

Filling and Decoration

2 c. whipping cream	3 oz. semi-sweet chocolate
½ c. granulated sugar	2 Tbsp. butter
1 Tbsp. vanilla	

Whip cream sugar and vanilla until soft peaks form. Place one cake layer on serving plate; spread one half of cream mixture on cake layer. Put second layer on top. Repeat cream mixture on second layer and place third layer on top. Melt chocolate over low heat; remove from heat and stir butter into melted chocolate. Drizzle cake with chocolate mixture; chill to set chocolate. Serves 8 to 10.

* * * * *

BAHAMA RUM CAKE

Rita Harris
Memphis, TN

½ c. chopped walnuts or
  pecans
1 c. butter
1 c. sugar
4 eggs
1 lime (grated peel and juice)

1 ½ c. sifted flour
1 tsp. baking powder
½ c. milk
½ c. dark rum
1 tsp. vanilla
½ c. raisins

Preheat oven to 325°. Grease and flour a tube or Bundt pan and line base with nuts. Cream butter and sugar together. Then beat in eggs and add lime. Mix in flour, baking powder and milk. Add rum, vanilla and raisins. Pour mixture into pan and bake 1 hour. Invert cake on a rack to cool.

Banana Rum Cake Glaze:

¼ c. butter
¼ c. water
¾ c. sugar

½ c. dark rum
½ tsp. vanilla

Melt butter in saucepan. Add water and sugar. Boil and stir 4 to 5 minutes. Remove from heat; add rum and vanilla. Pierce cake and brush glaze over top and sides. Repeat. Steep cake in pan. Serve with ice cream.

* * * * *

PUNCH BOWL CAKE

Mrs. Malinda's Recipe Collection

1 pineapple or lemon cake mix
2 small boxes instant vanilla pudding
2 cans cherry pie mix

2 cans crushed pineapple, drained
6 bananas, sliced
1 (12 oz.) Cool Whip
1 c. chopped nuts
1 (8 oz.) maraschino cherries

Cook cake mix according to directions; cool. Use a very big punch bowl to make punch bowl cake in. Crumble ½ of cake in bottom of punch bowl. Mix 1 box of pudding according to directions and spread over crumbled cake. Pour 1 can cherry pie mix over pudding; spread 1 can drained pineapple over pie mix. Spread 3 sliced bananas over pineapple; spread ½ box Cool Whip over bananas. Sprinkle ½ cup nuts over Cool Whip. Repeat the procedure.

* * * * *

CARROT CAKE

Balinda Moore
Memphis, TN

2 c. sifted flour	3 eggs
2 tsp. baking soda	1 tsp. vanilla
1 tsp. baking powder	2 c. shredded carrots
1 tsp. salt	1 c. shredded coconut
2 tsp. ground cinnamon	1 c. chopped walnuts
1 ¾ c. sugar	8 ¼ oz. can crushed
1 c. vegetable oil	pineapple, drained

Grease 13 x 9 x 2-inch baking pan. Dust lightly with flour.

Sift flour, baking soda, baking powder, salt and cinnamon into a large bowl. Make a well in center and add in order shown: sugar, oil, eggs and vanilla. Beat until smooth. Stir in carrots, coconut, walnuts and pineapple until well blended. Bake 45 minutes at 350°.

Creamed Cheese Frosting:

3 oz. cream cheese	½ tsp. vanilla
¼ c. softened butter	2 tsp. milk
2 c. confectioners sugar	

Beat cream cheese with softened butter in a medium size bowl. Beat in sifted confectioners sugar. Add vanilla. Add milk if necessary.

* * * * *

They shall know we are Christians by our love.

CHRISTMAS CAKE

¾ c. butter
3 eggs
3 c. flour
1 pkg. dates
½ c. nuts

2 c. sugar
1 c. water
1 tsp. soda
1 bottle cherries

Cream butter and sugar. Beat eggs and add to mixture. Sift flour and soda together and add alternately with water to egg mixture. Soak dates in water and stir in with cherries and nuts. Pour into a large ring mold and bake at 350° until a straw inserted in middle comes out clean.

Icing:

1 c. sugar
⅛ lb. butter
½ bottle maraschino cherries
¼ c. brandy
½ c. chopped pecans

1 c. water
2 Tbsp. flour
½ can coconut
½ box dates

Boil sugar and water. Mix flour with softened butter and add to water, then add remaining ingredients and cook until thick enough to spread.

* * * * *

CHRISTMAS FRUITCAKE

Mrs. Malinda's Recipe Collection

⅛ c. chopped dried cherries
⅛ c. chopped dried mango
¼ c. dried cranberries
¼ c. dried currants
2 Tbsp. chopped candied citron
¼ c. dark rum
½ c. butter
¼ c. packed brown sugar

1 egg
½ c. all-purpose flour
⅛ tsp. baking soda
¼ tsp. salt
¼ tsp. ground cinnamon
¼ c. unsulfured molasses
2 Tbsp. milk
¼ c. chopped pecans
¼ c. dark rum, divided

Soak cherries, mango, cranberries, currants and citron in ¼ cup rum for at least 24 hours. Cover tightly and store at room temperature.

Preheat oven to 325°F (165°C). Butter a 6 x 3-inch round pan and line with parchment paper.

In a large bowl, cream together butter and brown sugar until fluffy. Beat in egg. Whisk together flour, baking soda, salt and cinnamon. Mix into butter and sugar in 3 batches, alternating with molasses and milk. Stir in soaked fruit and chopped nuts. Scrape batter into prepared pan. Bake in preheated oven for 40 to 45 minutes. Cool in the pan for 10 minutes, then sprinkle with 2 tablespoons rum.

Cut out one piece of parchment and one piece of cheesecloth, each large enough to wrap around the cake. Moisten cheesecloth with 1 tablespoon rum. Arrange cheesecloth on top of parchment paper and unmold cake onto it. Sprinkle top and sides of cake with remaining rum. Wrap the cheesecloth closely to the surface of the cake, then wrap with paper. Place in an airtight tin and age for at least 10 weeks. If storing longer, douse with additional rum for every 10 weeks of storage.

* * * * *

Come let us reason together.

DUMP CAKE

Jeremy Johnson
Carson, CA

1 (No. 2) can crushed
  pineapple
1 can Angel Flake coconut

1 pkg. yellow cake mix
1 c. chopped nuts
1 ½ sticks oleo

Spread each of the ingredients evenly in oblong pan or Pyrex dish, one on top of the other, in the order listed (pineapple, coconut, cake mix, nuts and oleo). Do not mix. Bake 1 hour at 350°.

Deluxe Dump Cake: Same as before with additional ingredient of 1 can cherry pie filling as the first ingredient.

✝ MILLION DOLLAR POUND CAKE III ✝

Mrs. Malinda's Recipe Collection

3 c. sugar
1 lb. real butter, softened
6 eggs (room temperature)
4 c. plain flour or cake flour

¾ c. sweet milk
2 tsp. vanilla
1 c. chopped pecans
¾ c. coconut

Combine sugar and butter, creaming until light and fluffy. Add eggs, one at a time, creaming well after each addition. Add flour to mixture alternately with the milk, beating well after each addition. Stir in flavoring, pecans and coconut. Pour batter into a well-greased and floured 10-inch tube pan. Bake at 300° for 1 hour and 40 minutes or until done.

* * * * *

We will sit at the welcome table.

MOUNT CARAMEL ICING

Mrs. Malinda's Recipe Collection

2 c. white sugar
2 c. buttermilk
½ c. butter

1 tsp. soda
1 tsp. vanilla
8 to 10 marshmallows

Mix together and cook until it forms a soft ball in water. Add 8 to 10 marshmallows and vanilla. Beat the mixture until it is stiff. Spread on cake.

† SOUR CREAM POUND CAKE I †

Mrs. Malinda's Recipe Collection

2 sticks butter, softened
3 c. sugar
6 eggs
1 c. sour cream

¼ tsp. soda
3 c. all-purpose flour, sifted
1 tsp. lemon extract
1 tsp. almond extract

Sift flour and measure. Resift twice with soda. Set aside. Cream butter and add sugar slowly, beating constantly to cream well. Add eggs, one at a time, beating well after each addition. Stir in sour cream. Add flour mixture, ½ cup at a time, beating well and constantly. Stir in lemon extract and almond extract and turn batter into 10-inch tube pan, greased and floured well. Bake in moderate oven, 350°, about 1 ½ hours or until cake is done. Place pan on rack to cool 5 minutes. Loosen cake around edge of pan and edge of tube with dull side of knife. Press toward pan rather than toward cake. This protects crust. Turn cake onto rack to cool completely. Serve uniced.

Note: When freezing this cake, either whole or cut, wrap well in clear plastic or aluminum foil using several thicknessess.

PINEAPPLE COCONUT CAKE

Mrs. Malinda's Recipe Collection

2 ½ c. flour
4 ½ tsp. baking powder
1 tsp. salt
1 ½ c. sugar

2 c. Crisco
1 ¼ c. milk
1 tsp. vanilla

Filling:

1 (15 ½ oz.) crushed pineapple
⅓ c. sugar

1 Tbsp. flour

Sift together flour, baking powder, salt and 1 ½ cups sugar. Add Crisco, milk and vanilla. Beat for 1 ½ minutes. Add ⅔ cup egg whites, unbeaten. Beat for 1 ½ minutes. Bake in two 8 or 9-inch cake pans, greased and floured. Bake 30 minutes at 350°.

Can substitute pineapple flavored or yellow cake mix.

Mix filling; cook until thick. Let cool. Spread between layers.

Icing:

¾ c. sugar
1 c. white Karo
3 Tbsp. water

2 egg whites
½ tsp. vanilla

Cook the sugar, syrup and water until it forms soft-ball stage. Gradually pour over beaten egg whites. Beat 1 ½ minutes longer; add vanilla. Put coconut between layers and on top.

* * * * *

Bread of heaven feed me until I want no more.

PUNCH BOWL CAKE I

Mrs. Malinda's Recipe Collection

1 large angel food cake
1 can cherry pie filling
1 can blueberry pie filling
nuts (walnuts)

2 (5 oz.) instant vanilla pie
  filling and pudding
2 (8 oz.) Cool Whip
shredded coconut
maraschino cherries

Prepare pudding ahead of time. Tear angel food cake into small pieces. Layer on bottom of bowl. Spread a layer of pudding, a layer of pie filling (cherry and blueberry), Cool Whip, coconut and nuts. Continue with the layers. Top with whipped cream and nuts. Serve cold.

† PUNCH BOWL CAKE II †

Mrs. Malinda's Recipe Collection

1 can crushed pineapple
1 can sliced peaches
1 large can Baker's coconut
1 large container Cool Whip

1 pkg. frozen strawberries
1 large pkg. Jell-O instant
  pudding (vanilla)
1 box yellow cake mix

Prepare cake mix and cook 2 layers as directed on the box. Set aside to cool. Prepare pudding as directed and set aside. If the fruit is unsweetened, add sugar to taste and set aside. When the cake has cooled, break one layer up into the bowl. Spread all the pineapple over the cake layer. Spread ½ of the pudding mix over the pineapple, then spread ½ of the Cool Whip over the pudding mix. Sprinkle ½ the coconut over the Cool Whip. Now, repeat with the second cake layer, all the peaches, the remaining pudding mix, Cool Whip and coconut. Garnish with strawberries. Refrigerate.

MILLION DOLLAR CAKE

Mrs. Malinda's Recipe Collection

(Tastes Like A German Chocolate Cake)

2 sticks margarine
2 ½ c. sugar
2 eggs
2 tsp. vanilla
3 c. flour

2 tsp. baking soda
2 Tbsp. cocoa
½ tsp. salt
2 c. buttermilk

Frosting:

2 c. sugar
2 beaten eggs
⅔ c. Pet milk, mixed with ⅓ c.
  water

1 c. coconut
1 c. chopped pecans
1 tsp. vanilla

Cream together margarine and sugar. Add eggs; beat well. Add salt, soda, vanilla, cocoa and flour. Gradually add in milk until well blended. Makes 4 (9-inch) layers or 2 (13-inch) pans. Bake at 350°. Cool 20 minutes.

Frosting: Mix the first 4 ingredients together in heavy saucepan until well blended. Boil for 3 minutes or until thick. Add the coconut, pecans and vanilla. Spread on warm cake.

* * * * *

MILLION DOLLAR FRUITCAKE

Mrs. Malinda's Recipe Collection

2 c. sugar
1 pkg. (approximately 1 lb.)
  raisins
1 (1 lb.) jar mixed candied
  fruits
1 c. butter
1 tsp. cinnamon
2 c. boiling water

1 tsp. nutmeg
1 tsp. cloves
1 tsp. salt
1 tsp. baking soda
3 well beaten eggs
3 c. flour
1 c. chopped nuts

In large saucepan, combine the sugar, raisins, butter, water, cinnamon, nutmeg, cloves, baking soda, salt and candied fruit. Bring the mixture slowly to a boil. Reduce heat and simmer 10 minutes. Cool completely; overnight is best.

The next day, place the mixture in a large bowl and add the eggs and flour. Mix the batter well until smooth and well blended. Fold in the nuts. Pour into a well-greased and waxed paper lined 10-inch tube pan. Bake at 350° for 1 ½ hours or until the cake tests done. Brush heavily with rum or brandy. When cooled, wrap well and store a month before serving.

This cake also bakes well in smaller pans. Fill ½ full and test for baking time.

❉ ❉ ❉ ❉ ❉

PINTO BEAN CAKE

Barbara Tillman
Pasadena, CA

1 c. sugar
¼ c. butter
1 egg, beaten
2 c. pinto beans, cooked or
  mashed
1 c. flour
½ tsp. salt
½ tsp. allspice

2 c. raw apples, diced
2 c. nuts, chopped
1 tsp. vanilla
1 tsp. soda
½ tsp. cloves
1 tsp. cinnamon
1 c. raisins

Cream sugar and butter; add egg, then mashed beans. Sift all dry ingredients together. Add dry ingredients to sugar mixture. Add apples, raisins, nuts and vanilla. Pour in greased and floured pan. Bake at 375° for 45 minutes.

Caramel Frosting:

1 ½ sticks butter
3 c. brown sugar

¾ c. sweet milk
powdered sugar

Mix butter, brown sugar and sweet milk together. Boil for 2 minutes. Cool. Add powdered sugar for desired consistency.

* * * * *

Peace on earth, good will toward men.

PINEAPPLE COCONUT CAKE

Mrs. Malinda's Recipe Collection

2 c. sugar
2 c. flour
2 tsp. baking soda
2 eggs

1 (20 oz.) can pineapple (in its
   own juice)
1 c. coconut

Topping:

4 oz. cream cheese, softened
1 stick oleo

1 ½ c. powdered sugar
2 tsp. vanilla

Mix all at once with mixer. Add 1 cup chopped nuts; mix well. Bake in well-greased 9 x 13-inch cake pan for 25 to 30 minutes in 350° oven.

Topping: Mix well. Frost cake when cool. Do not refrigerate.

Pineapple-Coconut Cake Filling:

2 c. sugar
4 Tbsp. flour
1 (No. 2) can crushed
   pineapple

1 stick butter
1 fresh grated coconut

Mix sugar and flour. Add pineapple juice and coconut. Bring to a boil, then add coconut and pineapple. Boil until mixture thickens. Cool and spread on favorite cake layers.

* * * * *

Let there be peace, let it begin with me.

MILLION DOLLAR POUND CAKE II

Mrs. Malinda's Recipe Collection

3 c. sugar
6 eggs (room temperature)
¾ c. milk
1 tsp. almond extract
1 tsp. lemon extract

1 tsp. vanilla extract
1 tsp. yellow food coloring
1 lb. butter, softened
4 c. all-purpose flour or cake
  flour

Cream together sugar and butter until light and fluffy. Add eggs, one at a time, beating well after each addition. Add flour alternately to creamed mixture with milk, beating well after each addition. Stir in flavorings. Pour batter into greased and floured 10-inch tube pan. Bake at 350° for 1 hour and 40 minutes or until cake tests done.

† DUMP CAKE II †

Mrs. Malinda's Recipe Collection

1 can cherry pie filling
1 (No. 2) can crushed
  pineapple
1 can Angel Flake coconut

1 pkg. yellow cake mix
1 c. chopped nuts
1 ½ sticks butter or margarine

Spread ingredients evenly in oblong pan, one on top of the other in order: cherry pie filling, pineapple, coconut, cake mix, nuts and butter or margarine. Bake 1 hour; ½ hour at 350° and ½ hour at 325°.

* * * * *

Ain't going to study war no more.

HARTFORD ELECTION DAY CAKE

Mrs. Malinda's Recipe Collection

4 to 4 ½ c. flour
1 c. sugar
1 tsp. salt
1 ½ tsp. cinnamon
½ tsp. nutmeg
¼ tsp. cloves
¼ tsp. mace

2 pkg. active dry yeast
1 ½ sticks margarine
1 ½ c. very hot tap water
2 eggs, beaten
1 ½ c. seedless raisins
¾ c. chopped nuts
¼ c. chopped citron

Optional Glaze:

1 c. confectioners sugar
1 ½ Tbsp. orange juice

½ tsp. vanilla extract
pinch of salt

CAKE: In a large bowl, thoroughly mix 1 ¾ cups flour, sugar, salt, cinnamon, nutmeg, cloves, mace and undissolved active yeast. Add softened margarine. Gradually add very hot tap water to dry ingredients and beat 2 minutes at medium speed of electric mixer. Add eggs and ¾ cup flour or enough flour to make a thick batter. Beat at high speed for 2 minutes more, scraping bowl occasionally. Add raisins, nuts, citron and enough flour to make a stiff batter. Stir until well combined. Turn into a greased 10-inch tube pan. Cover until doubled in bulk, about 1 ½ hours. Bake at 350° for 1 ¼ hours or until done. Cake will be moist. Glaze or serve with whipped cream or ice cream.

GLAZE: Combine ingredients and pour over cake.

* * * * *

The Lord will provide.

JAM CAKE

Mrs. Malinda's Recipe Collection

1 c. sugar
1 tsp. baking powder
1 tsp. baking soda
3 eggs
2 c. cake flour, sifted
1 c. strawberry jam or
preserves

1 c. pecans, chopped
¾ c. butter or margarine
¾ c. buttermilk
½ tsp. cinnamon
¼ tsp. nutmeg

Beat butter and sugar. Add eggs, one at a time. Sift cake flour; measure, then sift flour, spices and baking powder together. Add to butter mixture. Mix buttermilk and baking soda together. Let it foam and add to flour mixture. Fold in jam or preserves with spatula and add nuts which have been mixed with a little of the flour mixture. Flour and grease 3 (8-inch) cake pans. Bake 35 to 40 minutes. Cool 10 minutes, then place on a cake rack to cool. After cooling, frost with Caramel Icing.

Caramel Icing:

2 ¾ c. sugar
¾ c. evaporated milk
1 stick butter or margarine

¼ tsp. salt
1 tsp. vanilla

Brown ¾ cup sugar in an iron skillet, stirring so as not to burn. Mix together 2 cups sugar and evaporated milk. Bring to a boil; then while it is boiling, stir in the caramelized sugar. Add butter and salt. Cook until it forms a soft ball (234°) when dropped in cold water.

* * * * *

Good bread, good meat, good God, let's eat.

MILKY WAY CAKE

Mrs. Malinda's Recipe Collection

6 Milky Way candy bars
1 c. butter or margarine (2 sticks), divided
2 c. sugar
4 eggs

2 ½ c. sifted flour
½ tsp. baking soda
1 ¼ c. buttermilk
1 tsp. vanilla extract
1 c. chopped nuts

Frosting:

2 ½ c. sugar
1 c. evaporated milk
1 c. chocolate chips
1 c. marshmallow cream

1 stick butter or margarine
chopped nuts (for garnish; optional)

To Make Cake: Combine chocolate bars and ½ cup butter or margarine in medium saucepan and melt over low heat. While candy is melting, prepare batter.

Cream ½ cup butter and sugar until mixture is light and fluffy. Add eggs, one at a time, beating well after each addition. Add flour and baking soda alternately with buttermilk, stirring until smooth. Add melted candy, mixing well. Stir in vanilla extract and nuts. Pour batter into greased and floured Bundt or 10-inch tube pan. Bake at 350° for 1 hour and 20 minutes or until done when tested with wooden pick. Remove from oven. Cool a few minutes and remove from pan.

To Make Frosting: Combine sugar and evaporated milk in saucepan and heat to soft-ball stage. Pour warm milk mixture over chips, marshmallow cream and butter. Beat mixture until it reaches a good spreading consistency. Spread frosting on cake and sprinkle with additional chopped nuts, if desired.

* * * * *

Rise, Peter, slay and eat.

ORANGE RUM LAYER CAKE

Mrs. Malinda's Recipe Collection

2 ⅔ c. sifted pastry flour
½ tsp. salt
pinch of powdered ginger
1 ⅓ c. sugar
1 ½ tsp. grated orange rind
¼ c. rum
3 egg whites, stiffly beaten

2 ½ tsp. baking powder
¼ tsp. soda
⅔ c. butter
3 egg yolks
¾ c. unstrained orange juice
½ tsp. each almond and
vanilla

Sift dry ingredients together twice. Cream sugar and butter. Add egg yolks one at a time, creaming well after each addition. With the last egg yolk, add the grated orange rind. Gradually add the flour mixture to the egg mixture, alternately with the orange juice and rum mixed. Beat the whole well. With a wooden spoon, stir in almond and vanilla flavoring and lastly, fold in the stiffly beaten egg whites. Divide the batter among 3 buttered cake pans and bake at 350° for 30 to 35 minutes. Turn the layers out on a wire rack cooler and when they are cold, put them together with Lemon Filling.

Lemon Filling:

2 egg yolks
1 whole egg
3 Tbsp. rum
⅓ c. lemon juice
4 Tbsp. butter

1 ⅔ c. sugar
4 Tbsp. flour
grated rind of 1 lemon
¼ tsp. salt

Place eggs in top of double boiler. Gradually beat in sugar sifted with the flour. Gradually beat in rum, mixed with lemon rind and juice. Cook the whole over hot water for about 15 to 20 minutes or until thick, stirring almost constantly. Remove from hot water and stir in butter. Return to hot water and cook 3 minutes longer. Cool and spread between layers and ice the cake.

PAULINE'S CARAMEL CAKE

Bettie Randle
Pauline Lenton

Cake:

¾ c. shortening
1 ¾ c. sugar
¾ c. milk
3 c. flour

3 tsp. baking powder
4 egg whites
1 tsp. vanilla

Icing:

2 c. light brown sugar
1 c. granulated sugar
1 tsp. salt

½ c. milk
2 Tbsp. butter
1 tsp. vanilla

Cream shortening and sugar together. Then add milk alternately with the sifted dry ingredients. Fold in the stiffly beaten egg whites to which vanilla has been added. Stir well, but never beat. Bake at 350° for 25 to 30 minutes.

Icing: Cook sugar, salt and milk together. Stir until all lumps are dissolved, then remove from heat. Add the shortening and cook at 110°. Beat hard until it will hold shape on cake. Add vanilla. If desired, decorate with halves of English walnuts or pecans.

* * * * *

Rub a dub dub, thank you for the grub.

PERFECT MAN IN A JAR

Pastor Balinda Moore
Memphis, TN

(Cookies)

gingerbread mix

70

You will need ribbon, pint size canning jars and lids and poem.

Put the dry ingredients for your favorite gingerbread man recipe into a canning jar. (May use box mix.) Add the directions and a gingerbread man cookie cutter; tie to ribbon. Attach poem to jar with ribbon. A great gift idea.

Some are sulky and some good sports.
Some are cute and some have warts.
Some are slow and some are fast.
Some are boring and some a blast.

Sometimes they're nice to have around,
But other times they just confound.
So when you feel lonely and forlorn,
Don't give up, but listen as I warn....

The perfect man is impossible to find,
But then this recipe comes to mind....
So if you ever do tire of being alone,
Just open this jar and bake your own!

* * * * *

BRIAN'S BUFFALO COOKIES

Mrs. Malinda's Recipe Collection

1 c. butter flavor Crisco shortening or 1 butter flavor Crisco stick, melted (plus additional for greasing)
1 c. granulated sugar
1 c. firmly packed brown sugar
2 Tbsp. milk
1 tsp. vanilla
2 eggs
2 c. all-purpose flour
1 tsp. baking powder

1 tsp. baking soda
½ tsp. salt
1 c. rolled oats (quick or old-fashioned, uncooked)
1 c. corn flakes, crushed to about ½ c.
1 c. semi-sweet chocolate chips
½ c. chopped pecans
½ c. flake coconut

Heat oven to 350°. Grease baking sheets with shortening. Place sheets of foil on countertop for cooling cookies.

Combine 1 cup shortening, granulated sugar, brown sugar, milk and vanilla in large bowl. Beat at low speed of electric mixer until well blended. Add eggs; beat at medium speed until well blended. Combine flour, baking powder, baking soda and salt. Add gradually to shortening mixture at low speed. Stir in oats, corn flakes, chocolate chips, nuts and coconut. Fill ice cream scoop that holds ¼ cup with dough (or use ¼ cup measuring cup; level with knife). Drop 3-inches apart onto prepared baking sheets. Bake at 350° for 13 to 15 minutes or until lightly browned around edges but still slightly soft in center. Do not overbake. Cool 3 minutes on baking sheets before removing to foil with wide thin pancake turner to cool completely. Makes about 2 ½ dozen cookies.

* * * * *

Weeping may endure for a night..
But joy cometh in the morning.

SUNSHINE PIE

A pound of patience, you must find
Mixed well with loving words, so kind
Drop in two pounds of helpful deeds
And thoughts of other people's deeds.

A pack of smiles, to make the crust,
Then stir and bake it well you must.
And now, I ask that you may try,
The recipe for this Sunshine Pie.
        Author unknown.

72

* * * * *

If you are willing and obedient,
You shall eat the Good of the Land.

ENGLISH TRIFLE 2

Mrs. Malinda's Recipe Collection

½ c. margarine
½ c. white sugar
2 eggs
1 ¾ c. all-purpose flour
½ tsp. baking powder
½ tsp. salt
1 pt. heavy cream
¼ c. white sugar
1 tsp. vanilla extract

1 (4.6 oz.) pkg. non-instant vanilla pudding mix
1 (8 oz.) jar seedless raspberry jam
½ c. sherry
4 fresh peaches, peeled, pitted and sliced
1 pt. fresh strawberries, rinsed and sliced
1 pt. blueberries

Preheat oven to 350°F (175°C). Grease and flour an 8 x 8-inch cake pan.

In a large bowl, cream together margarine and ½ cup sugar. Beat in eggs, one at a time. Combine flour, baking powder and salt. Fold dry ingredients into butter mixture. Pour into prepared pan. Bake 25 minutes or until cake springs back when lightly touched in center. Cool in pan for 5 minutes, then remove from pan and cool completely on wire rack. Cut into narrow pieces about 1 ½-inches by 4-inches. Set aside.

In large bowl, beat cream with electric mixer until soft peaks form. Beat in ¼ cup sugar and vanilla and continue to beat until stiff peaks form. Set aside.

Prepare vanilla pudding according to package directions. Set aside.

To Assemble Trifle: Brush each piece of cake with raspberry jam. Use half the cake pieces to line the bottom of a trifle bowl or other glass serving dish. Sprinkle half of the sherry over cake. Layer half the peaches, strawberries and blueberries on top. Cover with half the pudding and ⅓ of the whipped cream. Repeat layers with remaining cake, sherry, fruit and pudding. Top with remaining whipped cream. Chill in the refrigerator at least 30 minutes before serving.

POSSOM CREAM PIE

Mrs. Malinda's Recipe Collection

1 c. flour and crushed graham
  crackers
1 c. chopped pecans
1 stick margarine
1 (8 oz.) cream cheese
1 c. Cool Whip
1 c. powdered sugar

3 c. milk
1 pkg. instant vanilla pudding
1 pkg. instant chocolate
  pudding
¼ c. powdered sugar
1 tsp. vanilla flavoring

Bake flour, graham crackers, pecans and margarine 20 to 25 minutes at 325°. Cool.

Mix cream cheese, Cool Whip and powdered sugar; spread over crust. Spread milk, puddings, powdered sugar and vanilla mixture over creamed cheese mixture. Top with remainder of carton of Cool Whip and refrigerate.

MOLASSES CUSTARD PIE

First Lady Carolyn Green
Rialto, CA

1 c. molasses
1 c. sugar
3 eggs, beaten
2 Tbsp. flour

1 stick oleo, melted
1 tsp. vanilla
1 c. black walnuts (½ c. on top
  each pie)

Mix sugar with flour. Add molasses, beaten eggs, vanilla and oleo. Pour into unbaked pie crusts. Bake in a hot 400° oven for 10 to 15 minutes. Then bake at 350° to finish baking. Shake to see if center is firm. Delicious with black walnuts; then put Cool Whip on top. Makes 2 pies.

* * * * *

Name it and claim it.
Believe it and receive it.

BLACKBERRY ICE CREAM PIE

Mrs. Malinda's Recipe Collection

Crust:

9-inch Classic Crisco single crust

Filling:

1 (3 oz.) pkg. peach or berry
  flavor gelatin (not sugar-free)
1 c. boiling water
1 pt. vanilla ice cream,
  softened

1 ¾ c. fresh or frozen dry pack
  blackberries, partially
  thawed

For crust, prepare and bake (see Classic Crisco pie crust recipe). Cool.

For filling, combine gelatin and water in large bowl. Stir until dissolved. Cut ice cream into small chunks. Add to gelatin mixture, a spoonful at a time. Blend with wire whisk after each addition. Dry blackberries between paper towels. Fold into gelatin mixture. Spoon into cooled baked pie crust. Refrigerate or freeze several hours before serving. Makes one 9-inch pie, 8 servings.

* * * * *

MOLASSES REFRIGERATOR ICE CREAM

Mrs. Malinda's Recipe Collection

1 Tbsp. cornstarch
2 c. milk
2 eggs, separated
¼ c. sugar

⅓ c. molasses
1 tsp. vanilla
1 c. heavy cream

Combine cornstarch and ½ cup milk; mix smooth. Add remaining milk; cover over boiling water, stirring constantly, until slightly thickened. Beat egg yolks; add 2 tablespoons sugar. Add milk mixture; cook over hot water, stirring constantly, until mixture coats spoon. Add molasses and vanilla; chill. Beat egg whites stiff; gradually add remaining 2 tablespoons sugar, beating constantly. Whip cream; fold into molasses mixture with egg white mixture. Pour into tray of automatic refrigerator with cold control set at point recommended by manufacturer for freezing ice cream. Freeze to mush. Place in chilled bowl. Beat smooth; return to tray. Freeze firm. Makes about 1 quart.

* * * * *

CHOCOLATE FONDUE

Mrs. Malinda's Recipe Collection
(Grown Folks)

¾ c. heavy whipping cream
(reserve ¼ c. to thin if fondue
begins to thicken)
4 bittersweet chocolate bars,
chopped (3 ½ oz. each)

2 Tbsp. Frangelico or Amaretto
liqueur (optional)
¼ c. finely chopped hazelnuts
or almonds (optional)

Suggested Dippables*:

hazelnut or almond biscotti
salted pretzel sticks
cubed pound cake
sliced bananas

stem strawberries
sectioned navel oranges
ripe fresh diced pineapple

*Choose 3 or 4 selections.

Heat ½ cup cream in a heavy non-reactive saucepot over moderate heat until cream comes to a low boil. Remove the pan from the heat and add chocolate. Let the chocolate stand in hot cream 3 to 5 minutes to soften, then whisk chocolate together with the cream. Stir in liqueur and/or chopped nuts and transfer the fondue to a fondue pot or set the mixing bowl on a rack above a small lit candle. If fondue becomes too thick, stir in reserved cream, one tablespoon at a time, to desired consistency. Arrange your favorite dippables in piles on a platter alongside chocolate fondue with fondue forks, bamboo skewers or seafood forks, as utensils for dipping.

* * * * *

Oh how beautiful it is for brethren to dwell together in unity.

CHEESECAKE BAR

Lily Williams
Memphis, TN

1 pkg. Duncan Hines golden
  sugar cookie mix

1 Tbsp. water

78

Filling:

1 (8 oz.) cream cheese,
  softened
½ c. granulated sugar
1 egg

2 Tbsp. milk
1 Tbsp. lemon juice
½ tsp. vanilla

Preheat oven to 350°. Empty contents of the dry mix pouch and flavor packet into a large bowl. Add 1 tablespoon water. Mix until thoroughly blended. Save 1 cup of crumbs for topping. Press remaining crumb mixture into an ungreased 9 x 9 x 2-inch pan. Bake 12 to 15 minutes until lightly browned.

Filling: In a small bowl, blend softened cream cheese and sugar. Beat in egg, milk, lemon juice and vanilla. Beat until creamy. Pour over baked layer. Sprinkle with reserved crumbs. Return to oven and bake 25 minutes longer. Cool completely and cut into 18 bars. Store in the refrigerator.

* * * * *

DOWN HOME SWEET POTATO PIE

Mrs. Malinda's Recipe Collection

8 oz. cream cheese, softened
1 ¼ c. granulated sugar
2 large eggs
1 (15.5 oz.) can mashed yams
  or boil fresh yams until
  tender
1 (12 fluid oz.) can evaporated
  skim milk

1 Tbsp. pumpkin pie spice
2 (9-inch) deep-dish pie shells
2 c. coarsely chopped pecans
⅔ c. packed light brown sugar
4 Tbsp. melted butter
lightly whipped cream
  (optional)

Heat oven to 425°. Beat cream cheese with electric mixer until fluffy. Beat in sugar. Reduce mixer speed and add eggs, one at a time. Beat in yams, evaporated milk and pumpkin pie spice. Pour filling into pie shells. Bake pies 30 to 35 minutes until edges puff, crust browns and custard is set.

Meanwhile, mix the pecans, brown sugar and butter. Set aside. Remove pies from oven. Sprinkle with pecan mixture and return to oven 7 to 10 minutes longer, until topping is golden brown and crisp. Cool pies on rack completely. Garnish with whipped cream.

Note: If mashed yams are unavailable, puree a drained 16-ounce can of whole yams in a food processor until smooth.

* * * * *

EQUAL POTATO PIE

Mrs. Malinda's Recipe Collection

pastry for a single crust 9-inch
  pie
2 c. cooked mashed sweet
  potatoes
2 eggs, lightly beaten
1 c. Equal® Spoonful*
1 Tbsp. all-purpose flour

1 tsp. lemon juice
1 tsp. vanilla
½ tsp. ground cinnamon
½ tsp. ground nutmeg
½ tsp. salt
1 (12 fluid oz.) can evaporated
  fat-free milk

Roll pastry on a lightly floured surface into a circle 1-inch larger than inverted 9-inch pie pan. Ease pastry into pan; trim and flute edge.

Mix sweet potatoes with electric mixer in large bowl until smooth. Stir in eggs, Equal®, flour, lemon juice, vanilla, spices, salt and evaporated milk. Pour mixture into pastry shell. Bake in preheated 400° oven 40 to 45 minutes or until filling is set and sharp knife inserted into center comes out clean. Cool completely on wire rack. Refrigerate until serving time.

*May substitute 24 packets Equal® sweetener.

* * * * *

This little light of mine.
I'm going to let it shine.

AUNT BOBBIE'S BREAD PUDDING

Barbara Johnson-Simons
Los Angeles, CA

6 slices wheat bread
6 slices raisin bread
3 c. evaporated milk
1 box instant vanilla pudding
 (5 ½ oz.)
1 c. raisins
1 stick butter, melted

½ c. white sugar
6 slices white bread
6 eggs
2 tsp. vanilla flavoring
1 c. pecans
½ c. brown sugar

You will need a casserole dish.

Cut bread up in chunks. Mix vanilla pudding with milk, eggs and vanilla. Place 2 tablespoons melted butter in bottom of dish. Sprinkle 1 teaspoon brown sugar and 1 teaspoon white sugar over butter. Top with ½ of bread, raisins and pecans. Top with ½ pudding batter. Repeat remaining ingredients layered like a banana pudding. Place casserole in pan with 1-inch hot water in pan. Bake at 350° for 60 minutes. Makes 12 servings.

† KEY LIME PIE †

Mrs. Malinda's Recipe Collection

Crust:

1 ⅔ c. crushed graham
 crackers

¼ c. sugar
¼ c. soft butter or margarine

You will need an 8-inch pie pan. Combine ingredients and chill.

Filling:

2 eggs, separated
1 can Eagle Brand milk

½ c. fresh lime juice
1 grated lime rind

Beat yolks until light. Add milk and beat well. Fold in lime juice and rind. Beat egg whites until stiff; fold into lime filling. Pour into crust. Freeze.

KENTUCKY PIE

Mrs. Malinda's Recipe Collection

¾ c. semi-sweet chocolate
  chips
1 c. English walnuts, chopped
2 eggs, beaten
1 c. sugar

1 stick oleo, melted and
  cooled
½ c. flour
1 tsp. vanilla

82

Mix all together and pour into an unbaked pastry shell. Bake at 350° for 30 minutes.

† PECAN SLICES †

Diane "Mrs. Chicken" Ivy
Memphis, TN

1 pkg. Duncan Hines golden
  sugar cookie mix

1 egg
¼ c. sour cream

Topping:

2 beaten eggs
1 ½ c. brown sugar
1 c. chopped pecans
¼ c. coconut

2 Tbsp. flour
½ tsp. baking powder
¼ tsp. salt
1 tsp. vanilla

Preheat oven to 350°. Empty contents of the dry mix pouch and flavor packet into a large bowl. Add 1 egg and sour cream. Mix until thoroughly blended. Spread dough into an ungreased 9 x 13-inch pan. Bake 18 to 20 minutes or until lightly browned.

Mix topping ingredients together and spread over baked crust. Return to oven and bake 25 minutes. Cut into bars while warm.

* * * * *

Be blessed!

LEMON ICEBOX PIE

Mrs. Malinda's Recipe Collection

1 (8 oz.) can Borden Eagle
Brand milk
1 (9-inch) prepared graham
cracker pie crust

⅓ c. lemon juice
1 ½ c. Cool Whip
few drops yellow food coloring
(added to filling; optional)

Mix milk, lemon juice and Cool Whip in large bowl until smooth. Pour into pie crust. Chill in the refrigerator for 1 hour before serving.

† POLLY'S BLUEBERRY PIE †

Mrs. Malinda's Recipe Collection

1 c. sugar
1 tsp. cinnamon
3 Tbsp. cornstarch
blueberries (coat with sugar)

½ stick butter, cut up and put
on berries
1 tsp. nutmeg

Crust:

2 c. flour
2 Tbsp. Wesson oil

3 Tbsp. milk

Chill crust.
Pour blueberry mixture in pie crust. Sprinkle pinched off crust from sides on top and brown. Cook 30 minutes at 400° until berries bubble and crust browns.

* * * * *

I have never seen the righteous forsaken, nor his seed begging bread.

EASY OLD FASHION EGG CUSTARD (PIE)

Bettie Randle

84

3 eggs
1 c. sugar
1 c. milk
1 (9-inch) unbaked pie crust

1 Tbsp. butter
1 tsp. flour
1 Tbsp. vanilla extract

Beat eggs, sugar and flour. Gradually add vanilla. Cook in unbaked pie shell in oven at 350° until firm.

CHRISTMAS FRUIT COOKIES

Mrs. Malinda's Recipe Collection

3 c. flour
1 c. brown sugar
½ c. or 1 stick butter
4 eggs, well beaten
1 tsp. soda
3 Tbsp. buttermilk
1 tsp. nutmeg
1 tsp. cinnamon

½ c. whiskey
1 tsp. vanilla
1 lb. seedless white raisins
1 lb. candied pineapple
1 lb. candied cherries (red and green)
1 ½ lb. lb. pecans, chopped

Cut fruit in tiny pieces; add chopped pecans and raisins. Sprinkle with ¾ cup of the flour; toss to mix well and coat all fruit.

In separate bowl, cream butter and sugar. Add beaten eggs. Add remainder of flour and dry ingredients gradually. Add whiskey while beating, then vanilla. Pour batter over fruit and stir until all fruit is coated. Spoon with a teaspoon onto ungreased cookie sheet. Bake 15 minutes at 350° or until brown.

* * * * *

NORTH CAROLINA GRATED SWEET POTATO PUDDING

Mrs. Malinda's Recipe Collection

5 c. coarsely grated raw sweet
  potatoes
¾ c. brown sugar, packed
1 ½ c. milk
½ c. melted butter
3 eggs, well beaten
¼ tsp. powdered nutmeg
½ tsp. powdered cinnamon

¼ tsp. powdered allspice
¼ tsp. ground cloves
½ c. seedless raisins
½ c. shredded coconut
½ c. chopped pecans
½ tsp. grated orange or lemon
  rind

Mix all ingredients and pour into a buttered medium size casserole dish or skillet. Bake in a preheated 400° oven for 50 to 60 minutes.

As crust forms around edges, remove from oven and stir pudding well to mix crust throughout. Do this several times until baking is finished. Serve warm or cold; plain or topped with whipped cream or ice cream. Yield: 8 servings.

BANANA PUDDING

Mrs. Malinda's Recipe Collection

3 c. milk
1 large pkg. instant vanilla
  pudding
1 can Eagle Brand milk

1 large carton Cool Whip,
  divided
1 box vanilla wafers
4 large bananas

Mix milk and instant pudding until thick. Add Cool Whip (½ carton) and Eagle Brand milk; mix well. Lay vanilla wafers, bananas and pudding mixture. Top with Cool Whip.

MILE HIGH LEMON PIE

Mrs. Malinda's Recipe Collection

8 egg yolks, beaten
1 c. sugar
1 envelope unflavored gelatin
½ c. water
1 Tbsp. grated lemon peel

½ c. lemon juice
¼ tsp. salt
8 egg whites
¼ tsp. cream of tartar
1 c. sugar

Mix egg yolks, 1 cup sugar, gelatin, water, lemon peel, lemon juice and salt. Cook over medium heat, stirring constantly, just until mixture boils. Chill in the refrigerator, stirring once, until mixture mounds slightly when dropped from a spoon. Beat egg whites and cream of tartar until stiff and glossy. Add 1 cup sugar; beat again. Fold meringue into lemon mixture; pile into baked pie shell. Chill until set.

TEXAS COOKIES

Mrs. Malinda's Recipe Collection

1 ⅓ c. plain flour
3 Tbsp. sugar
¼ lb. oleo (room temperature)

1 can vanilla sour cream
    frosting
almond extract

Mix flour, sugar and oleo together until it forms a soft dough; roll into 1-inch balls. Place on ungreased cookie sheet. Press down each ball with your thumb to make an indentation. Bake at 250° for 20 minutes. Mix can of vanilla sour cream frosting with 1 cap almond extract. Tint to desired color and frost each indentation.

＊ ＊ ＊ ＊ ＊

SUN-MAID RAISIN CUPCAKES

Mrs. Malinda's Recipe Collection

1 c. Sun-Maid puffed raisins	1 ¾ c. flour
¼ c. butter	3 tsp. baking powder
¾ c. sugar	½ c. milk
1 egg	1 tsp. lemon extract

Slice or chop raisins. Cream butter with sugar; add beaten egg. Sift flour with baking powder and add alternately with milk to creamed mixture, mixing thoroughly. Add raisins and lemon extract; blend well. Fill greased muffin pans ½ full. Bake about 20 minutes in a moderate oven, 375° to 400°. This will make 12 to 14 medium sized cupcakes.

* * * * *

MAMA'S LEMON PIES

Mrs. Malinda's Recipe Collection

3 c. water
2 c. sugar
6 Tbsp. plain flour
4 egg yolks

2 lemons, grated rind and
  juice
pinch of salt
1 Tbsp. butter or margarine

Meringue:

4 egg whites
¼ tsp. cream of tartar

8 Tbsp. sugar

Bring water to a boil. Mix sugar, flour and salt thoroughly and pour slowly into boiling water, stirring constantly (be careful at this tends to lump). Cook slowly for 10 minutes. Add lemon rind and juice. Add about 1 to 1 ½ cups of hot mixture to egg yolks, then add this back to rest of hot mixture. Cook 5 minutes longer. Remove from heat and cool a few minutes. Pour into baked pie crusts. Put meringue on pies and bake at 300° until brown.

Meringue: Beat egg whites until really stiff. Add cream of tartar as whites begin to form stiff peaks. Add sugar, one tablespoon at a time, and beat until very stiff. Test by pressing between fingers or tasting to see if sugar particles are dissolved. Spread on pies.

Note: This recipe makes 2 pies.

≈ ❊ ❊ ❊ ❊

MAMA'S BEST PEACH COBBLER

Mrs. Malinda's Recipe Collection

4 to 5 large fresh peaches
2 Tbsp. sugar

1 ¼ tsp. nutmeg

Custard:

¼ c. brown sugar
¼ c. white sugar
1 heaping Tbsp. cornstarch
½ c. cold water

1 Tbsp. lemon juice
2 to 3 drops yellow food
   coloring

Topping:

1 ½ c. flour
½ c. sugar

½ c. milk
¼ c. soft margarine

Peel and slice peaches and arrange on bottom of a 2-quart baking dish. Set aside.

Custard: In saucepan, mix brown sugar and white sugar. Add cornstarch and cold water. Cook until thick and add lemon juice. Add food coloring. Pour custard over sliced peaches. Set aside.

Topping: Mix flour and sugar along with milk and soft margarine. Mix well. Spoon over top of peach cobbler.

In a small bowl, mix 2 tablespoons sugar and 1 ¼ teaspoons nutmeg. Sprinkle this over top of cobbler. Bake at 375° for 40 to 50 minutes.

* * * * *

MOMMA'S CHESS PIES

Mrs. Malinda's Recipe Collection

1 c. raisins
1 c. sugar
¼ c. butter or oleo
1 c. evaporated milk
1 c. water

1 Tbsp. flour
2 egg yolks (reserve whites)
1 c. chopped walnuts
1 tsp. vanilla

Combine raisins, sugar, butter or oleo, milk, water, flour and egg yolks; cook until thick. Cool. Add walnuts and vanilla. Make pie crust for 2-crust pie. Line 18 muffin cups with crust. Bake. Fill crust with cooked and cooled mixture. Beat egg whites until stiff. Add 2 tablespoons sugar and top pies. Brown.

* * * * *

There is a brighter day ahead.

SWEET POTATO AND PECAN PIE

Sis. Sheryl Scott

Layer 1:

1 (9-inch) ready-made pie crust

2 medium sweet potatoes, baked (1 c.)

¼ c. packed light brown sugar

2 Tbsp. sugar

½ egg, beaten well

1 Tbsp. heavy cream

1 Tbsp. unsalted butter, softened

1 Tbsp. vanilla extract

¼ tsp. salt

½ tsp. cinnamon

⅛ tsp. allspice

⅛ tsp. nutmeg

Layer 2:

¾ c. sugar

¾ c. dark corn syrup

2 small eggs

1 ½ Tbsp. butter, melted

2 tsp. vanilla extract

pinch of salt (only if using unsalted butter)

pinch of cinnamon

¾ c. pecan halves

In a bowl, combine all the first layer ingredients. Beat the mixture on medium speed for 2 minutes. Do not overbeat; set aside. Combine all of the second layer ingredients, except for the pecans, in another bowl. Mix well on low speed with an electric mixer until the mixture is opaque (1 minute). Slowly stir in the pecans and set aside.

To assemble, spoon the sweet potato mixture into the pie crust evenly. Pour the pecan mixture on top. Bake at 325° for 1 hour and 45 minutes or until toothpick inserted in middle comes out clean. Eat within 24 hours or refrigerate.

* * * * *

According to your faith it shall be done unto you.

BANANA PUDDING II

Mrs. Malinda's Recipe Collection

⅔ c. sugar
3 Tbsp. plus 2 tsp. all-purpose
   flour
dash of salt
1 (14 oz.) can sweetened
   condensed milk
2 ½ c. milk

4 eggs, separated
2 tsp. vanilla extract
1 (12 oz.) pkg. vanilla wafers
6 large bananas
¼ c. plus 2 Tbsp. sugar
½ tsp. banana extract

Combine ⅔ cup sugar, flour and salt in a heavy saucepan. Combine both milks and egg yolks; stir well. Add to dry ingredients. Cook over medium heat, stirring constantly, until smooth and thickened. Remove pudding mixture from heat; stir in vanilla. Arrange ⅓ of wafers in the bottom of a 3-quart baking dish. Slice 2 bananas and layer over wafers. Pour ⅓ of pudding mixture over bananas. Repeat layers twice, arranging remaining wafers around outside edge of dish. Beat egg whites (at room temperature) at high speed of an electric mixer until soft peaks form. Gradually add ¼ cup plus 2 tablespoons sugar, 1 tablespoon at a time, beating until stiff peaks form. Fold in banana extract. Spread meringue over pudding, sealing to edge of dish. Bake at 425° for 6 to 8 minutes or until meringue is golden brown. Yield: 8 to 10 servings.

* * * * *

PEANUT BUTTER CHOCOLATE CHIP COOKIES OF LOVE

Dorothy Milton
Pasadena, CA

1 c. peanut butter
1 c. butter or margarine
2 eggs
1 tsp. vanilla flavoring
1 c. sugar

1 c. brown sugar, firmly
  packed
2 ½ c. flour
½ tsp. salt
½ tsp. baking soda
¾ c. chocolate chips

Cream peanut butter and margarine. Add sugars; blend well. Add vanilla flavoring. Mix flour, salt and baking powder together (until well mixed). A little at a time, add to peanut butter mixture. Fold in chocolate chips. Place in sealed container. Leave in the refrigerator 2 hours or overnight. Drop by teaspoon onto cookie sheet (ungreased). Bake in 375° oven 10 to 12 minutes.

TOMATO PIE

Mrs. Malinda's Recipe Collection

3 c. sliced green tomatoes
1 ½ c. sugar
3 Tbsp. flour
¼ tsp. salt

3 Tbsp. lemon juice
4 tsp. grated lemon rind
1 recipe plain pastry
3 Tbsp. butter or margarine

Combine tomatoes, sugar, flour, salt, lemon juice and grated rind and pour into a pastry-lined pie plate. Dot with butter. Add top crust. Bake for 10 minutes in very hot oven, 450°, then at 350°, moderate, for 30 minutes or until the tomatoes are tender. Serve with a wedge of mild cheese and plenty of black coffee. Delicious.

DOUBLE LAYER PUMPKIN PIE

Sister Shirley Bickham
Lancaster, CA

4 oz. Philadelphia cream cheese, softened
1 Tbsp. milk
1 Tbsp. sugar
1 Honey Maid graham crust (6 oz.)
1 (8 oz.) tub Cool Whip, thawed and divided
1 c. milk
1 (15 oz.) can pumpkin
2 small pkg. Jell-O vanilla instant pudding and pie filling
1 tsp. ground cinnamon
½ tsp. ground ginger
¼ tsp. ground cloves

Mix cream cheese, 1 tablespoon milk and sugar in large bowl with wire whisk until well blended. Gently stir in half of the whipped topping. Spread into the crust. Pour 1 cup milk into large bowl. Add pumpkin, DRY pudding mixes and spices. Beat with wire whisk until well blended. Mixture will be thick. Spread over cream cheese layer. Refrigerate 4 hours or until set. Top with remaining whipped topping. Makes 10 servings. Prep time: 20 minutes plus refrigeration.

CHEESECAKE COOKIE CUPS

Mrs. Malinda's Recipe Collection

12 pieces Nestlé Toll House refrigerated chocolate chip cookie bar dough
1 (8 oz.) pkg. cream cheese, softened
½ c. Carnation sweetened condensed milk
1 large egg
1 tsp. vanilla extract
1 (21 oz.) can cherry pie filling

Preheat oven to 325°. Paper line 12 muffin cups.

Place 1 piece of cookie dough in each prepared muffin cup. Bake for 10 to 12 minutes or until cookie has spread to edge of cup. Beat cream cheese, sweetened condensed milk, egg and vanilla extract in medium bowl until smooth. Pour about 3 tablespoons cream cheese mixture over each cookie in cup. Bake for an additional 15 to 18 minutes or until set. Cool completely in pan on wire rack. Top with pie filling. Refrigerate for 1 hour.

GOOEY BABY RUTH BROWNIES

Mrs. Malinda's Recipe Collection

1 (18.25 oz.) pkg. chocolate
  brownie mix
3 (2.1 oz.) Nestlé Baby Ruth
  candy bars, chopped

1 (8 oz.) pkg. cream cheese
  (at room temperature)
½ c. granulated sugar
1 large egg
2 tsp. milk

Preheat oven to 350°. Grease 13 x 9-inch baking pan. Prepare brownie batter according to package directions; stir in chopped Baby Ruth. Pour into prepared pan. Beat cream cheese and sugar in small mixer bowl until smooth. Beat in egg and milk. Using knife or spatula, swirl cream cheese mixture into brownie batter to create a marbling effect. Bake for 35 to 40 minutes or until wooden pick inserted in center comes out almost clean. Cool completely in pan on wire rack. Cut into bars using wet knife.

GRANNY SMITH APPLE PECAN PIE

Balinda Moore
Memphis, TN

½ c. brown sugar
2 c. pecans
1 bottom and 1 top pie crust
4 to 6 Granny Smith's apples,
  peeled and sliced

½ lemon, juiced
1 tsp. cinnamon
2 c. caramel

Slice and peel apples. Coat with lemon juice and cinnamon. Place pecans flat side up in brown sugar in pie pan. Place 1 pie crust over pecan mixture. Fill with half of the apples. Cover with half of the caramel. Fill with remaining apples. Cover with remaining caramel. Top with last pie crust. Cook at 350° for 50 minutes. Cool 5 minutes (only). Place plate over pie and invert onto another plate.

COCONUT PIES

1 Tbsp. Crisco
2 c. sifted flour
2 tsp. sugar
1 Tbsp. flour

1 tsp. salt
1 stick butter
4 Tbsp. ice water

Cut shortening into dry ingredients until the consistency of coarse meal. Stir in ice water and work dough with hands. Chill in the refrigerator. Roll out on a floured board and cut into circles about 3 ½-inches in diameter. Put a spoonful of the Coconut Filling in the center of each and fold over. Seal together with the tines of a fork. Bake at 350° for about 25 minutes or until brown. Sprinkle with powdered sugar while hot.

Filling:

2 c. grated coconut
¼ c. toasted almonds
3 egg yolks

½ c. sugar
½ c. water
2 tsp. whiskey

Boil sugar and water to a syrup. Add coconut and cook until a little dry. Beat egg yolks and fold in the coconut after it has cooled. Add almonds and whiskey to taste. Makes 18 pies.

* * * * *

COOKIE ON A STICK

Mrs. Malinda's Recipe Collection

1 (18 oz.) pkg. Nestlé Toll House refrigerated chocolate chip cookie dough or 1 batch chocolate chip cookies

1 container decorator icing (various colors; optional)
1 pkg. candies (optional)
1 melted chocolate (optional)

You will need 8 wooden craft sticks.

Preheat oven to 375°. Shape cookie dough into 8 (2-inch) balls. Place 4 balls at a time onto an ungreased baking sheet. Insert wooden sticks into each ball to resemble a lollipop; flatten dough slightly. Bake for 13 to 15 minutes or until edges are crisp. Cool on baking sheet for 1 minute; remove to wire racks to cool completely. Decorate as desired. Tie ribbons around sticks and give as a cookie bouquet.

JIM'S OLD FASHIONED SPICED PEACH PIE

Jimmy Lenton
for Bettie Randle
Memphis, TN

pastry for 2-crust 9-inch pie
¾ c. sugar
¼ c. flour
1 tsp. cinnamon
¼ tsp. nutmeg
⅛ tsp. salt

6 c. sliced peeled peaches (about 7 peaches)
1 egg, lightly beaten
1 c. heavy cream or light cream

In large bowl, combine sugar, flour, cinnamon, nutmeg and salt. Add peaches and toss until peaches are coated. Spoon into pastry shell. Blend egg with cream and pour over peaches. Roll remaining pastry to cover pie; trim edges and flute to seal. Prick top of pastry to let steam escape. Bake in a preheated 425° oven for 10 minutes; reduce heat to 350° and bake for 25 minutes or longer.

LEMON ICEBOX PIE II

Pastor Beatrice Davis, '92 Silver, '96 Gold
Olympic Track and Field Medalist, Coach
Memphis, TN

98

1 (8 or 9-inch) graham cracker
crust
1 (14 oz.) can sweetened
condensed milk

1 (6 oz.) can frozen lemonade
concentrate, thawed
1 small carton nondairy
whipped topping, thawed

Beat milk and lemonade until thick. Fold in nondairy topping and pour into pie shell. Top with whipped cream if desired. Serves 8.

MINCEMEAT PIE WITH TOPPING

Mrs. Malinda's Recipe Collection

1 (9-inch) pie shell (unbaked)

1 large jar mincemeat

Topping:

¼ c. margarine, softened
½ c. all-purpose flour
⅓ c. coconut

½ c. brown sugar
½ c. pecans, chopped

Pour mincemeat into pie shell. In a mixing bowl, cut margarine and flour together with a pastry blender. Add rest of ingredients; mix well. Sprinkle topping on pie. Bake in a 400° oven 20 to 25 minutes or until brown. Serves 8 to 10.

* * * * *

Love thy neighbor as thyself.

MOLASSES PIE

Mrs. Malinda's Recipe Collection

2 c. dark molasses
½ tsp. soda
1 tsp. butter

3 eggs, beaten lightly
¼ c. sugar
½ tsp. vanilla

Warm molasses. Add soda and stir until foams. Combine sugar and beaten eggs and blend into molasses. Add butter and vanilla and pour into unbaked pastry shell. Put into a 450° oven for 15 minutes, then reduce to 325° for about 35 minutes or until filling is set.

OATMEAL COOKIES

Mrs. Malinda's Recipe Collection
(Alternate Dessert)

1 c. shortening
2 c. flour
3 c. 3-minute oats
1 tsp. baking powder
1 tsp. cinnamon
1 c. chopped dates

1 c. sugar
2 eggs, beaten
¼ c. milk
½ tsp. soda
¼ tsp. salt
1 c. chopped nuts

Cream shortening and sugar; add eggs. Mix the rest of the dry ingredients and sprinkle over the dates and nuts. Combine the mixtures, adding only enough milk to make a stiff dough. Drop on a greased tin 1-inch apart. Bake 10 to 12 minutes at 350°. Makes 4 dozen.

* * * * *

Do unto others as you would have them do unto you.

PEACH COBBLER

Mrs. Malinda's Recipe Collection

½ c. sugar
1 Tbsp. cornstarch
¼ tsp. ground cinnamon
4 c. sliced peaches
  (approximately 6)
1 Tbsp. lemon juice

3 Tbsp. shortening
1 c. all-purpose flour
1 Tbsp. sugar
1 ½ tsp. baking powder
½ tsp. salt
½ c. milk

Heat oven to 400°. Mix ½ cup sugar, cornstarch and cinnamon in 2-quart saucepan. Stir in peaches and lemon juice. Cook, stirring constantly, until mixture thickens and boils. Boil and stir 1 minute. Pour into ungreased 2-quart casserole. Keep peach mixture hot in oven. Cut shortening into flour, 1 tablespoon sugar, baking powder and salt until mixture resembles fine crumbs. Stir in milk. Drop by 6 spoonfuls onto hot peach mixture. Bake until topping is golden brown, approximately 25 to 30 minutes. Serve warm, and if desired, with whipped cream.

SHOO-FLY PIES

Mrs. Malinda's Recipe Collection

2 (9-inch) pie crusts
3 c. flour
½ c. sugar
½ c. shortening

1 c. Grandma's molasses
1 c. hot water
1 Tbsp. baking soda

Make 2 pie crusts. Mix together flour, sugar and shortening; crumble. Mix molasses and water, then add baking soda. Pour molasses mixture, alternately with crumbled flour, ending with flour mixture into unbaked pie shells. Bake at 350° for 30 minutes. Makes 2 pies.

SOUTHERN PEACH FRIED PIES

Mrs. Malinda's Recipe Collection

3 c. fresh peach slices (about
  5 peaches)**
½ c. sugar
2 Tbsp. butter or margarine
1 ½ tsp. vanilla
½ tsp. ground nutmeg

1 ½ c. all-purpose flour
¾ tsp. salt
½ c. lard or shortening
5 Tbsp. cold water
cooking oil (for shallow frying)

**When fresh peaches aren't available, you can substitute unsweetened frozen sliced peaches.

In a large heavy saucepan, combine the sliced peaches, sugar, butter or margarine, vanilla and nutmeg. Bring the peach mixture to boiling; reduce heat. Boil gently, uncovered, about 1 hour or until of jam consistency, stirring occasionally. Cool 1 hour.

Combine the flour and salt. With a pastry cutter or 2 knives, cut in large until pieces are the size of small peas. Sprinkle 1 tablespoon of water over part of the mixture; gently toss with a fork. Push to side of bowl. Repeat until all is moistened. Form into a ball.

On a lightly floured surface, roll the dough to ⅛-inch thickness. Cut the dough into 5-inch circles. Place about 1 rounded tablespoonful of the peach mixture on half of each circle. Fold circle in half; seal well with tines of a fork.

In a skillet, heat ¼-inch cooking oil to 375°. Fry the peach pies for 3 to 4 minutes or until golden, turning pies once. Drain the fried pies on paper towels. Serve the pies warm or cool. Makes 8 to 10 fried pies.

* * * * *

SOUTHERN PECAN PIE

Mrs. Malinda's Recipe Collection

1 (9-inch) pie shell (unbaked)
¼ c. butter
1 c. sugar
1 c. white corn syrup

1 c. pecan halves
3 eggs, well beaten with a fork
1 tsp. vanilla
¼ tsp. salt

Cream butter and sugar together until fluffy. Add white corn syrup, pecan halves, well beaten eggs, vanilla and salt. Pour into unbaked pie shell. Bake in 450° oven for 10 minutes. Reduce temperature to 350°. Bake 35 minutes longer or until knife inserted comes out clean. Serves 8.

SPECIAL PEACH COBBLER

Mrs. Malinda's Recipe Collection

2 ½ c. fresh peaches, sliced
    and peeled
1 c. sugar
1 stick butter (½ c.)

1 ¼ c. flour
2 tsp. baking powder
¾ c. milk
pinch of salt

Place 1 stick of butter in a baking dish and melt it. Prepare batter from remaining ingredients, adding some of the melted butter. Pour it into baking dish over the remaining melted butter. Do not stir. Arrange fruit on top; again, do not stir. Bake at 350° for 45 minutes or until top is brown and crisp. Batter rises to top during baking.

Use a 9 x 13-inch pan.

* * * * *

TASSIES OR MINIATURE PECAN PIES

Mrs. Malinda's Recipe Collection

Crust:

1 stick butter or oleo

1 (3 oz.) pkg. cream cheese

Filling:

¾ c. brown sugar
1 Tbsp. soft oleo
1 egg

1 tsp. vanilla
1 c. nuts, chopped

Crust: Cream butter or oleo and cream cheese. Stir in flour. Mix well. Chill. When ready to use, shape into 24 (1-inch) balls. Put in ungreased muffin tins and shape.

Filling: Cream sugar and oleo. Add egg and vanilla. Mix well. Add nuts. Put mixture into the uncooked shells. Bake at 325° for 20 to 25 minutes. Makes 24 (1 ½-inch) pies.

TEA CAKES

Mrs. Malinda's Recipe Collection

2 c. self-rising flour
1 c. sugar
1 tsp. vanilla extract

2 eggs
½ c. margarine

Mix together all ingredients. Dough needs to be cold or use butter out of the tub instead of melted butter. Roll in teaspoon size balls. Put on cookie sheet and mash down. Bake at 375° for 10 minutes or until they are slightly brown on bottom.

* * * * *

LEMON SUGAR COOKIES

Mrs. Malinda's Recipe Collection

½ c. margarine
1 c. sugar
1 egg
1 egg yolk
1 ½ c. sifted flour

1 tsp. baking powder
½ tsp. salt
¼ c. lemon juice
grated rind of 1 lemon

Cream margarine. Work in sugar until mixture is smooth. Beat the whole egg and the extra egg yolk slightly and stir into the sugar combination. Sift flour, baking powder and salt together. Add it alternately with the lemon juice, beating hard after each addition. Mix in lemon rind. Set oven to 350° and grease cookie sheet. Drop batter by teaspoonfuls on cookie sheet and bake 10 minutes. Remove.

* * * * *

CHOCOLATE CARAMEL PECAN PIE

Shirley Bickham
Lancaster, CA

3 c. Planters pecan pieces, divided
¼ c. (½ stick) butter or margarine
1 pkg. (8 sq.) Baker's semi-sweet baking chocolate

¼ c. powdered sugar
¼ c. granulated sugar
⅔ c. whipping cream, divided
½ tsp. vanilla

Preheat oven to 350°. Place 2 cups of pecans in food processor. Cover processor until finely ground, using pulsing action. Mix with granulated sugar and butter. Press into 9-inch pan. Bake 12 minutes until lightly browned. Cool completely. (If crust puffs up during baking, gently press down with back of spoon.)

Microwave caramels and ⅓ cup of whipping cream in microwavable bowl on High for 3 minutes or until caramels melt (stirring after each minute). Pour into crust. Chop remaining 1 cup pecans and sprinkle over pie.

Place chocolate, remaining whipping cream, powdered sugar and vanilla in saucepan. Cook and stir on low heat until chocolate is melted. Pour over pie. Gently spread to cover top of pie. Refrigerate at least 2 hours. Makes 10 servings. Prep: 30 minutes plus refrigeration.

✿ ✿ ✿ ✿ ✿

PIE CRUST

For 2 (9-Inch) Pies or 1 (2-Crust) Pie:

1 ⅔ c. all-purpose white flour   ¾ c. shortening
½ tsp. salt   ⅓ c. whole-wheat flour

For 4 (9-Inch) Pies or 5 (8-Inch) Pies:

3 ⅓ c. all-purpose white flour   1 ½ c. shortening
1 tsp. salt   ⅔ c. whole-wheat flour

Cut shortening into larger quantity of flour and salt until pieces are size of small peas. Measure smaller amount of flour into separate bowl. Stir water in this flour to form a paste. Pour flour paste over shortening and flour mixture. Mix with fork until dough comes together into a ball. Divide into number of pies being made. Roll to about ⅛-inch thick.

For Baked Pie Crust Only: Bake at 350° around 15 minutes. To prevent shrinkage, crust can be put on outside of pie pan. Pack. Bake with pie pan upside down.

* * * * *

COCONUT LOG

Sean Boston
Carson, CA

1 lb. box vanilla wafers
1 can Eagle Brand milk
2 c. chopped pecans

1 c. raisins
1 can coconut

Crush vanilla wafers until fine (rolling wafers between waxed paper with rolling pin is an easy way). Pour into large bowl; add other ingredients and mix well with large spoon or faster by hands. It will be a very stiff mixture. Form into logs any size you choose by putting margarine on your hands to make them roll out smoothly. Powdered sugar can be added to the rolls to handle better (so they will not be tacky). They can then be wrapped tightly in Saran Wrap, waxed paper or foil and stored in the refrigerator. They slice like a jelly roll after chilling and can be made days or weeks ahead of a special occasion.

* * * * *

Come let us reason together.

CHEESECAKE COOKIES

Ms. Toria S. Randle
Memphis, TN

Crust:

½ c. brown sugar, packed
¾ c. all-purpose flour

½ c. chopped nuts
⅓ c. melted butter

Preheat oven to 350°. Grease an 8-inch square baking pan; set aside.

In small bowl, mix sugar, flour and nuts until blended, then stir in butter until well mixed. Reserve ⅓ cup of crumbs. Pat remaining crumbs into pan. Bake 15 minutes.

Filling:

1 (8 oz.) pkg. softened cream
    cheese
½ c. sugar

2 Tbsp. milk
1 egg
1 tsp. vanilla extract

Beat cream cheese and sugar at high speed until smooth. Beat in remaining ingredients. Pour over crust and sprinkle with reserved crumbs. Bake 25 minutes until set. Cool on a wire rack. When cool, cut into 2-inch squares and cut each square diagonally in half. Makes 32 triangle cookies.

PEANUT BRITTLE

Mrs. Malinda's Recipe Collection

2 c. sugar
1 c. white Karo
2 tsp. soda

3 c. raw peanuts
c. water

Place sugar, peanuts, Karo and water in saucepan. Cook to 290° on candy thermometer. Remove from fire and add soda. Pour onto a well-greased cookie sheet. When cool, break into pieces.

SOUR CREAM PECAN PIE

Mrs. Malinda's Recipe Collection

2 eggs, beaten
1 c. sour cream
¼ tsp. lemon extract
¼ tsp. cloves
½ pt. cream, whipped

1 c. sugar
1 tsp. flour
½ tsp. cinnamon
1 c. nuts
pastry shell (unbaked)

Beat eggs and add rest of the ingredients. Line pastry shell with nuts. Pour custard over and bake at 450° for 10 minutes, then lower heat to 325° and bake for about 40 minutes or until firm. Serve with whipped cream.

BOILED CUSTARD ICE CREAM

Mrs. Malinda's Recipe Collection

12 eggs
2 ½ to 3 c. sugar
2 qt. whole milk
1 pt. cream

1 can sweetened condensed
 milk
¾ tsp. salt
3 Tbsp. cornstarch
3 Tbsp. vanilla extract

Separate the eggs; beat yolks well, adding sugar, cornstarch and salt. Start heating the milk, then add the beaten yolk mixture to it slowly, stirring constantly. Cook in top of double boiler or in saucepan over direct heat. Continue stirring. Cook custard until mixture thinly coats spoon. Never let it boil. Remove pan from heat and stir in beaten egg whites, beaten light and fluffy. Let custard cool, then stir in vanilla and add cream and condensed milk. Fill gallon freezer only about ¾ full of custard to allow for expansion. Don't be skimpy with salt. Use at least ¾ of a box, alternating with a layer of ice and layer of salt.

ORANGE BASKETS

Mrs. Malinda's Recipe Collection

Cut a large orange in shape of a basket, leaving a handle. Scoop out the interior and fill with creme de menthe, sherbet or ice cream. A Japanese umbrella looks very pretty stuck into the ice cream.

GERMAN CHOCOLATE PIES

Mrs. Malinda's Recipe Collection

3 pie crusts	1 stick margarine
3 c. sugar	1 tall can evaporated milk
7 Tbsp. cocoa	2 c. coconut
pinch of salt	1 c. pecans
4 eggs	1 tsp. vanilla

Melt margarine over low heat. Stir in beaten eggs, sugar, cocoa, salt, evaporated milk, coconut, pecans and vanilla; mix well. Pour into 3 unbaked pie shells. Bake at 350° for approximately 45 minutes. Pies will feel firm when done.

OLD-FASHIONED CUSTARD ICE CREAM

Mrs. Malinda's Recipe Collection

2 qt. milk	12 egg yolks
1 c. sugar	2 tsp. vanilla
1 pt. heavy cream	½ pt. single cream

Beat the egg yolks until light. Add sugar. Gradually stir in milk. Cook in a double boiler until the custard coats the spoon. Cool. Add vanilla and cream. Freeze in a gallon freezer.

FRESH FRUIT ICE CREAM

Barbara Tillman
Pasadena, CA

3 c. half and half (1 ½ pt.)
1 (14 oz.) can Eagle Brand
  condensed milk
1 c. pureed or mashed fresh
  fruit

1 Tbsp. vanilla extract
peaches, strawberries,
  bananas, etc.*

*For vanilla ice cream, omit fruit; use 4 cups half and half.

In ice cream freezer, electric or hand-crank type, combine all ingredients; mix well. Pour into ice cream container. Freeze according to manufacturer's instructions. Freeze leftover. Makes 1 ½ quarts. Triple to make 5 quarts. Hum Hum Good.

BUTTER PECAN ICE CREAM

Mrs. Malinda's Recipe Collection

3 Tbsp. margarine
1 c. chopped pecans
4 eggs
2 c. sugar

3 tsp. vanilla
1 (13 oz.) can evaporated milk
1 can Eagle Brand milk
½ gal. sweet milk

Melt margarine. Add pecans; set aside. Beat eggs with sugar. Add vanilla. Mix all ingredients and pour into freezer can. Add sweet milk. Makes 1 gallon.

* * * * *

We will sit at the welcome table.

UNCLE JOHN'S ICE CREAM

Mrs. Malinda's Recipe Collection

1 ½ c. sugar
2 to 3 Tbsp. cornstarch
1 tsp. salt
10 beaten eggs
1 can sweetened condensed
  milk

1 (13 oz.) can evaporated milk
1 c. milk
2 c. cold milk
½ tsp. almond extract
2 to 4 Tbsp. vanilla

For a 4 to 5-quart freezer.

Mix in a large saucepan. In a double boiler, bring to a boil the sugar, cornstarch and salt, stirring constantly. When it starts to thicken, remove from heat. Immediately add 2 cups cold milk, almond extract and vanilla. Pour into freezer can and finish filling to fill line with milk (or half and half). Freeze according to freezer directions.

* * * * *

Bread of heaven feed me until I want no more.

PEACHY KEEN ICE CREAM

Mrs. Malinda's Recipe Collection

2 lb. ripe peaches
1 Tbsp. lemon juice
¾ c. sugar

1 c. milk
3 c. heavy cream
1 Tbsp. pure vanilla extract

Peel, pit and slice peaches, reserving peels and pits. Combine the peach slices, lemon juice and ¼ cup sugar; then set aside.

In a saucepan, combine the milk, cream, remaining sugar, vanilla and peach peels and pits; cook, stirring over medium heat, for 10 minutes. Do not boil. Remove from heat. Place yolks in a bowl and whisking constantly, pour in 1 cup of the hot milk mixture; continue whisking until smooth. Slowly pour the egg mixture back into the hot milk mixture in the saucepan, whisking constantly until smooth. Place the saucepan over medium heat and stir the mixture constantly until it is thick enough to coat the back of a spoon (6 to 8 minutes). The mixture should never boil. Cool to room temperature and then strain into a bowl. Puree the reserved peaches in a food processor until smooth. Stir into the milk mixture and freeze in an ice cream maker according to the manufacturer's instructions. Makes about 2 quarts to serve 16.

BLACK WALNUT CANDY

Mrs. Malinda's Recipe Collection

2 ½ c. sugar
½ c. water
2 egg whites

½ c. white Karo
3 c. black walnuts, chopped
1 tsp. vanilla

Mix sugar, Karo and water and let stand 30 minutes. Put egg whites in bowl with a pinch of salt. Put syrup on to boil and when it sticks in cold water, pour half of it over stiffly beaten egg whites. Return rest of syrup to the fire and as soon as it crystallizes in water, pour into egg mixture which has been beaten continuously. Beat all 1 hour or more. Add vanilla and nuts last. Pour into pan to harden.

YOUR FAVORITE RECIPES

Recipe

Breads

&

Vegetables

Baking Tips

COMMON PROBLEMS (Common Failures)	CAUSES OF PROBLEMS (Causes of Failures)

Biscuits

Rough biscuits	Insufficient mixing
Dry biscuits	Baking in too slow an oven and handling too much
Uneven browning	Cooking in dark surface pan, too high a temperature and rolling the dough too thin

Breads (yeast)

Porous bread	Over-rising or cooking at too low a temperature
Crust is dark and blisters just under the crust	Under-rising
Bread does not rise	Over-kneading or using old yeast
Bread is streaked	Under-kneading and not kneading evenly
Bread bakes unevenly	Using old, dark pans, too much dough in pan, crowding the oven shelf or cooking at too high a temperature

Cakes

Cracks and uneven surface	Too much flour, too hot an oven and sometimes from cold oven start
Dry cakes	Too much flour, too little shortening, too much baking powder or cooking at too low a temperature
Heavy cakes	Too much sugar or baking too short a period
Sticky crust	Too much sugar
Coarse grained cake	Too little mixing, too much shortening, too much baking powder, using shortening too soft, and baking at too low a temperature
Fallen cakes	Using insufficient flour, under baking, too much sugar, too much shortening or not enough baking powder
Uneven color	Cooking at too high a temperature, crowding the shelf (allow at least 2 inches around pans) or using dark pans
Uneven browning	Not mixing well

Cookies

Uneven browning	Not using shiny cookie sheet or not allowing at least 2 inches on all sides of cookie sheets in oven
Soggy cookies	Cooling cookies in pans instead of racks
Excessive spreading of cookies	Dropping cookies onto hot cookie sheets; not chilling dough; not baking at correct temperature

Muffins

Coarse texture	Insufficient stirring and cooking at too low a temperature
Tunnels in muffins, peaks in center and soggy texture	Over-mixing

Pies

Pastry crumbles	Over-mixing flour and shortening
Pastry tough	Using too much water and over-mixing the dough
Pies do not brown (fruit or custard)	Bake at constant temperature (400-425 degrees) in Pyrex or enamel pie pan

Breads & Vegetables

HUSH PUPPIES

Mrs. Malinda's Recipe Collection

2 c. corn meal
salt and pepper to taste

onion, finely chopped to taste
hot water

To corn meal, add salt, pepper and finely chopped onion. Add enough hot water to make stiff dough. Mold with hands into small pones. Fry in deep hot oil until done. Good with fish or turnip greens.

* * * * *

THE BISHOP'S SUGAR CRISP ROLLS

Bishop T.E. Medlock
Presiding Bishop
Pasadena, CA

(Makes 1 ½ Dozen)

2 to 2 ½ c. unsifted flour	¼ c. water
1 ¼ c. sugar	¼ c. margarine
½ tsp. salt	1 egg (at room temperature)
1 pkg. active dry yeast	¼ c. milk

In a large bowl, thoroughly mix ¾ cup flour, ¼ cup sugar, salt and undissolved active dry yeast.

Combine milk, water and ¼ cup margarine in a saucepan. Heat over low heat until liquids are warm. (Margarine does not need to melt.) Gradually add to dry ingredients and beat 2 minutes at medium speed of electric mixer, scraping bowl occasionally. Add egg and ¼ cup flour or enough flour to make a thick batter. Beat at high speed 2 minutes, scraping bowl occasionally. Stir in enough additional flour to make a soft dough. Turn out onto lightly floured board; knead until smooth and elastic, about 8 to 10 minutes. Cover and let rise in a warm place, free from draft until doubled in bulk, about 1 hour. Punch down and let rise an additional 30 minutes. Punch dough down; turn out onto lightly floured board. Roll dough as if making biscuits, then cut out with biscuit cutter and place on a well-greased baking sheet. Cover and allow to rise in a warm place, free from draft until double in bulk, about 30 minutes. Bake in a moderate oven at 375° about 10 to 15 minutes or until done.

* * * * *

JAYBO'S MOMMA'S MONKEY BREAD

Jeremiah Johnson
Los Angeles, CA

This is one of the greatest baked breads of all time. It takes time and it's good for big meals around the holidays or special occasions. It has simple ingredients. This dish gives you RESPECT in the kitchen. Make sure you have 6 hours to hang around the house to make this bread. It takes about 90 minutes of work and 6 hours of attention. It is well worth the time. Go for it!

5 lb. all-purpose flour
1 c. sugar
2 eggs
3 pkg. yeast
1 lb. butter

1 Tbsp. salt
3 drops yellow food coloring
4 c. plus ¾ c. hot water (not boiling)

You will need a 9 x 16 x 2 baking pan, mixer, large bowl, pastry brush and pizza cutter.

In large mixing bowl on slow speed, add sugar, salt and ½ pound of softened butter. Add eggs and 4 cups of hot water and mix well. Add flour, 2 cups at a time, until you have a liquid texture similar to pancake mix.

In separate small bowl, use ¾ cup of hot water (not boiling) and the entire 3 packs of yeast. Mix until yeast has completely dissolved. Add yeast mixture to large bowl; mix well. The mixture should have a grayish look. Now is the time to add food coloring. Mix well. This will give it a buttery look.

Continue to add flour until you have a firm dough ball. Soon after adding flour, the mixture will become difficult to mix. Remove mixer from bowl. Use large spoon and fold flour in until you have a firm dough ball.

Sprinkle dough ball with a small amount of flour to keep from sticking to side of bowl. Cover bowl with large piece of plastic wrap. Make sure wrap is touching dough ball. Place in warm atmosphere (on top of refrigerator). Let it sit for approximately 2 hours.

Brush pan with butter. Use enough butter to cover pan sides and bottom. Melt remaining butter (reserve).

The dough should rise over the top of large bowl. Clear an area large enough to spread the contents of the bowl (add small amount of flour to cover counter to keep dough from sticking). Roll out dough to approximately ¼-inch or a little thinner is okay. Use pizza cutter and cut dough into 1-inch squares. Place squares into large pan, covering the bottom completely. Keep the squares close together. Use pastry brush with melted butter to cover any exposed floured dough.

Place enough plastic wrap over pan to completely cover pan. Let bread rise again in warm atmosphere, approximately 1 hour.

Preheat oven to 400°. Remove plastic and place pan in oven for 20 minutes. Check after 12 minutes; you may have to rotate pan to make sure it browns evenly. When bread is golden brown, remove from oven and brush lightly with butter while it's still hot. Pull bread apart. Go ahead, taste this bread, make a Monkey out of yourself.

* * * * *

Peace on earth, good will toward men.

FRENCH TOAST WITH CINNAMON SYRUP

Mrs. Malinda's Recipe Collection

1 large egg
2 large egg whites
¾ c. milk
2 Tbsp. sugar
1 tsp. vanilla
¼ tsp. cinnamon

pinch of baking powder
8 slices Texas toast or French
  bread, sliced ½-inch thick
2 tsp. grapeseed oil
1 tsp. butter

Cinnamon Syrup:

½ c. sugar
¼ c. corn syrup

¼ tsp. cinnamon
¼ c. evaporated skim milk

French Toast: In a medium-sized bowl, whisk together egg, egg whites, milk, sugar, Watkins vanilla, cinnamon and baking powder until well blended. Place bread slices in a large, shallow baking dish and pour egg mixture over the top; turn to coat evenly. Press a piece of wax paper directly on the bread to cover it, then cover dish with plastic wrap. Refrigerate overnight.

Cinnamon Syrup: In a small saucepan, stir together sugar, corn syrup, cinnamon and ¼ cup sugar. Bring the mixture to a boil over medium-high heat, stirring constantly. Boil for 2 minutes. Remove from heat and stir in evaporated skim milk. Let cool. Transfer to a small pitcher.

To Cook French Toast: Heat 1 teaspoon oil and ½ teaspoon butter in a 12-inch nonstick skillet over medium-high heat. Add 4 of the soaked bread slices to the pan and cook until golden on both sides, 2 to 3 minutes per side. Transfer to a platter and keep warm in a preheated low oven. Cook the remaining slices in the same manner, using the remaining 1 teaspoon oil and ½ teaspoon butter. Serve with Cinnamon Syrup.

HONEY-RAISIN BREAD

Mrs. Malinda's Recipe Collection

about 4 c. unbleached flour
scant ¼ c. clover honey
1 ½ tsp. salt
2 pkg. yeast
½ c. milk
½ c. water

4 Tbsp. butter, softened
2 eggs
1 tsp. vanilla
2 to 3 c. dark seedless raisins
1 egg white
2 tsp. water

120

Mix 1 ¼ cups flour with salt and undissolved yeast in large electric mixer bowl. Heat milk, water and butter until just warm enough to melt butter. Add honey. Slowly stir into dry mixture; beat on medium speed for 2 minutes. Beat in eggs, one at a time. Add vanilla and ¾ cup flour. Beat at high speed 2 minutes. By hand, stir in raisins and remaining flour. Turn onto lightly floured surface; knead 5 minutes. Put dough into greased bowl; turn, cover and allow to rise until double, about 1 hour. Punch down; let rest 5 minutes, covered. Divide dough in half; form into 2 loaves. Put in greased loaf pans; cover and let rise about 25 minutes. Make egg wash of 1 egg white mixed with 2 teaspoons water. Brush gently over tops of loaves. (This gives a professional, glazed look.) Bake at 375° for 25 to 30 minutes. Remove from pan and brush with soft butter, if desired. Cool on wire racks.

= * * * *

Let there be peace, let it begin with me.

BUTTERMILK BISCUITS

Mrs. Malinda's Recipe Collection

2 c. all-purpose enriched flour,
  sifted
2 tsp. baking powder
¼ tsp. soda

1 tsp. salt
¼ c. vegetable shortening
1 c. buttermilk

Sift flour and measure. Sift again with baking powder, soda and salt. Cut in shortening with pastry blender or knife and fork until mixture resembles coarse corn meal. Add buttermilk all at once and stir mixture into soft ball of dough. Knead lightly. See directions under sweet milk biscuits. Yields about 20 biscuits.

CLOVER LEAF BISCUITS

Mrs. Malinda's Recipe Collection

2 c. sifted flour
2 tsp. double-acting baking
  powder
¾ c. milk

½ tsp. salt
¼ c. shortening
2 Tbsp. butter

Sift flour once; measure. Add baking powder and salt and sift twice. Cut in shortening until the mixture resembles coarse meal. Add milk all at once; mix until all flour is dampened. Flour hands. Shape dough into small balls. Place 3 balls in each greased, medium-sized muffin pan. Dot with butter. Bake at 450° until golden brown. Makes 18 biscuits.

* * * * *

Ain't going to study war no more.

WHIPPING CREAM BISCUITS

Mrs. Malinda's Recipe Collection

1 c. whipping cream
(unwhipped)

2 c. self-rising flour

Mix flour and whipp ng cream together, then place dough on a floured pastry board. Roll out dough; cut out biscuits and place on a greased cookie sheet. Bake at 350° for 12 minutes.

BROCCOLI CORNBREAD

Mrs. Malinda's Recipe Collection

2 sticks margarine
4 large beaten eggs
1 (10 oz.) pkg. chopped,
  thawed broccoli
1 medium chopped onion

8 oz. cottage cheese
2 pkg. Jiffy corn muffin mix
1 c. grated sharp cheese
  (optional)

Preheat oven to 375°. In 9 x 13-inch pan, melt the margarine in oven while mixing the remaining ingredients. Stir until well mixed, then add melted margarine but do not scrape pan. This remainder will keep bread from sticking. Stir again until all ingredients are well combined. Bake at 375° for 30 to 40 minutes (until lightly browned). Serve warm. Can be frozen and reheated.

VARIATION: Can substitute 8 ounces of sour cream for cottage cheese.

* * * * *

The Lord will provide.

104   Breads & Vegetables

CORNMEAL BREAD

Mrs. Malinda's Recipe Collection

1 pkg. yeast	¼ c. water
2 c. scalded milk	⅓ c. sugar
⅓ c. shortening	1 Tbsp. salt
3 c. sifted flour	2 eggs
1 c. yellow cornmeal	4 to 4 ½ c. sifted flour

Soften yeast in warm water. Combine milk, sugar, shortening and salt. Mix well. Cool to lukewarm. Add 3 cups flour, softened yeast and eggs. Beat until smooth. Add cornmeal and remaining flour to make a soft dough. Place on a lightly floured surface; knead 10 minutes. Cover and let rise until double in bulk. Punch down; let rest 10 minutes. Divide dough and shape into 3 loaves. Cover and let rise until double. Sprinkle with cornmeal. Bake in greased 9 x 4 ¾ x 2 ¾-inch loaf pans at 350° for 45 minutes.

* * * * *

Good bread, good meat, good God, let's eat.

MOLASSES DUMPLINGS

Mrs. Malinda's Recipe Collection
(From the Year 1776)

2 c. flour	2 tsp. cream of tartar
1 tsp. salt	¾ c. milk
1 tsp. soda	kettle of hot fat (for frying)
2 tsp. fat	kettle of boiling molasses

Mix dumpling ingredients and roll to 1-inch thickness. Cut with small cutter. Drop 2 or 3 at a time in hot fat. Have ready another kettle of boiling molasses. As soon as fried, drop into molasses. Remove and drain.

Molasses Sauce:

Dumplings	cinnamon to taste
1 c. sugar	2 Tbsp. cornstarch or 4 Tbsp.
1 c. molasses	flour, dissolved in ½ c. water
2 c. water	applesauce (homemade or
1 Tbsp. vinegar	bottled)

Serve over Dumplings and applesauce.

Make your favorite steamed or baked dumplings. (I use one on Bisquick box.) Boil sugar, molasses, water and vinegar together. Thicken with cornstarch and water. Should be consistency of a thick white sauce. Before serving, add piece of butter the size of a walnut and cinnamon to taste. Serve dumpling covered with applesauce and Molasses Sauce poured over top. Good on a cold winter's night.

* * * * *

MEXICAN CORNBREAD

Mrs. Malinda's Recipe Collection

1 c. cornmeal mix
1 c. cream-style corn
1 c. yellow cheese, grated
½ c. onions, chopped

½ c. oil
3 eggs, beaten slightly
1 tsp. red pepper or 1 hot
   green pepper, chopped

Mix all ingredients together until well blended. Bake in 425° oven until brown. Goes good with fish, also fresh mustard greens.

NANCY'S GREATEST HOT WATER CORNBREAD

Mrs. Malinda's Recipe Collection

1 c. cornmeal
1 c. flour
1 tsp. salt

2 Tbsp. sugar
2 tsp. baking powder

Mix all ingredients together. Add enough hot water to create dropping consistency. Have grease very hot. Drop by tablespoons; fry to golden. Yum, yum.

SAUSAGE CORNBREAD

Mrs. Malinda's Recipe Collection

2 pkg. yellow cornbread
1 can creamed corn
1 onion (medium), chopped

2 lb. Owens sausage (hot or
   regular)
1 small jar pimentos
sharp Cheddar cheese, grated

Mix cornbread according to package directions. Add corn. Brown onions with sausage. Layer ½ cornbread and corn mixture, then add sausage and onion mixture. Sprinkle pimentos on top of sausage and onion mixture. Cook with grated cheese, then top with other half of cornbread mixture. Bake at 350° for 20 to 25 minutes. Do not overcook.

SOUTHERN CORNBREAD

Diane "Mrs. Chicken" Ivy
Memphis, TN

2 ½ c. self-rising meal
1 c. buttermilk
4 Tbsp. cooking oil

2 eggs
2 Tbsp. sugar
½ stick butter or margarine

Preheat oven to 350˚. Put 4 tablespoons oil in hot skillet. Mix all ingredients until thoroughly blended (add more milk if needed). Bake until golden brown. Spread margarine or butter on top of the cornbread while still hot. "Enjoy."

HOT CAKES

Mrs. Malinda's Recipe Collection

1 c. flour
3 eggs
½ tsp. salt
6 oz. milk

2 Tbsp. baking powder
2 Tbsp. maple syrup
1 tsp. sugar
2 Tbsp. melted butter

Sift dry ingredients. Mix alternately with milk into well beaten eggs. Last, add syrup and butter. It is very important to have the griddle the right temperature. To begin with, grease the griddle lightly, then it is not necessary to grease it again. Spread about 2 tablespoons of batter on griddle. When holes appear in top, flip over and lightly brown the other side. Serve with a pitcher of melted butter and a pitcher of hot maple syrup. Makes 22 cakes.

* * * * *

Rub a dub dub, thank you for the grub.

108   Breads & Vegetables

MONKEY BREAD

Mrs. Malinda's Recipe Collection

1 pkg. dry yeast
1 c. milk
⅓ c. butter
⅓ c. sugar

3 eggs, beaten (at room
   temperature)
1 tsp. salt
4 ½ c. flour
½ c. melted butter

Heat milk and add butter, sugar and salt. Stir to dissolve. When mixture is lukewarm, add yeast and beaten eggs. Add flour slowly and beat well. Place in warm area to rise. Knead on board and roll ¼-inch thick. Cut in diamond shapes. Dip in melted butter and overlap in greased Bundt pan. Allow to rise 30 minutes. Bake at 350° for 30 minutes. Let cool on rack. Remove from pan and serve upside down.

SOUTHERN WAFFLES

Pamela J. Johnson
Carson, CA

2 c. flour
1 tsp. sugar
1 c. milk
¾ c. water

1 egg
1 tsp. salt
¾ c. Wesson oil

Mix flour, salt, sugar, milk and water. Beat until quite light. Add oil and beaten egg. Add more water to make a thin batter. About 5 minutes before cooking, add 2 rounded teaspoonful baking powder. Bake in hot waffle iron.

* * * * *

Weeping may endure for a night..
But joy cometh in the morning.

CARROT BREAD

Mrs. Malinda's Recipe Collection

1 c. sugar
¾ c. vegetable oil
2 beaten eggs
1 ½ c. flour
1 tsp. soda

½ tsp. salt
1 tsp. cinnamon
1 c. grated carrots
1 c. chopped pecans

128

Mix sugar, oil and eggs. Sift in flour, soda, salt and cinnamon. Add grated carrots and nuts. Carrots may be grated in a blender. Pour in floured, ungreased loaf pan, 9 x 5 x 3-inches. Bake at 325° for 1 hour or until done. Cool. May be frozen. Makes 1 loaf.

CRANBERRY BANANA LOAF

Mrs. Malinda's Recipe Collection

1 (16 oz.) can cranberry jelly
  sauce
1 medium apple, pared and
  grated
2 medium bananas, mashed

⅓ c. sifted confectioners sugar
1 tsp. vanilla
¼ c. chopped nuts
1 c. whipping cream, whipped

Beat cranberry sauce until smooth; stir in grated apple. Pour into 11 x 7 x 1 ½-inch pan. Fold bananas, sugar, vanilla and half the nuts into whipped cream. Spread over cranberry sauce layer. Sprinkle with remaining nuts. Freeze until firm. Let stand at room temperature before serving. Cut into squares. Serves 8.

* * * * *

ZUCCHINI BREAD

Chaplain Rev. Angela Duncan
Richmond, VA

3 eggs, beaten
2 c. sugar
1 c. vegetable oil
2 c. raw grated unpeeled
zucchini
2 c. sifted flour*
1 c. grated carrots

1 ¼ tsp. baking soda*
1 tsp. salt*
2 tsp. cinnamon
¼ tsp. baking powder
2 tsp. vanilla
1 c. chopped pecans

Add sugar and oil to beaten eggs; mix well. Add zucchini. Sift dry ingredients. Add to zucchini mixture. Mix well and add remaining ingredients. Bake 1 hour at 325°.
*May substitute self-rising flour. Omit salt and baking powder.

HOTEL PEABODY VANILLA MUFFINS

Mrs. Malinda's Recipe Collection

4 eggs
2 c. sugar
4 c. flour
1 Tbsp. baking powder

1 stick butter
2 c. milk
1 tsp. vanilla

Beat eggs and sugar. Add flour, baking powder, butter, milk and vanilla. Mix thoroughly. Pour into well-greased muffin pan. Bake at 375° for 20 to 25 minutes.

A bit of nostalgia for those who may remember the old Hotel Peabody in Memphis, Tennessee.

* * * * *

If you are willing and obedient,
You shall eat the Good of the Land.

SOUR CREAM YEAST ROLLS

Sis. Sheryl Scott

1 pkg. active dry yeast
¼ c. warm water
2 c. sour cream

2 Tbsp. sugar
¼ tsp. baking soda
5 ½ c. biscuit mix, divided

130

Let the yeast stand in the warm water while combining sour cream, sugar and baking soda in a big bowl. Add in 2 cups of the biscuit mix and the yeast water; mix it well. Add in 3 more cups of biscuit mix and stir. Use the last ½ cup of biscuit mix to dust onto counter. Turn the dough onto the counter. Knead the dough until it is smooth. Shape the dough into small balls the size of a walnut. Put them close together in a well buttered 9 x 13-inch pan. Allow it to set and rise until double in size. Preheat the oven to 375° and bake for 15 to 17 minutes. Makes 72 bite-size rolls.

= * * * *

Name it and claim it.
Believe it and receive it.

BUTTER ROLLS

Reverend and Mrs. Dangerfield Sr.
Chicago, IL

1 stick margarine or butter
2 c. flour
2 tsp. baking powder
½ tsp. salt
4 c. milk
¾ c. cold water

2 tsp. vanilla extract
1 stick margarine or butter
  (reserved)
2 pinches of nutmeg
  (reserved)
½ c. sugar (reserved)

Put baking powder, salt and margarine in flour. Add ¾ cups cold water to the mixture; mix well. Roll your dough out very thin. Use a saucer turned upside down to cut your dough into round shapes. Add a spoonful of margarine, a teaspoon of sugar and 2 pinches of nutmeg in the center of cut out dough of the rolls. Put them in your pan, folded side down (use a pan that is a little deep). Pour 4 cups milk, ½ cup sugar and 2 teaspoons vanilla extract in a mixing bowl; mix well. Pour the mixture over the rolls in the pan. Let cook for 350° for approximately 1 hour or until brown. Makes about 8 delicious rolls.

FRIED OKRA AND GREEN TOMATOES

Mrs. Malinda's Recipe Collection

1 lb. okra, sliced
2 medium green tomatoes,
  diced

1 c. diced onions

In a heavy skillet, pour about ½-inch cooking oil and heat. Coat okra, tomatoes and onions in seasoned mixture of ½ flour and ½ corn meal (season with paprika, salt, pepper, garlic and onion salt). Add vegetables to hot oil and brown. Cook on low heat until vegetables are done.

FRIED CORN TENNESSEE-STYLE

Mrs. Malinda's Recipe Collection

6 ears fresh corn
4 slices bacon
½ c. milk

1 tsp. salt
¼ tsp. black pepper
pinch of sugar

132

With sharp knife, cut corn kernels from cob. Also, scrape pulp out with back of knife. Set aside. Cut bacon in half and fry in heavy iron skillet until crisp. Drain on paper toweling. Discard all but 4 tablespoons bacon fat. Add corn. Cook, without stirring, until bottom is browned (lift corn from the side with a spatula to check). When well browned, add milk and seasonings, stirring until well combined. Cover and cook over low heat 10 minutes longer. Arrange bacon over the top and serve. Serves 4.

GREENS WITH TURNIPS

Mrs. Malinda's Recipe Collection

6 lb. mixed greens (turnip and kale or mustard)
4 smoked ham hocks (plus 1 other seasoning meat of your choice)

2 whole dried red peppers
1 bay leaf
8 small turnips, pared and quartered

Wash greens thoroughly to remove all sand and grit. (Wash in at least 5 clean pans of water.) Remove thick center rib, if necessary. Place ham hocks in large kettle with whole red peppers, bay leaf and enough water to cover. Cook until tender, about 1 ½ hours. Add greens and cook over low heat for 25 to 30 minutes. Add turnips and continue cooking until turnips are tender, about 25 to 30 minutes. Remove bay leaf. Serves 8 to 10.

MRS. ELLA MAE'S BROCCOLI POTATO BAKE

Mrs. Ella Mae Alexander
Memphis, TN

1 bunch broccoli (florets only)
1 can cream of mushroom
  soup
1 c. plus ⅓ c. grated cheese
salt and pepper to taste

1 can white potatoes, sliced
1 c. whole milk
½ stick butter
¾ c. bread crumbs

Blanche vegetables (put in hot water 3 minutes). Drain. Combine 1 cup grated cheese, butter, salt and pepper and milk. Heat. Layer hot vegetables in casserole dish. Pour heated milk mixture over vegetables. Top with bread crumbs and ⅓ cup cheese. Bake at 350° for 30 minutes or until golden brown.

YELLOW COCONUT RICE

Mrs. Malinda's Recipe Collection
(Tanzania)

This is rich but really delicious! You may, if you like, add ½ cup grated coconut to give it a stronger coconut flavor.

2 c. coconut milk
3 c. milk
2 c. rice
1 tsp. salt
½ tsp. ground turmeric

¼ tsp. ground cinnamon
¼ tsp. ground cloves
¼ tsp. ground cardamom
  (optional)
2 Tbsp. butter

In a 2-quart saucepan, prepare the coconut milk. Add 3 cups milk and bring to boiling point. Add rice, salt, turmeric, cinnamon, cloves and cardamom. Cover and cook until rice is absorbed, about 20 minutes. Add the butter. Serve as vegetable with fish or chicken. Yield: 8 portions.

BAKED SWEET POTATOES WITH RAISINS AND PECANS

Mrs. Malinda's Recipe Collection

5 sweet potatoes, peeled and cubed
1 oz. raisins
1 oz. chopped pecans
¼ c. butter, melted
½ c. maple syrup
½ c. water

Preheat oven to 400°F (200°C). Spread sweet potatoes in a single layer in a 9 x 13-inch baking dish. Sprinkle with raisins and chopped pecans. In a small bowl, mix the butter, syrup and water. Pour the mixture over potatoes. Cover the baking dish with aluminum foil. Bake in the preheated oven 50 to 60 minutes until sweet potatoes are tender. Makes 12 servings.

PINTO BEANS AND HOCKS

Mrs. Malinda's Recipe Collection

2 lb. pinto beans, washed (but don't soak)
6 c. chicken broth
6 c. water
3 ham hocks
¾ tsp. leaf oregano
5 cloves garlic, chopped
1 large onion, chopped
2 stalks celery, chopped
2 carrots, chopped
½ c. parsley, chopped
salt and pepper
1 dry red pepper
basil

Wash beans; place in stainless steel pot or Dutch oven. Add liquid; saute garlic, onion, vegetables and spices in 1 tablespoon oi until onion is transparent. Add this, plus hocks, to beans and bring to a boil. Reduce heat to low setting and cook for 6 to 8 hours. Serve with hot sauce and cornbread.

LOUISIANA RED BEANS AND RICE

Jeremiah Johnson
Carson, CA

1 lb. dry kidney beans
¼ c. olive oil
1 large onion, chopped
1 green bell pepper, chopped
2 Tbsp. minced garlic
2 stalks celery, chopped
6 c. water
2 bay leaves

½ tsp. cayenne pepper
1 tsp. dried thyme
¼ tsp. dried sage
1 Tbsp. dried parsley
1 tsp. Cajun seasoning
1 lb. andouille sausage, sliced
4 c. water
2 c. long grain white rice

Rinse beans and then soak in a large pot of water overnight. In a skillet, heat oil over medium heat. Cook onion, bell pepper, garlic and celery in olive oil for 3 to 4 minutes. Rinse beans and transfer to a large pot with 6 cups water. Stir cooked vegetables into beans. Season with bay leaves, cayenne pepper, thyme, sage, parsley and Cajun seasoning. Bring to a boil and then reduce heat to medium-low. Simmer for 2 ½ hours. Stir sausage into beans and continue to simmer for 30 minutes.

Meanwhile, prepare the rice. In a saucepan, bring water and rice to a boil. Reduce heat, cover and simmer for 20 minutes. Serve beans over steamed white rice.

SOUTHERN BLACK-EYED PEAS

Mrs. Malinda's Recipe Collection

1 can jalapeno black-eyed peas
1 can plain black-eyed peas
1 can stewed tomatoes

1 medium chopped onion
⅔ c. cooked white rice
2 Tbsp. bacon drippings
salt and pepper to taste

Combine peas, tomatoes, onion, rice, bacon drippings, salt and pepper. Pour into baking dish and bake at 350° for 30 minutes.

HOPPING JOHN

Mrs. Malinda's Recipe Collection

Eat Hopping John on New Year's Day and you'll have good luck.

1 c. dry black-eyed peas
6 c. water
6 slices bacon, cut up or 4 oz. salt pork, diced
4 c. water
¾ c. chopped onion
1 stalk celery, chopped
1 ½ c. salt
½ tsp. ground red pepper
1 c. long grain rice

Rinse dry peas. In Dutch oven, combine peas and water. Bring to boiling. Reduce heat. Simmer 2 minutes. Remove from heat. Cover and let stand 1 hour or soak peas overnight in covered pan. Drain peas and rinse.

In same saucepan, cook bacon or salt pork until crisp. Drain, reserving about 3 tablespoons fat. Add peas, 4 cups water, onion, celery, salt and red pepper. Bring to boiling. Cover. Reduce heat. Simmer 30 minutes. Add uncooked rice. Cover; simmer 20 minutes more or until peas and rice are tender, stirring occasionally. Serves 8.

ARKANSAS DOWN-HOME FRIED CORN

Mrs. Malinda's Recipe Collection

1 Tbsp. bacon drippings or butter
4 c. corn (6 to 7 ears)
4 tsp. sugar
1 tsp. salt
1 c. water

In large skillet, heat bacon drippings or butter over medium heat. Add corn, sugar, salt and water. Saute 5 to 7 minutes. Serve hot. Makes 8 servings.

≈ * * * *

Be blessed!

PIZZA STRING BEANS ITALIAN-STYLE

Mrs. Malinda's Recipe Collection

½ envelope onion soup mix
  (any kind)
margarine or butter

3 cans string beans
parsley
tomato paste

Empty onion soup mix into saucepan. Add approximately 1 tablespoon of margarine or butter. Heat; stir and brown a little (few seconds). Add string beans including the water. Add 2 tablespoons tomato paste and a little parsley flakes. Stir it all up and simmer for 4 hours. Stir occasionally and keep checking and stirring.

STUFFED GREEN PEPPERS

Mrs. Malinda's Recipe Collection

4 medium green peppers
1 (26 oz.) pkg. frozen Sloppy
  Joes sauce with beef
1 ½ tsp. leaf basil

¾ c. quick-cooking rice
  (uncooked)
¾ c. water

Remove frozen Sloppy Joes mixture from foil pan. Place in 2-quart casserole, breaking mixture in half, if necessary. Cook, covered, 6 to 7 minutes or until thawed, turning over twice. Add basil, uncooked rice and water; stir until mixed. Cut green peppers in half lengthwise, removing core and seeds. Place in shallow casserole. Fill with Sloppy Joes mixture. Cook, covered, with waxed paper, 10 minutes. Let stand 2 minutes before serving. Makes 8 stuffed pepper halves.

* * * * *

BETTIE'S SPICY CARROTS

Bettie Randle
Memphis, TN

4 or 5 large carrots, cut in
  julienne strips
½ c. sugar

1 tsp. salt
¼ c. cinnamon
2 Tbsp. butter, cut in pieces

138

Place carrots, sugar, salt and cinnamon in 1-quart casserole. Toss to combine. Dot with butter. Cover. Microwave 7 to 8 minutes on High until carrots are tender-crisp. Serves 4.

ALICE'S CORN-ON-THE-COB

Alice Higgins
For Bettie Randle
Memphis, TN

Corn may be cooked right in the husk in your microwave oven. Place on paper towel, turn ears over and rearrange after ½ of the cooking time. Wrap corn in a tea towel as soon as it comes out of the oven for 5 minutes. Because all of the heat is contained in the food, it continues to cook when covered even after it comes out of the oven. Cook 1 ear 1 ½ minutes, 2 ears 4 minutes, 3 ears 6 minutes, 4 ears 8 minutes and 6 ears 9 minutes.

* * * * *

PEA GARDEN

Balinda Moore
Memphis, TN

FOR THE GARDEN OF YOUR DAILY LIVING, PLANT THREE ROWS OF PEAS:
1. Peace of mind
2. Peace of heart
3. Peace of soul

PLANT FOUR ROWS OF SQUASH:
1. Squash gossip
2. Squash indifference
3. Squash grumbling
4. Squash selfishness

PLANT FOUR ROWS OF LETTUCE:
1. Lettuce be faithful
2. Lettuce be kind
3. Lettuce be patient
4. Lettuce really love one another

NO GARDEN IS WITHOUT TURNIPS:
1. Turnip for meetings
2. Turnip for service
3. Turnip to help one another

TO CONCLUDE OUR GARDEN WE MUST HAVE THYME:
1. Thyme for each other
2. Thyme for family
3. Thyme for friends

WATER FREELY WITH PATIENCE AND CULTIVATE WITH LOVE. THERE IS MUCH FRUIT IN YOUR GARDEN BECAUSE YOU REAP WHAT YOU SOW.

STIR-FRY CABBAGE

Pamela Johnson
Carson, CA

2 small cabbage
1 small red pepper, diced
1 small white onion, diced
2 carrots, grated

bacon ends
seasoned salt
black pepper
2 Tbsp. cooking oil

Cut up bacon ends. Place bacon ends, onion and bell pepper into skillet with oil. Saute over a medium fire. While these are cooking cut cabbage in half. Place flat side down on cutting board and make ½-inch slices in each half. Place half the amount of cabbage and carrots in skillet and begin seasoning. Turn fire up high (not enough to burn skillet). Stir cabbage, not letting it stick or burn. Add more cabbage and carrots as cabbage cooks down. When cabbage is done, place a lid on it for 5 minutes before you serve. Preparation and cooking time is 20 minutes. Excellent with rice.

YELLOW SQUASH CASSEROLE

Mary J. Lewis
Los Angeles, CA

3 boxes frozen yellow squash
  or 2 ½ to 3 lb. fresh
½ c. margarine
1 c. sour cream
1 (10 ¾ oz.) can cream of
  chicken soup (undiluted)
2 onions, chopped

1 (5 oz.) can water chestnuts,
  drained and sliced
1 (2 oz.) jar pimiento, chopped
1 (8 oz.) pkg. herb seasoned
  stuffing mix, divided into 2
  parts
salt and pepper to taste

Save ½ of stuffing mix for topping. Cook squash until tender; drain and reserve 1 cup of liquid. Season with salt, pepper and margarine; mash. Combine remaining liquid (if needed) and other ingredients into drained squash. Pour into 2 ½-quart casserole. Top with remaining stuffing mix. Bake at 350° for 30 minutes. Serves 12 to 15.

CAJUN BUTTER

Mrs. Malinda's Recipe Collection

½ tsp. oregano
¼ tsp. cumin
dash of red pepper

⅛ tsp. thyme
½ c. butter, softened

Combine spices with ½ cup softened butter. Brush on foods (meat, fish, poultry and vegetables) before and during cooking.

CORN ROASTED IN HUSKS

Mrs. Malinda's Recipe Collection

Remove silks from roasting ears. Twist husks tightly around ears. Soak in salted water for ½ hour. Roast on grill, turning to roast evenly until the husks are steaming hot (about 15 minutes).

CABBAGE

Mrs. Malinda's Recipe Collection

1 lb. country sausage (hot)
1 bell pepper, chopped
1 onion, chopped

1 medium head cabbage, chopped
1 qt. tomatoes
salt and pepper

Brown sausage, bell pepper and onion in skillet. Partially cook cabbage in a quart of water. Add tomatoes and sausage mixture. Add salt and pepper. Cook for 30 minutes to an hour.

POTATO FAT RASCALS

Mrs. Malinda's Recipe Collection

5 medium baking potatoes,
  grated
5 Tbsp. shredded cheese
  (Cheddar)
½ tsp. salt

vegetable oil
2 Tbsp. all-purpose flour
2 eggs, beaten
dash of cayenne pepper

Combine all ingredients, except oil, in large mixing bowl; mix well. Drain liquid that may accumulate. Pour oil into large skillet to the depth of ½-inch. Heat oil to 350°. Drop potato mixture into hot oil ¼ cup at a time. Flatten slightly with a spatula, forming circle. Cook 3 minutes on each side or until potatoes are brown. Add oil as necessary. Yield: 8 to 10 servings.

GREENS WITH SMOKED TURKEY TAILS

Barbara Johnson-Simons
Los Angeles, CA

9 bunches greens (collards,
  mustard or turnips)
6 turkey tails
½ c. maple bacon drippings
4 garlic cloves, chopped

3 c. water
1 Tbsp. chicken bouillon
1 onion (white/Spanish),
  chopped
2 Tbsp. sugar

Pick and cut greens (remove stems). Wash in warm water. Add all ingredients except greens. Let boil for 30 minutes. Add greens; cook until tender, 1 ½ to 2 hours. Makes 10 to 12 servings.

= * * * *

Oh how beautiful it is for brethren to dwell together in unity.

MR. FRED'S COUNTRY-STYLE PEAS AND BUTTER BEANS

Mrs. Malinda's Recipe Collection

1 lb. pkg. frozen speckled
  butter beans
1 lb. pkg. frozen black-eyed
  peas
1 lb. smoked neck bones or
  ham hocks
1 small onion
1 tsp. Accent

dash of red pepper (optional)
1 tsp. garlic salt (optional)
1 tsp. seasoned salt (optional)
okra (optional)
2 Tbsp. flour
water
1 Tbsp. sugar

Cook smoked meat until tender. Add peas, beans and onion. Season to taste. Cook for 1 hour. Serve with corn muffins and rice. Add okra the last 20 minutes. Last 15 minutes. To thicken, mix 2 teaspoons flour and ½ water. Slowly stir into vegetables. Continue cooking.

CREAM CHEESE AND ONION MASHED POTATOES

Mrs. Malinda's Recipe Collection

1 (7 ¾ oz.) pkg. instant
  mashed potato flakes
3 ½ c. water
1 c. skim milk
1 (8 oz.) pkg. cream cheese,
  cubed and softened

⅔ c. green onions, chopped
1 tsp. salt
1 tsp. black pepper
½ tsp. Cajun King Spice Blend
  seasoning

Cook mashed potato flakes with water and skim milk. Add remaining ingredients to mashed potatoes and blend.

* * * * *

BAKED POTATOES IN A POT

Mrs. Malinda's Recipe Collection

5 lb. potatoes
½ lb. butter
1 bunch green onions

1 pt. sour cream
2 c. Cheddar cheese, grated
1 jar Hormel bacon bits

Peel potatoes and cut as if to mash. Cook until tender. Drain and return to pot. Chop green onions in ¼ pieces, tops included. Mix all ingredients in pot with potatoes while potatoes are still hot. Serve hot. Serves 12 to 16.

ITALIAN BAKED EGGPLANT

Mrs. Malinda's Recipe Collection

4 eggplants, peeled and
  cubed
2 lb. hamburger
1 large onion, chopped
½ green pepper, chopped
½ tsp. salt
½ tsp. paprika
¼ tsp. pepper

2 cans tomato sauce special
½ tsp. oregano
1 Tbsp. Lea & Perrins
1 Tbsp. sugar
Italian seasoning
1 tsp. Accent
½ c. Italian bread crumbs

Cook eggplants in boiling water until tender. Brown meat, onion and green pepper in skillet. Drain eggplants and mash. (Drain any grease off of meat.) Combine all ingredients except the bread crumbs. Mix well. Place in a casserole. Top with the bread crumbs. Bake, covered, at 350° for 30 minutes.

* * * * *

CANDIED YAMS II

Mrs. Malinda's Recipe Collection

1 lb. unsalted butter
2 lb. sweet potatoes, peeled and coarsely chopped
2 c. water
1 c. sugar
1 c. packed brown sugar
2/3 unpeeled orange, sliced and seeded (stem slice discarded)

2/3 unpeeled lemon, sliced and seeded (stem slice discarded)
2 sticks cinnamon
1 Tbsp. vanilla extract
1/2 tsp. ground mace

Heat the butter in a 4-quart saucepan over high heat. When about half melted, add the remaining ingredients. Stir, cover and cook over high heat until mixture comes to a strong boil, about 10 minutes. Stir, then reduce heat and simmer, covered, for 20 minutes. Remove cover and continue cooking until sweet potatoes are very tender, about 20 minutes, stirring occasionally. Remove from heat and discard cinnamon sticks. Serve immediately, undrained.

EGGPLANT ROUNDS

Mrs. Malinda's Recipe Collection

1/2 c. cornmeal
1/2 tsp. chili powder
1/4 tsp. dried oregano
salt to taste

1 eggplant, sliced into 1/2-inch rounds
1 qt. vegetable oil (for frying)

In a shallow dish, combine corn meal, chili powder, oregano and salt. Dredge each eggplant slice in this mixture until coated on both the sides. Shake off excess. Heat a small layer of oil in a large skillet. When the oil is hot, arrange a layer of the eggplant rounds in the oil and fry, uncovered, for 2 to 3 minutes. Flip the rounds over and fry until golden brown. Continue adding oil and frying the rounds until they are all fried. Serve either hot or cold.

BUDDY'S MEDLEY

Uncle Buddy
94 Years Old
Los Angeles, CA

1 bag cauliflower (frozen)
1 bag carrots (frozen; sliced or
  baby)
3 c. water

1 bag broccoli (frozen)
butter
season to taste

Place all vegetables in pot with water. Add seasonings. Bring to a boil. Reduce heat; cook 10 minutes or until tender. Drain. Butter and serve hot.

GREEN BEAN MEDLEY

Mrs. Malinda's Recipe Collection

¼ c./60 mL mushroom soup
  base
1 ¼ c./325 mL milk
¾ c./180 mL water
⅛ tsp./0.6 mL black pepper
2 tsp./10 mL Worcestershire
  sauce (optional)

2 (9 oz./255 g) pkg. frozen
  French-cut green beans,
  thawed and drained*
1 (2.8 oz./79 g) French fried
  onion rings

*Or 2 (14.5 ounce/411 g) French-cut green beans, drained.

Combine first 4 ingredients in large saucepan; mix well. Place over medium heat and bring mixture to a hard boil, stirring constantly. Stir in Worcestershire sauce, beans and ½ can of the onion rings. Place mixture in a 1.5-quart/ liter casserole and bake, uncovered, at 350°F/180°C for 30 minutes or until heated through; stir. Top with remaining onion rings and bake an additional 5 minutes or until onions are golden. Makes 6 servings.

"AT THE CROSS" COLLARD GREENS

Mrs. Malinda's Recipe Collection

2 smoked ham hocks	salt
1 other seasoning meat	3 to 4 bunches collard greens
(smoked turkey leg or tail,	hot pepper part
pig tail, streak of lean pork,	2 tsp. sugar
etc.)	bay leaf

Place ham hocks and other choice of seasoning meat in large pot. Add enough water to cover meat. If your meats are not smoked, add a few drops of liquid smoke. Cook, covered, for at least 30 minutes. Pick greens (remove stems and any spots). Check for insects and grit. Break or cut leaves in pieces. Wash greens in warm, salted water. Wash at least 4 times until water runs clear when rinsed. No grit or debris should be in rinse water. Check meat at this point; if excess salt is in the water, the meat can be rinsed and drained. Add new water to meat. Bring to boil. Add enough greens to fill pot. Cover and let greens cook at high heat and shrink. Add more greens, stirring occasionally, moving them from the bottom to the top of the pot, until all greens are added. If you know greens are extremely bitter, you may parboil them in a separate pot and discard water. Add greens to pot with meat. Add sugar, bay leaf and pepper part. Cook for 1 ½ to 2 ½ hours until tender. Lower heat halfway through cooking cycle. Check to see if more salt is needed. Remove pepper and bay leaf. Serve.

You can cook greens in larger batches and put in freezer bags. These make great gifts for city visitors. Keeps up to a year in the freezer. Greens are best when served with sweet potatoes and corn bread. No other meat is really needed. An old chitterling bucket of frozen greens is just the right amount for a family size Thanksgiving or Christmas Day dinner.

If you are wondering what "At The Cross Collard Greens" means: "The secret to good greens is crossing up the seasoning meats."

TURNIP GREENS WITH CORN MEAL DUMPLINGS

Mrs. Malinda's Recipe Collection

ham hocks
3 to 4 lb. well cleaned turnip
  greens
1 ½ c. boiling water

1 c. water-ground corn meal
1 tsp. sugar
1 egg
¼ tsp. salt

In a large pan, cover ham hocks in boiling water; simmer 30 minutes. If ham is salty, pour off water and add fresh water. Simmer 40 minutes. Add greens and cook until tender.

To make dumplings, add corn meal all at one time to 1 ½ cups water; stir vigorously until mush is formed. Add sugar and salt. Cool. Add egg and beat well. Drop by tablespoon onto floured board. Roll into small balls; flatten and dredge lightly with flour. Drop dumplings into boiling greens liquid. Lower heat and cook about 15 minutes.

TEXAS SAUSAGE, BEANS 'N RICE

Mrs. Malinda's Recipe Collection

1 lb. dried pinto beans
1 ham bone
2 large onions, chopped
1 medium green pepper,
  chopped
2 stalks celery, chopped

3 cloves garlic, crushed
1 bay leaf
½ tsp. salt
¼ c. chopped parsley
1 lb. hot bulk sausage
1 lb. mild bulk sausage

Look and wash pinto beans; place in large pot with ham bone. Cover with water and cook until just done. Stir in onions, green pepper, celery, garlic, bay leaf, salt and parsley and let simmer while you cook the sausage. Drain sausage and add to beans. Stir and let simmer 5 minutes to blend aromas. Remove bay leaf and serve with cooked rice.

FRIED CAULIFLOWER

L. H. Dangerfield Jr.
Chicago, IL

1 large head cauliflower
2 c. cooking oil
salt and pepper

2 egg yolks
½ c. flour
½ c. milk or water

Remove old leaves from cauliflower; rinse. Soak flower side down in a bowl of cold salted water to cover (at least 2 hours). Parboil in pan for 10 minutes. Drain well and pat dry. Break into florets or slice and cool. Make a pancake-like batter of last 3 ingredients. Coat cauliflower with batter. Heat oil; fry until golden brown or until they float on top of oil. Drain, season and serve with hot sauce. Good with fish.

* * * * *

YOUR FAVORITE RECIPES

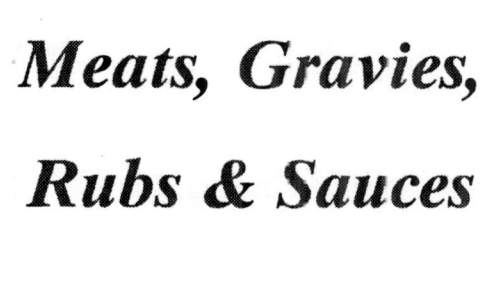

Meats, Gravies, Rubs & Sauces

Meat Cooking Chart

Roasting	Weight	Minutes Per lb.	Oven Temp.	Internal Temp.
FRESH PORK				
Rib and loin	3-7 lb.	30-40	325 F	175 F
Leg	5 lb.	25-30	325 F	170 F
Picnic shoulder	5-10 lb.	40	325 F	175 F
Shoulder, butt	3-10 lb.	40-50	325 F	170 F
Boned and rolled				
Shoulder	3-6 lb.	60	325 F	170 F
BEEF				
Standing ribs - rare	3-7 lb.	25	325 F	135 F
- medium	3-7 lb.	30	325 F	165 F
- well done	3-7 lb.	35	325 F	170 F
For rolled and boned roasts, increase cooking time 5 to 12 minutes				
LAMB				
Shoulder- well done	4-10 lb.	40	325 F	190 F
- boned and rolled	3-6 lb.	40	325 F	182 F
Leg- medium	5-10 lb.	40	325 F	175 F
- well done	3-6 lb.	40-50	325 F	182 F
Crown- well done	3-6 lb.	40-50	325 F	182 F
SMOKED PORK				
Shoulder and picnic hams	5 lb.	30-40	325 F	170 F
	8 lb.	30-40	325 F	175 F
Boneless butt	2 lb.	40	325 F	180 F
	4 lb.	25	325 F	170 F
Ham	12-20 lb.	16-18	325 F	170 F
	Under 10 lb.	20	325 F	175 F
	Half Hams	25	325 F	170 F
VEAL				
Loin	4-6 lb.	35	325 F	175 F
Leg	5-10 lb.	35	325 F	175 F
Boneless shoulder	4-10 lb.	45	325 F	175 F
POULTRY				
Chicken	3-5 lb.	40	325 F	170 F
Stuffed	over 5 lb.	30	325 F	170 F
Turkey	8-10 lb.	20	325 F	175 F
	18-20 lb.	14	325 F	175 F
Duck	5-10 lb.	30	325 F	175 F

Meats, Gravies, Rubs & Sauces

SMOTHERED CHICKEN

Mrs. Malinda's Recipe Collection

chicken, cut in frying size and
   seasoned with salt and
   pepper
flour
hot oil

½ onion
bell pepper
celery stalk
1 small can tomatoes
water

Cut chicken in frying size and season with salt and pepper. Roll in flour and brown in hot oil. Remove chicken and drain off all of the oil except for 1 tablespoon. Brown 2 tablespoons flour and add ½ onion, some bell pepper, celery stalk, tomatoes and enough water to make a gravy. Put chicken back into the gravy and season to taste. Cover and cook over low heat for 30 minutes.

POLYNESIAN POT ROAST

Mrs. Malinda's Recipe Collection

3 to 4 lb. boneless pot roast
4 oz. can mushrooms
1 c. pineapple juice
¼ c. soy sauce
1 ½ tsp. ground ginger

½ tsp. salt
1 large onion
1 Tbsp. cornstarch
2 Tbsp. water

152

Place roast and mushrooms in a large Dutch oven. Combine pineapple juice, soy sauce, ginger and salt. Mix well and pour over roast. Let stand 1 hour at room temperature, turning once. Add onion. Place over high heat and bring to a boil. Reduce heat. Cover and simmer 2 ½ to 3 hours or until roast is tender. Remove roast and vegetables to warm serving dish. Combine cornstarch and water, mixing well. Stir into pan drippings. Cook mixture over medium-high heat, stirring constantly, until thickened and bubbly. Ladle sauce over roast.

* * * * *

This little light of mine.
I'm going to let it shine.

CAPON

8 thin slices salt pork	3 Tbsp. truffles
2 carrots, sliced	2 onions, sliced
3 sprigs parsley	4 cloves garlic
2 bay leaves	1 ½ c. consomme
1 capon	½ c. rum
1 c. Burgundy or Claret wine	salt
flour	pepper

Line the bottom of a heavy pot with slices of salt pork. Lay the carrots and onions on the pork, also parsley, cloves and bay leaves. Rub the capon with salt and pepper, inside and out. Sprinkle the outside of the bird with flour and put it in the pot on top of the pork and vegetables. Cover the pot. Cook 25 minutes over strong heat. Turn the bird over once during this time. Now, add ½ cup consomme; cover and cook slowly for 1 ½ hours. Turn the bird several times. At the end of 1 ½ hours, it should be tender and brown, but you can continue cooking for ½ hour more if necessary. Add 2 more tablespoons consomme if the pot gets dry. Cut the truffles in long thin slivers. (I prefer the white truffles for flavor.) Mix the wine and rum and soak the truffles for 30 minutes. When the capon is ready to take up, place on a warm platter and keep it warm.

Sauce: Skim off the fat and strain liquid from the pot. Thicken with a little flour, then add the truffles, wine and rest of consomme. Boil up and serve. There should be about 2 cups of sauce.

* * * * *

I have never seen the righteous forsaken, nor his seed begging bread.

TOMATO POT ROAST

Maurice Brown
Inglewood, CA

4 lb. pot roast
2 Tbsp. shortening
1 (10 ¾ oz.) can tomato soup
¼ c. Burgundy or dry wine
4 onions

1 clove garlic
1 bay leaf
1 tsp. oregano
⅛ tsp. pepper

Brown beef; pour off fat. Stir in soup, wine and seasonings. Cover and cook 2 ½ to 3 hours. May be served with mushrooms and noodles. Makes 6 to 8 servings.

† SWEET AND SOUR POT ROAST †

Mrs. Malinda's Recipe Collection

3 to 4 lb. beef arm or blade
  roast
¼ c. flour
1 tsp. salt
pepper to taste
½ tsp. celery seed

2 Tbsp. cooking oil
⅓ c. vinegar
2 Tbsp. brown sugar
¼ tsp. nutmeg
vegetables of choice
¼ c. water

Combine flour, salt, pepper and celery seed. Dredge pot roast in seasoned flour. Brown in cooking oil in skillet on top of stove. Pour off drippings. Combine the vinegar, brown sugar, water and nutmeg. Pour mixture over roast. Cover tightly and cook slowly in a 325° oven for 1 hour. Add vegetables of choice (onions, celery, carrots, potatoes, etc.) and cook an additional 1 ½ to 2 hours or until meat is tender and vegetables are done. Thicken the liquid with flour for gravy. Serves 6 to 8.

* * * * *

SMOTHERED RABBIT

Mrs. Malinda's Recipe Collection

1 rabbit
corn oil
1 whole onion, sliced
seasoned salt

seasoned pepper
garlic powder
Cavender's Greek seasoning

Cut rabbit into pieces; season with seasonings to taste. Dip in flour and sear both sides of the rabbit. Saute onions in a separate skillet. Make a gravy using some of the seasonings mentioned. Pour gravy and sauteed onions over the rabbit. Bake in the oven at 250° for 2 ½ to 3 hours.

* * * * *

BABY LOIN BACK RIBS

Mrs. Malinda's Recipe Collection

(Makes 4 Servings)

2 (2 lb.) slabs baby loin back ribs

3 Tbsp. Dry Spices (see below)

1 c. Basting Sauce (see below)

1 c. Sweet Sauce (see below)

Dry Spices:

3 Tbsp. paprika
2 tsp. seasoned salt
2 tsp. garlic powder
2 tsp. ground black pepper

1 tsp. dry mustard
1 tsp. ground oregano
1 tsp. ground red pepper
½ tsp. chili powder

Basting Sauce:

¼ c. firmly packed brown sugar
1 ½ Tbsp. Dry Spices
2 c. red wine vinegar

2 c. water
¼ c. Worcestershire sauce
½ tsp. hot sauce
1 small bay leaf

Sweet Sauce:

1 c. ketchup
1 c. red wine vinegar
1 (8 oz.) can tomato sauce
½ c. honey mustard
½ c. Worcestershire sauce
¼ c. butter or margarine
2 Tbsp. brown sugar
2 Tbsp. hot sauce

1 Tbsp. seasoned salt
1 Tbsp. paprika
1 Tbsp. lemon juice
1 ½ tsp. garlic powder
⅛ tsp. chili powder
⅛ tsp. ground red pepper
⅛ tsp. ground black pepper

Combine all Dry Spices ingredients in a small bowl.

Stir together all Basting Sauce ingredients; cover and let stand 8 hours. Remove bay leaf. (Sauce is intended for basting ribs only.)

Bring all Sweet Sauce ingredients to a boil in a Dutch oven. Reduce heat and simmer sauce, stirring occasionally, 30 minutes.

Place ribs in a large, shallow pan. Rub Dry Spices evenly over ribs. Cover and chill 3 hours.

Prepare a hot fire by piling charcoal or lava rocks on one side of grill, leaving other side empty. (For gas grill, light only one side.) Place food rack on grill. Arrange ribs over unlit side. Grill ribs, covered with grill lid, over medium heat (300° to 350°) for 2 to 2 ½ hours, basting every 30 minutes with Basting Sauce and turning occasionally. Brush ribs with Sweet Sauce the last 30 minutes.

SIZZLIN BARBECUE

Mrs. Malinda's Recipe Collection

1 pork shoulder, trim off skin or
   excess fat
2 Tbsp. salt
2 Tbsp. black pepper
2 Tbsp. sugar

2 c. cider vinegar
1 c. drippings
⅓ c. ketchup
⅓ c. favorite barbecue sauce

Place pork shoulder in crock-pot. Add vinegar, salt, pepper and sugar. Cook on low heat for 12 hours. Remove shoulder from crock-pot and let cool for ½ hour. Slice and chop meat. Mix drippings left in pot, ketchup and barbecue sauce. Pour over chopped meat.

* * * * *

He's still able and available.

PORK HAWAIIAN

Mrs. Malinda's Recipe Collection

3 lb. pork tenderloin, cut into
  bite size chunks
1 ½ tsp. ground ginger
1 ½ Tbsp. Kitchen Bouquet
½ c. vegetable oil
1 ½ c. pineapple chunks,
  diced (reserve juice)
1 (9 oz.) can mushrooms,
  sliced (reserve juice)

1 (12 oz.) jar sweet gherkin
  pickles, sliced (reserve juice)
3 tsp. salt
3 green peppers, sliced
3 Tbsp. cornstarch
5 Tbsp. water
rice

158

Cut pork into bite size pieces and put in bowl. Add ginger and gravy sauce over pork and stir. In a large skillet, add vegetable oil and heat, then sauté meat, about 5 minutes. In a 2-pint measuring cup, pour juice from pineapple chunks. Add juice from mushrooms, pickle juice and add water to make 1 ½ pints. Add cornstarch to juices. Mix until smooth and cook until thick. Then pour over meat and add salt. Cover and simmer on low heat until meat is tender, approximately 10 minutes. Add pineapple chunks, cut up, mushrooms and pickles, cut. Cover and simmer for 5 more minutes. Add sliced green peppers and cook an additional 5 minutes. Serve over rice. Serves 9.

* * * * *

BEE'S BAKED HAM

Josie B. Dangerfield
Chicago, IL

25 to 35 lb. ham	16 oz. can pineapple slices
1 to 1 ½ c. vinegar	1 liter ginger ale
24 oz. honey	16 oz. can cherries

Let the ham sit in hot water for 4 to 6 hours (remove from the plastic wrapping) to take the salt out. Remove the ham from the water. Line roast pan with aluminum foil and add about 1 to 1 ½ cups vinegar; the vinegar will help tenderize the ham. Place the ham with the fat side up; remove the skin before soaking the ham. Pour about ¼ honey over the ham. Take the large can of pineapple, drain the juice off and reserve juice. Then take the pineapple slices and place them on the ham. Next, take the large can of cherries, drain the juice off, reserve the juice and place the cherries on the ham. Pour about a liter of ginger ale on the ham. Drain the juice off the ham. Add more honey along with the cherry juice and the pineapple juice after the ham begins to brown to your preference. Continue to baste it so that the honey, cherry juice and pineapple juice penetrate the meat. Cook at 350° without the roast pan top for about 2 ½ to 3 hours (after the ham cooks for about 1 ½ hours, reduce your heat to 250° because you do not want it to burn; you want a well cooked ham.) Remove the ham from the oven and let sit in the roaster. It is now ready to serve at a nice sized family gathering. What a ham! Just try it!

* * * * *

There is a brighter day ahead.

BAKED HAM

Mrs. Malinda's Recipe Collection

ham	1 doz. cloves
2 c. granulated sugar	6 allspice berries
1 c. cider vinegar	brown sugar
1 stick cinnamon	1 c. pineapple juice

Place ham in roasting pan with lid. Add granulated sugar, cider vinegar, cinnamon, cloves and allspice berries. Fill the pan with water. Place the lid on tight. Put into 350° oven and cook 20 minutes per pound. Turn ham often. If ham is tenderized, cook only 12 minutes to pound. Cool in liquid. When cool, remove top skin, leaving all possible fat. Stud ham with cloves. Cover with brown sugar. Place in fresh pan without lid. Pour pineapple juice into pan. Cook in a very slow oven, 250°, for 1 hour. After ½ hour, baste ham every 10 minutes for last ½ hour.

* * * * *

According to your faith it shall be done unto you.

BAKED HICKORY SMOKED HAM IN A BROWN PAPER BAG

Pastor Balinda Moore
Memphis, TN

ham
1 c. brown sugar
½ c. honey

2 Tbsp. orange juice
1 tsp. lemon juice

Remove wrappings. Soak ham in bucket of water 3 hours. Remove and pat dry. Place in a plain brown grocery bag, fat side up. Twist ends of bag together as tightly as possible; place in a deep broiler-type pan. Bake in a slow oven at 300°, uncovered, for 30 minutes per pound, allowing an extra 30 minutes for the ham to heat through and through. Example: 8 pound ham would be in oven for 4 ½ hours. At the end of cooking, the brown bag will be greasy and there will be liquid in the bottom of the pan. Carefully tear bag open and discard (don't get steamed fingers). Cut away the hard skin; discard this too and score the fat on both sides of the ham. Mix sauce and spoon over top side of the ham. Return it to oven at 375° to 400° for 10 to 15 minutes of browning. Take out; turn the ham over and repeat the sauce and browning on that side. This will be golden brown and luscious tasting!

This will be thick; stir and mix well. Spoon over ham.

* * * * *

FIREHOUSE MEAT LOAF

Mrs. Malinda's Recipe Collection

1 egg, beaten
1 c. soft bread crumbs
½ c. bottled pasta sauce with
 vegetables and/or herbs
1 to 2 cloves garlic, minced
½ tsp. dried rosemary, crushed
8 oz. Italian sausage, pork
 sausage links or ground beef

1 lb. ground beef
2 oz. Provolone or Mozzarella
 cheese, cubed
2 Tbsp. bottled pasta sauce
 with vegetables and/or herbs
2 Tbsp. shredded Provolone or
 Mozzarella cheese

162

In a large bowl, combine egg, bread crumbs, the ½ cup pasta sauce, garlic and rosemary. Remove casings from sausage, if using. Add ground beef and sausage; mix well. Press ⅔ of the mixture evenly in the bottom of an 8 x 4 x 2-inch loaf pan.

Make a ½-inch indentation down the center of the meat mixture. Place the cheese cubes in indentation. Pat remaining meat mixture evenly over top. Bake, uncovered, in 350° oven for 55 to 60 minutes until no pink remains and until a thermometer inserted in the thickest part of the loaf registers 170°. Let stand for 10 minutes.

To serve, transfer meat loaf to a platter. Drizzle top with the 2 tablespoons pasta sauce. Sprinkle with the 2 tablespoons shredded cheese. If desired, garnish with fresh rosemary sprigs. Makes 6 servings.

To Make Ahead: Prepare meat loaf as directed, except do not bake. Cover and chill for up to 24 hours. To serve, bake meat loaf, uncovered, about 1 hour or until no pink remains and a thermometer inserted into the thickest part of the meat registers 170°.

* * * * *

PORK CHOPS AND TOMATO GRAVY

Mrs. Malinda's Recipe Collection

approximately 6 pork chops
2 Tbsp. oil
1 can stewed tomatoes (16 oz.)

2 Tbsp. cornstarch
½ c. water

Brown pork chops in the 2 tablespoons oil. Pour the stewed tomatoes into the same frying pan. Bring tomatoes to a simmer. Let simmer for 30 minutes. Remove pork chops from pan. Thicken the tomato gravy with the cornstarch and water to the desired consistency. Serve gravy over the chops.

FIREHOUSE CHILI

CAPT. JBO
Venice Beach, CA

1 ½ lb. ground beef
2 c. chopped onions
1 medium green pepper, chopped
2 large cloves garlic, chopped
1 (28 oz.) can whole tomatoes
1 (8 oz.) can tomato sauce
2 c. water

2 Tbsp. chili powder
1 Tbsp. salt
1 Tbsp. sugar
½ tsp. hot pepper sauce
1 chili brick
1 bay leaf
2 (15 oz.) cans pinto beans

Brown beef, onions, green pepper and garlic in Dutch oven or large skillet. Stir in tomatoes, sauce, chili powder, salt, chili brick, sugar and hot sauce. Cook, covered, over low heat 1 ½ hours. Add beans. Cook 30 minutes longer. Makes 6 servings.

* * * * *

Love thy neighbor as thyself.

BARBEQUE SAUCE

Jeremiah Johnson
Carson, CA

2 Tbsp. fresh lemon juice
1 onion, peeled and sliced
¼ c. distilled white vinegar
½ c. water
2 Tbsp. brown sugar
1 Tbsp. prepared mustard
½ tsp. ground black pepper

1 ½ tsp. salt
¼ tsp. cayenne pepper
¼ c. vegetable oil
½ c. ketchup or 1 can tomato
   sauce
2 Tbsp. Worcestershire sauce
1 ½ tsp. liquid smoke flavoring

In a medium saucepan, mix lemon juice, onion, distilled white vinegar, water, brown sugar, prepared mustard, ground black pepper, salt, cayenne pepper and vegetable oil. Bring to a boil, then simmer, uncovered, 20 minutes. Stir ketchup, Worcestershire sauce and liquid smoke flavoring into the mixture. Return to boil, then remove from heat. Refrigerate until ready for use.

STRAWBERRY GAME HENS

Rochelle Stevens, '92 Silver and '96 Gold
Olympic Track and Field Medalist
Memphis, TN

4 Cornish game hens
salt and pepper to taste
4 c. strawberries (fresh or
   frozen)

3 Tbsp. cornstarch
½ c. water
⅔ c. orange juice
2 Tbsp. lemon juice

Preheat oven to 350˚. Wash game hens and season with salt and pepper. Place hens in roasting pan. Mash strawberries and combine cornstarch and water; mix until smooth. Add strawberry pulp, orange juice and lemon juice. Pour over game hens and roast, basting frequently, with sauce for 1 ½ hours or until done.

GAME HENS WITH FLAMING CHERRY SAUCE

Balinda Moore
Memphis, TN

2 Rock Cornish game hens
salt and pepper
2 Tbsp. butter, melted
½ tsp. seasoned salt

½ tsp. ground ginger
½ tsp. paprika
slices of orange
2 Tbsp. brandy (optional)

Cherry Sauce:

1 (8 oz.) pitted dark sweet
  cherries
⅔ c. water
1 chicken bouillon cube

1 small onion, cut in wedges
8 whole cloves
¼ tsp. ground cinnamon

Sprinkle hens inside with seasoned salt and pepper. Place in roasting pan, breast up. Combine butter with seasoned salt, ginger and paprika; brush over hens. Bake, uncovered, at 350° for 1 hour. During last ½ hour, baste with pan drippings. When roasted, discard fat from pan juices and stir juices into Cherry Sauce. Arrange on platter; garnish with orange slices. Keep warm.

To flame birds, add brandy to Cherry Sauce. Warm, ignite and spoon sauce over birds. Serve.

Cherry Sauce: Drain the cherries, reserving ⅓ cup syrup. In pan, combine reserved syrup with water, bouillon cube, onion wedges, cloves and cinnamon. Bring to a boil; simmer 10 minutes and discard onions and cloves. Stir 1 tablespoon of each of cornstarch and water together. Stir into sauce and cook until it thickens. Stir in cherries, grated lemon peel and 1 tablespoon lemon juice. Flame and pour on birds.

* * * * *

Do unto others as you would have them do unto you.

PORK TENDERLOIN SKEWERS

Mrs. Malinda's Recipe Collection

1 pork tenderloin
½ c. honey
½ c. Dijon mustard
2 Tbsp. balsamic vinegar
2 Tbsp. Howlin Hollar hot sauce

5 sprigs fresh parsley
1 fresh golden pineapple
2 summer squash
2 zucchini

Slice pork tenderloin into ½-inch slices. Mix honey, Dijon mustard, vinegar and Howlin Hollar hot sauce. Coat pork slices with honey Dijan mixture and refrigerate at least 4 hours. Slice squash, zucchini and pineapple into ½ slices. Place a piece of squash, pineapple, zucchini and pork onto a metal skewer alternating items until you have used all of your items. Remove rosemary from stems and coat skewers with rosemary.

Okay, now it's time for some grillin! Place your skewers onto a grill; turn frequently. Cook 15 to 18 minutes. Serve skewers over rice pilaf and top with the mint chutney.

PAPA'S RECIPE FOR COUNTRY SAUSAGE

Mrs. Malinda's Recipe Collection

18 lb. lean pork
6 lb. pork fat
2 oz. sage
1 ½ c. pepper

½ c. salt
1 Tbsp. crushed dried red
  pepper
1 Tbsp. sugar

Have meat ground fine (twice is not too much). Combine all ingredients. Mix well with hands. Shape into patties and fry in skillet.

HOMEMADE SAUSAGE

Mrs. Malinda's Recipe Collection

2 ½ lb. boneless pork shoulder
½ lb. pork fat
2 tsp. salt
½ tsp. cayenne
1 tsp. powdered sage

½ tsp. fresh ground pepper
½ tsp. dried thyme
½ tsp. dried savory
¼ tsp. powdered bay leaf
pinch of allspice

Cut meat and put through meat grinder with all other ingredients. Cook small piece to taste for seasoning. Add more sage and cayenne if you prefer hot sausage. To cook, shape into patties and fry until crispy.

BARBEQUED COON

Mrs. Malinda's Recipe Collection
(Oven Baked)

2 medium sized coons, kernels
   removed
2 apples
2 onions

3 sweet potatoes, peeled
cracked red pepper
⅔ bottle Wicker's barbecue
   sauce

Cut each coon into 8 pieces. Place in large roasting pan (or tinfoil baking pan). Quarter apples, sweet potatoes and onions and place around and over coon. Shake well and pour Wicker's over coon. Sprinkle red pepper on top. (Use your own judgement.) Cover with aluminum foil tightly. Bake at 375° for 4 hours. Serve over coon and sweet potatoes. Enjoy, Enjoy, Enjoy.

* * * * *

HOW TO COOK COON WITH SWEET POTATOES

Mrs. Malinda's Recipe Collection

salt
coon
1 c. broth

sweet potatoes
sage

168

Skin coon of course Cut up and boil in water with a little salt until tender. Place in shallow pan. Sprinkle with a little sage. Add 1 cup of broth. Precook about 5 medium-size sweet potatoes Cut in half and place around coon. Bake in hot oven for 20 minutes.

* * * * *

HOW TO COOK A HUSBAND

Mrs. Malinda's Recipe Collection

Be careful about your selections. Do not choose them too young or too old. (Best to let them select you.) Cover them in prayer. Let God clean them up. Let God take away bad habits. Be happy yourself before you try to make someone else happy. Love and appreciate your self. Then love and appreciate him. Know who you are. Now discover who he is. Don't choose on looks alone. Looks change, hair fades. Beware if he wants to change you. He may be wrong for you. If he doesn't like your God and your mama, leave him where you found him. Wait on God. No good thing will be withheld from you. Don't be in a hurry to cook a husband. Cook slowly.

Once you have settled on your selection, devote yourself to preparation. Others are always getting them in hot water. This makes them sour, hard to get along with and sometimes bitter. Sprinkle with love and kindness. Even poor varieties can be made sweet, tender and good by garnishing them with patience and sweetening with kisses. Wrap them in a mantle of love. Keep warm with a steady fire of domestic devotion. Serve with Peaches and Cream.

Follow these directions and they will keep well for years.

* * * * *

MARYLAND PORK CHOPS

Mrs. Malinda's Recipe Collection

4 pork chops
4 slices onion
4 strips red pepper
chopped celery
1 tsp. Kitchen Bouquet

4 slices tomato
4 strips green pepper
4 Tbsp. uncooked rice
1 c. water

Have pork chops cut 1-inch or more thick. Brown slightly in skillet on both sides. Place in shallow baking pan. Then on each chop, place a slice of tomato, slice of onion, strip of red pepper, strip of green pepper and top with a tablespoon of uncooked rice. Fill spaces in between the pork chops with chopped celery. Pour over water with Kitchen Bouquet dissolved in it. Bake for 3 hours at 350°.

FORGOTTEN CHICKEN

Mrs. Malinda's Recipe Collection

2 c. Minute rice (uncooked)
1 can cream of celery soup
1 can cream of chicken soup
1 soup can water

1 envelope dry onion soup mix
about 2 c. leftover chicken or
   turkey

Butter a 9 x 13-inch pan. Combine the celery and chicken soups with 1 soup can of water and heat to blend. Put rice into casserole and place pieces of meat on top. Pour over this the heated soups. Shake envelopes of dry soup mix well to break up lumps and sprinkle over top of rice mixture. Cover tightly and bake for ½ hour in a 350° oven.

Southern Style
COOKING

with a dash of
MRS. MALINDA'S™
Inspirational
Reflections & Meditations

Meet... -Mrs. Malinda- Johnson Dangerfield

Mrs. Malinda was born in Webb, Mississippi, February 25, 1925. She was the second child born to Dobie and Ruth Parker-Ford. At the tender age of 14, she gave her life to the Lord.

She married Fred Johnson of Bobo, Mississippi. They were blessed with Eleven children: Earthia (deceased); Fred; Ruth; Debora; Joseph (deceased); Balinda; Jeremiah; Barbara; Rita; Horace and Sandra. She has many grandchildren and great-grandchildren; Brothers & Sisters-in-law; Nieces; Nephews; one Aunt, and many friends.

She relocated to Memphis with her family in the late 1940's. They lived on E.H. Crump Boulevard in Memphis. They soon moved to North Memphis in the Douglas-Crump Neighborhood. Their family was very active in Church, and participated in many community and school programs, including extra-curricular activities. She was a very Spiritual and dedicated Christian woman.

Her husband, Fred Sr., retired from International Harvester Company, after more than 25 years of service. They were married for 50 years. He preceded her in death on April 1, 1992. Mrs. Malinda was mostly a homemaker, occasionally working outside the home as a cook and a housekeeper.

In December, 1995, she married Mr. Ervin Dangerfield. They enjoyed nine years together, until her passing on August 20, 2004. Mr. Dangerfield later passed away on January 2, 2005.

Her hobbies included: Cooking; Baking; Ceramics; Sewing; Gardening; Canning; Embroidery; Reading; Praying; Bible-Study and Traveling. She was a devoted worker in the Missionary society at her Church. She was also a Sunday School Teacher and Usher, attending the National Baptist Convention annually for over 40 years. She was also the founding president of the Home Industrial Ladies Club for 50 years. She, along with Delores Washington, led the Morning Prayer Line for some 28 years.

HOW TO COOK A WIFE

**BY Jeremiah Johnson
Carson, CA**

Cooking a wife is a rare science. If you want a wife she's got to be cooked. It takes a good man to cook a wife. So man if this is what you want, you will need all the utensils, seasonings and appliances in the kitchen. Remember," When a man chooses a wife he chooses a good thing."

A wife should be spiritually chosen. You need to be guided by the Spirit of God in you. To properly season this wife she has to be pampered and catered to. This is very important step in the cooking process. To make her right for you it is important that you simply look and listen to her cares and needs. Don't just listen...respond to her with love, strength and patience. The woman you choose to be your wife needs to be empowered by you. Then She can give the kind of support you need in building your family Kingdom.. Godly wisdom lets you know you've have made the right choice. *Spice* thing up and *Enjoy* being with her.

Keep in mind: She 's chosen, seasoned and She's yours. Just don't bore her, *Love* and adore her.   *Sprinkle* her with kind thoughts and slow kisses. She can be sweetened, peppered, salted, dry rubbed, baked or boiled. Your wife can be your main dish and side dish too. She is not just an appetizer. Your wife is all for you. If you want to keep her, be there for her too. *Plant* joy in her heart. *Cover* her with your strong protection. *Tenderize* the tough days by taking thyme for your wife.. Court her mind and her body. Give her kisses like a hot toddy. Her look of contentment will let the world know she's got a *Man*. That's how you COOK A WIFE.

MOM & DAD

THE JOHNSON BROTHERS

PICTORIAL
REVIEW

THE CHILDREN & MOMMA 19

HNSON FORD FAMILY REUNION 2001

JOE

DOROTHY & JOE

PINEAPPLE-ONION SMOTHERED CHICKEN

Maurice Brown
Inglewood, CA

2 Tbsp. oil
2 ½ to 3 lb. cut up chicken
1 envelope Lipton onion soup
  mix

1 can pineapple chunks,
  drained
2 ¼ c. water
2 Tbsp. flour

Brown chicken well in oil. Add soup mix, pineapple and water. Simmer, covered, 45 minutes. Remove chicken. Add flour and a little water to pan to make gravy.

* * * * *

✝ SMOKIN GOOD CHICKEN WINGS ✝

William Woodland
Memphis, TN

10 lb. chicken wings or you
   may also use chicken thighs
½ c. oliver oil
1 c. cider vinegar
¼ c. balsamic vinegar
¼ c. Grey Poupon mustard
1 egg, beaten well

2 Tbsp. Spittin Fire Hot Sauce
2 Tbsp. kosher salt
1 ½ Tbsp. poultry seasoning
4 to 5 cloves garlic, minced
   fine
¼ tsp. white pepper

Mix olive oil, mustard and egg in a large stainless steel bowl with a wire whisk. While continuing to whisk slowly, add cider and balsamic vinegar; whisk until mixed well. Add rest of the ingredients and mix. Place chicken into 2 heavy-duty 2-gallon Ziploc bags and add the marinade mixture. Place bag in a large bowl and refrigerate 24 hours, rotating bag every so often so all chicken pieces sit in the marinade evenly.

Okay, some of you fans out there may have noticed that the marinade for the chicken is the same for months. Well it is cause I just love this stuff, but we are going to do a little different procedure this time! For these wings, we are just using a simple inexpensive backyard smoker. I'm just using lid with a small fire pan and water pan type of smoker.

Now, we're ready for some smokin. I prefer to use apple wood, soaked for 24 hours. I use natural hardwood charcoal. Set up smoker and start the coals. When hot and glowing, add your soaked apple wood. Place marinated wings in and smoke for 2 to 3 hours. Make sure fire box is not too hot as it will dry out the wings and thighs. Remove chicken and place on a hot gas grill for about 10 minutes, turning often. This will crisp up the outside a bit. Serve with Zesty Blue Cheese Dip!

Zesty Blue Cheese Dip:

1 c. mayonnaise
¾ c. sour cream
1 Tbsp. Worcestershire sauce
½ Tbsp. lemon juice
1 tsp. fresh garlic, minced fine

1 ½ c. crumbled Blue cheese
¼ c. half and half
1 Tbsp. Spittin Fire or Spittin Fire
   XXX

Combine all ingredients and serve with the Smokin Good Chicken.

---

† MR. COOTS' GOOD COON †

Mrs. Malinda's Recipe Collection

1 large coon
3 large chopped onions
2 tsp. salt
3 tsp. Chinese red pepper

3 tsp. black pepper
5 tsp. wild sage, crumbled
2 c. Crisco

Cut up coon. Melt Crisco in large iron pot. Add onions, coon, salt, both peppers and sage. Cover with water. Cook 3 to 4 hours until it falls off the bone, then stir every 10 to 15 minutes until the coon is light brown.

---

† CHICAGO CHICKEN LEGS †

Mrs. Malinda's Recipe Collection

1 lb. pork
1 lb. beef steak
½ c. flour
4 Tbsp. Crisco

3 Tbsp. chopped onions,
    celery and green peppers
¼ Tbsp. paprika
2 to 3 c. water
salt and pepper

Have the butcher cut steak into 1-inch square pieces. Alternate with pork and beef on wooden or metal skewers. Roll in flour and brown in fat. Put in roast pan. Add the rest of the ingredients. Cook 1 hour.

* * * * *

They shall know we are Christians by our love.

† ROAST DUCK †

Mrs. Malinda's Recipe Collection

2 wild ducks
1 onion
¼ tsp. thyme
3 pods garlic
1 (6 oz.) can frozen orange
  juice
1 tsp. ginger
2 Tbsp. honey

2 c. water
1 apple
½ tsp. caraway seed
¼ tsp. celery seed
½ c. red wine
B & B sliced mushrooms
½ tsp. marjoram
1 tsp. Kitchen Bouquet

Salt and pepper ducks well. Stuff each with ½ of apple and ½ an onion. Cook in pressure cooker for 30 minutes. Remove and place in shallow roaster. Make a sauce with all the spices, water, wine and concentrated orange juice. Place duck in 325° oven and baste frequently with sauce. Roast for 1 ½ hours.

† FLAMING DUCK †

Mrs. Malinda's Recipe Collection

2 (5 lb.) ducklings
orange peel (from 2 large
  oranges)

salt and pepper
½ lb. butter
4 soup spoons Grand Marnier

Roast the ducklings without stuffing. While they are roasting, prepare a mixture of butter, salt, pepper and the finely chopped peel of the oranges. When ducklings are roasted, spread the mixture on a copper or earthenware platter and melt the mixture over a low flame. Add the Grand Marnier. Place roasted ducklings on platter and baste with the mixture for 10 minutes over low heat. Sprinkle on Grand Marnier and flame. Carve on the platter and serve very hot with gravy.

✝ VENISON POT ROAST (DEER MEAT) ✝

Mrs. Malinda's Recipe Collection

1 Tbsp. flour	¼ c. vinegar
1 (4 lb.) venison pot roast	¼ c. lemon juice
1 c. water	¼ c. ketchup
2 cloves garlic	2 Tbsp. brown sugar
1 Tbsp. salt	1 Tbsp. Worcestershire sauce
½ tsp. pepper	1 tsp. mustard
1 c. sliced onions	¼ tsp. paprika

Rub flour on meat; brown well on all sides in heavy kettle. Slip rack under meat. Add tomatoes, water, garlic, salt and pepper. Cover and simmer 2 hours. Combine remaining ingredients. Pour over meat; cover and simmer until tender, about 1 ½ hours.

* * * * *

Oh taste and see that the Lord is good.

† TURKEY, CORNBREAD DRESSING AND † GRAVY

Mrs. Malinda's Recipe Collection

176

12 lb. turkey	2 c. diced celery
10 c. stale cornbread	2 bunches green onions
3 c. toast, stale bread or biscuits	1 large onion, chopped
1 green pepper	2 hard-boiled eggs

Wash bird and salt on the insides; grease the outside with Crisco. Place on rack in roasting pan with breast side up. Wrap baking pan and bird in heavy foil, sealing all sides. Bake in oven at 325° according to the chart.

For 8 to 11 pounds, bake 3 hours.

For 11 to 14 pounds, bake 3 ½ hours.

For 14 to 18 pounds, bake 4 hours.

Drain off liquid in roaster pan and reserve for gravy. Stuff bird with prepared dressing. Return to pot; place extra dressing around the bird and cook about 25 minutes to brown. Crumble toast and cornbread into a large pan. Set aside. Boil the liver, gizzard and turkey neck slowly in 2 quarts of water until tender. Strip the neck meat and chop with the gizzard and add the bread crumbs. Save liver for gravy. Use broth of boiled meat and add bread crumbs (about 3 ½ cups). Add plain water if more juice is needed. Salt and pepper to taste. Cook chopped celery, pepper and onions in 4 tablespoons oleo until tender. Take out ⅓ cup of this mixture and set aside for the gravy. Stir the rest into cornbread mixture and mix well. Stuff the cooking turkey with dressing and return to oven, uncovered, to brown, about 25 minutes. If the craw spice is filled with foil before the bird is cooked, it will be full and the foil can be removed and the cavity can be filled with more dressing without the skin breaking.

Turkey Gravy: Brown 3 tablespoons flour in 2 tablespoons of oleo or fat drippings from turkey broth. Add broth drained from roasting pan when you remove the bird to stuff (2 ½ cups). Mash egg yolks and liver to a smooth paste in about ¼ cup of broth or water. Mash egg whites with fork. Put the cooked celery, onion and pepper

† 158 †   Meats, Gravies, Rubs & Sauces

you saved from the dressing into the gravy mix and cook about 10 minutes over slow fire. Stir in egg whites, yolk and liver mixture. Salt and pepper to taste. Some people like to add 1 tablespoon white wine just before removing from fire. If gravy seems too thin, add about 2 tablespoons of dressing to it and stir well.

✝ MEAT BALLS IN BUTTERMILK SAUCE ✝

Mrs. Malinda's Recipe Collection

1 ½ lb. ground beef
1 small onion, finely chopped
3 Tbsp. chopped green pepper
⅓ c. sliced celery
1 c. cooked rice
1 tsp. salt
½ tsp. pepper

1 egg
1 (10 ½ oz.) can mushroom soup
1 soup can of buttermilk
1 (2 oz.) can mushroom stems and pieces

Put the ground beef, onion, green pepper, celery, rice, salt, pepper and egg into a large bowl. Work together with hands until well mixed. Divide into 12 portions; roll each into a ball. Place in a greased 2-quart casserole. Place the soup, buttermilk and liquid from the mushrooms in a bowl. Beat until smooth. Pour over the meat balls, along with the mushrooms. Bake in a moderate 350° oven for 1 hour. The extra gravy is good to spoon over baked potatoes. Yield: 6 servings.

* * * * *

Come let us reason together.

✝ BOILING FRIED CHICKEN ✝

Mrs. Malinda's Recipe Collection

(Southern Fried Chicken)

chicken parts	Season-All and pepper
cooking oil	garlic powder
hot boiling water	2 c. flour

Wash chicken. Dip pieces of chicken in boiling water; immediately coat with seasoned flour. Quickly place in hot skillet, 300°, skin side down. Cover; fry 5 minutes. Remove cover and cook 4 minutes longer. Turn chicken; cover 5 minutes longer. Remove cover and cook 4 minutes. By now the chicken should be brown, crunchy and done. Do not overcook.

✝ FRIED CHICKEN ✝

Mrs. Malinda's Recipe Collection

2 lb. frying chicken, skinned	¼ tsp. onion powder
1 ½ c. buttermilk	dash of salt
2 eggs	2 c. flour
¼ tsp. garlic powder	

Mix buttermilk, eggs, onion powder, garlic powder and salt. Dip chicken in this mixture, then roll the chicken in the flour. Fry in 2-inches of cooking oil. Turn once only. This makes a very tasty, crisp crust. Can be served hot or cold.

* * * * *

We will sit at the welcome table.

✝ DEEP-FRIED CHITTERLINGS ✝

Mrs. Malinda's Recipe Collection

1 lb. chitterlings
1 c. meal
2 Tbsp. self-rising flour
2 eggs, beaten

I oz. Lea & Perrins sauce
I oz. Tabasco sauce
pepper and salt to taste

Put chitterlings in hot salted water. Remove lining and fat. Rinse and boil chitterlings at least 1 hour. Drain and cool. Mix ingredients thoroughly. Add 1 cup white wine. Soak chitterlings for 1 hour. Drop in Fry Daddy until they come to top. Very good with pinto or white beans.

✝ 5 MEAT CHILI BEST YET ✝

Pastor Balinda Moore
Memphis, TN

2 lb. chorizo sausage
2 lb. Italian sausage
2 lb. round steak, tenderized
2 lb. smoked sausage
2 lb. pork sausage

2 large cans stewed tomatoes
2 tsp. cumin
chili powder to taste
1 bunch cilantro, chopped
½ gal. salsa

In large pot, mix ½ of salsa, cumin and cilantro. Bring to boil and simmer. Remove all meat casings. In large skillet or pot, brown all meats. Cut round steak in 1 to 2-inch pieces before browning. Drain meats. Add tomatoes. Simmer for 15 minutes. Add this mixture to pot. Add chili powder and remaining salsa as needed. Simmer for 30 to 60 minutes. Stir often. Serve with Mexican or crackling cornbread.

* * * * *

Bread of heaven feed me until I want no more.

✝ DRY RUB ✝

Willie Wiley
Palo Alto, CA

½ c. paprika
3 Tbsp. cayenne pepper
5 Tbsp. freshly ground black
    pepper
6 Tbsp. garlic powder

3 Tbsp. onion powder
6 Tbsp. salt
2 ½ Tbsp. dried oregano
2 ½ Tbsp. dried thyme

In a medium bowl, combine the paprika, cayenne pepper, ground black pepper, garlic powder, onion powder, salt, oregano and thyme. Mix well and store in a cool, dry place in an airtight container.

✝ HOT SAUCE ✝

Mrs. Malinda's Recipe Collection

4 qt. ripe tomatoes
1 c. vinegar
3 bell peppers
1 ½ c. chopped onions
4 or 5 hot chili peppers
    (jalapeno)

4 yellow chili peppers
    (banana)
6 garlic cloves, chopped
2 stalks celery
2 Tbsp. canning salt
1 ½ Tbsp. chili powder
1 Tbsp. Tabasco

Cook together until ½ down from top the vinegar and tomatoes. Chop bell peppers, onions, chili peppers, garlic cloves and celery. Mix together all of these with cooked tomatoes and vinegar. Bring all to a boil. Cook 5 minutes longer. Then add remaining ingredients. Stir good. Put in jars. Hot water bath for 30 minutes. Makes 12 pint jars.

Joy to the world the Lord is come.

✝ 162 ✝   Meats, Graves, Rubs & Sauces

† CHEESEBURGER LOAF †

Mrs. Malinda's Recipe Collection

2 lb. ground beef
1 (1 ³/₈ oz.) envelope onion
  soup mix
½ c. quick cooking oats
⅛ tsp. pepper

1 egg, beaten
½ c. milk
½ lb. Cheddar cheese, sliced
¼ c. chili sauce
½ tsp. dry mustard

Combine ground beef, soup mix, oats, pepper, egg and milk in large mixing bowl; mix well. Pack half of meat mixture into a 9 x 5 x 3-inch loaf pan. Place cheese slices on top of meat mixture. Spoon remaining meat mixture over cheese, covering cheese layer and pressing lightly on sides to seal; set aside. Combine chili sauce and mustard; mix well. Spread sauce mixture over top of meat loaf. Bake at 350° for 1 hour and 20 minutes. Yield: 8 to 10 servings.

† BIG MATCH ATTACK †

Jarren Leach
Memphis, TN

(Big Mac)

hamburger patties
toasted buns
shredded lettuce

cheese slices
pickles
chopped onion

Special Sauce:

1 c. Miracle Whip salad
  dressing
⅓ c. bottled creamy French
  dressing

¼ c. sweet pickle relish
1 Tbsp. sugar
¼ tsp. pepper
1 tsp. dry minced onion

Combine Miracle Whip with remaining ingredients. Blend well using fork rather than mixer. Keep refrigerated in covered container until time to serve. Makes about 2 cups sauce.

† SMOKED TURKEY LEGS †

Mrs. Malinda's Recipe Collection

6 turkey legs
3 Tbsp. Worcestershire sauce
1 Tbsp. vegetable oil
Dry Rub (recipe follows)
Mop (recipe follows)

your favorite BBQ sauce (as
needed; recommended
North of the Border Chipotle
BBQ Sauce)

Several hours before planning on barbecuing, loosen skin on the turkey legs by running your fingers under it as far as possible without tearing the skin.

Combine the Worcestershire sauce and the oil. Coat your fingers with the mixture and rub really well into the turkey legs, getting as much as you can under the skin. Sprinkle the Dry Rub over the skin liberally, rubbing into the turkey legs and under the skin. Place the legs in plastic bags and refrigerate.

Prepare the smoker for barbecuing, bringing the temperature to 200° to 220°. Remove the turkey legs from the refrigerator and let them sit at room temperature for about 30 minutes.

Re-warm the Mop mixture over low heat.

Transfer the turkey legs to the smoker. Cook until the legs are very tender and the juices run clear, about 3 ½ to 4 hours. Mop the legs at 45 minute intervals in a wood burning pit or as appropriate for your style of smoker. Serve the legs hot, to be eaten with your fingers, with a side of barbecue sauce.

Dry Rub:

¼ c. chipotle seasoning
(recommended: North of the
Border Chipotle Seasoning)

1 to 2 Tbsp. mild dried ground
red chili or paprika
1 Tbsp. packed brown sugar

Mix ingredients together in a small bowl.

Mop:

1 c. white vinegar
1 Tbsp. BBQ sauce
(recommended: North of the
Border Chipotle Barbecue
Sauce)

1 Tbsp. vegetable oil

Combine the Mop ingredients in a small saucepan and warm the mixture over low heat.

† TURKEY MEAT LOAF †

Mrs. Malinda's Recipe Collection

2 lb. ground turkey
1 pkg. meat loaf seasoning
  mix
1 small can tomato sauce

1 egg, beaten
½ c. bread crumbs
1 pkg. onion soup mix

Mix all ingredients together well. Shape into loaf and bake in oven for 1 hour or until done at 375°.
Microwave: Place container on rotating tray or turn every 5 minutes without turntable on High setting for 22 minutes. Let stand for 5 minutes before serving.

† MOLASSES CHICKEN †

Mrs. Malinda's Recipe Collection

chicken pieces or 1 cut up
  fryer
2 Tbsp. mustard

¾ c. molasses
4 tsp. cider or tarragon
  vinegar

Place chicken pieces in baking dish. Spread with mustard. Pour molasses over chicken. Pour 1 teaspoon vinegar in 4 corners of dish. Bake at 275° for 1 ½ to 2 hours. Preparation time: 2 minutes.

† CHICKEN FINGERS †

Mrs. Malinda's Recipe Collection

1 pkg. Lipton onion soup
1 Wish-Bone Russian dressing
1 Smucker's apricot preserves

3 lb. chicken wings or
  drummettes

Mix soup, dressing and preserves in 9 x 13-inch roasting pan. Add chicken and coat well. Bake at 350° for 1 hour.

✝ GRANDMA'S TOMATO GRAVY ✝

Mrs. Malinda's Recipe Collection

2 Tbsp. bacon drippings
1 medium onion, minced

3 Tbsp. flour
1 large can tomatoes

184

Brown onion in bacon drippings until golden brown. Add flour and stir until smooth. Add tomatoes and let cook until thick, stirring constantly. Serve with pot roast or meat loaf.

✝ SILTA OR HEAD CHEESE ✝

Mrs. Malinda's Recipe Collection

Cook pork shoulder until it falls apart. Layer meat, fat and onion; sprinkle allspice, layer it. Put rag in bowl first, then layer. Tie rag tight and put something heavy on top so it sets. Put in cool place until it sets.

* * * * *

He is Lord.

† BAKED BOLOGNA †

Mrs. Malinda's Recipe Collection

1 (6 ½ lb.) all beef bologna
½ c. Dijon mustard
1 ½ c. golden brown sugar

1 loaf sliced white bread
1 jar yellow mustard

Preheat the oven to 250°. Line a large roasting pan with foil to cover well. Using a small sharp knife, score the top of the bologna, cutting about ¼-inch deep to create a diamond design. Place the bologna, cut side down, in the foil lined pan and spread a thin layer of mustard on the exposed areas. Using your hands, press the brown sugar onto the Dijon mustard to create a coating. Carefully turn the bologna over so that the cut side is facing up and spread the top and sides with the remaining Dijon mustard. Press the remaining brown sugar onto the mustard to coat the entire bologna well. Place the bologna in the top third of the oven. Bake for 5 hours, rotating the bologna slightly during cooking to keep the bottom from burning. Remove the bologna from the pan and place it on a large platter. Slice the bologna ¼ to ½-inch thick and make sandwiches on fresh white bread with yellow mustard....just the way Emeril likes it!

* * * * *

Peace on earth, good will toward men.

✝ BIRD IN A BAG ✝

Mrs. Malinda's Recipe Collection

1 Tbsp. flour
1 medium onion, sliced
2 stalks celery, sliced
1 (4 lb.) roasting chicken
salt and pepper

lemon pepper
tarragon vinegar
1 Tbsp. vegetable oil
3 to 4 red potatoes
5 to 6 carrots

You will need 1 large 14 x 20-inch Reynolds oven cooking bag. Preheat oven to 350°. Shake 1 tablespoon flour in bag. Place bag in large shallow pan. Make 3 to 4 slits in top of bag. Remove giblets from chicken. Wash and dry chicken. Inside of chicken, sprinkle lemon pepper and tarragon vinegar. Place half of the onions and celery in cavity. Brush chicken with oil and season with lemon pepper, salt and pepper. Place chicken in bag. Add remaining onions and celery in bag. Cut up potatoes and carrots and place in bag. Close bag. Bake 1 ½ hours. Serves 3 to 4.

✝ FRIED BOLOGNA WITH MELTED CHEESE ✝ SANDWICH

Mrs. Malinda's Recipe Collection

2 slices round bologna
2 pieces bread

1 slice Velveeta cheese

Heat skillet until hot. Fry bologna on both sides. Put cheese on one slice; add second slice on top. Heat until cheese is melted. Put between 2 slices of bread and eat.

✳ ✳ ✳ ✳ ✳

Let there be peace, let it begin with me.

Meats, Gravies, Rubs & Sauces

✝ BARBEQUE BRATWURSTS ✝

Mrs. Malinda's Recipe Collection

Get the most from your marinade injector. Tasty bratwursts that are injected with barbeque sauce before grilling.

4 fresh bratwurst sausages   **½ c. barbeque sauce**

Preheat grill for high heat. Fill a marinade injector with barbeque sauce. Inject sauce into each bratwurst until the skin is tight. Place bratwurst on the grill and cook for 10 minutes, turning once. Serve on buns. Makes 4 servings.

* * * * *

Ain't going to study war no more.

† CHITTERLINGS (CHITLIN'S) †

Pastor Balinda Moore
Memphis, TN

30 lb. frozen chitterlings
1 large green bell pepper
1 c. salt (to wash in)
garlic powder
½ pt. vinegar (optional)
3 Tbsp. salt (to season)

½ onion (reserve)
2 tsp. sage
10 garlic cloves
crushed red pepper
2 large onions, chopped

Let meat unthaw in the refrigerator for 2 days or unthaw at room temperature overnight.

Drain water from buckets. Pour meat in sink or tub of warm to hot water. Sprinkle with ½ cup salt. This will loosen fat from chitterlings. Discard fat and debris. Empty water and refill sink with hot water. Sprinkle remaining salt over chitterlings. This cleans and bleaches spots from meat. Pick through meat again; rinse with warm water. Meat should be clear and white to pink in color. This does not make meat salty. When you remove the lining and debris, the salt comes out. Drain water. Place ⅓ of chitterlings in large pot. Do not add water. Sprinkle that layer of meat with ⅓ garlic cloves, bell pepper chopped coarsely and crushed red pepper. Repeat layering in pot 2 times. Place all of the chopped onion on top of meat. Add remaining seasonings. Put lid on pot. Cut 1 onion in half. Place on top of lid. This will keep down the odor of cooking meat. Bring to boil; reduce heat to medium and cook 2 hours. Skim water and fat from pot. Cover and cook on low 2 more hours. Remove excess water and fat. Remove chitterlings; cut to bite size pieces. Return to liquid. Season to taste. Serve hot. Great with cole slaw and spaghetti.

Meats, Gravies, Rubs & Sauces

✝ PRIZE WINNING BABY BACK RIBS ✝

Mrs. Malinda's Recipe Collection

1 Tbsp. ground cumin
1 Tbsp. chili powder
1 Tbsp. paprika

salt and pepper to taste
3 lb. baby back pork ribs
1 c. barbeque sauce

Preheat grill for high heat. In a small jar, combine cumin, chili powder, paprika, salt and pepper. Close the lid and shake to mix. Trim the membrane sheath from the back of each rack. Run a small, sharp knife between the membrane and each rib and snip off the membrane as much as possible. Sprinkle as much of the rub onto both sides of the ribs as desired. To prevent the ribs from becoming too dark and spicy, do not thoroughly rub the spices into the ribs. Store the unused portion of the spice mix for future use. Place aluminum foil on lower rack to capture drippings and prevent flare-ups. Lightly oil grate and lay ribs on top rack of grill. Reduce heat to low; close lid and leave undisturbed for 1 hour. Do not lift lid at all. Brush ribs with barbeque sauce and grill an additional 5 minutes. Serve ribs as whole rack or cut between each rib bone and pile individually on a platter.

* * * * *

The Lord will provide.

† BIG DADDY'S MEMPHIS SHOULDER †
LEAN ON ME!

Horace Ford Johnson
Los Angeles, CA

10 to 14 lb. pork shoulder
1 small bottle liquid smoke

2 Tbsp. minced garlic
BBQ sauce

Dry Rub:

4 oz. cumin
4 oz. garlic powder
4 oz. lemon pepper

4 oz. paprika
4 oz. Montreal steak seasoning

Mix all Dry Rub ingredients together.

Wash meat. In meat preparation, don't cut the fat. Let the shoulder soak for 30 minutes in Worcestershire sauce and vinegar (equal amounts) in enough to cover bottom of pan. Add 1 whole bottle of liquid smoke. Rub Dry Rub all over shoulder. Massage it in. Add 2 tablespoons minced garlic. Rub on top. Put shoulder in a big roast pan with liquid.

For the sippin' saints, put a little beer in there. Now, you can either bake in an oven at 350° for 3 hours and 15 minutes; overnight real slow. Or the next day, you can drain it and lay meat on grill fat side down. Smoke for about 3 hours. Rotate. Let the heat and smoke get to it. Take it out. Let it stand 45 minutes. Pull meat off bone. Put meat into a food processor or shred or chop with a knife. Do not grind it. Add your favorite BBQ sauce (1 ½ to 2 bottles). Mix it in good. Now, get a big burger bun (toasted, of course), some cole slaw and an iced cold Coke. Enjoy!

* * * * *

Good bread, good meat, good God, let's eat.

† SPICY PRIME RIB ROAST †

Mrs. Malinda's Recipe Collection

¼ tsp. white pepper
¼ tsp. garlic salt
¼ tsp. salt
¼ tsp. onion powder

¼ tsp. oregano
2 bay leaves
6 to 8 lb. prime rib roast

Sprinkle seasonings on both sides of roast; cover and place in the refrigerator for 24 hours before cooking so roast will absorb spices. Lightly rinse roast with water. Baste outside of roast with butter. Grill for 20 minutes for each pound. Serves 10 to 12.

* * * * *

Rise, Peter, slay and eat.

† SUCKLING PIG BBQ †

1 (15 to 20 lb.) suckling pig   8 c. Marinade (recipe follows)

Break the spine of the pig with a cleaver from head to tail to allow the animal to lie flat on the grill. Marinate the pig for 2 hours before placing it over the coals.

Prepare the barbeque pit with coals. The coals are ready when they glow and are covered with a white ash. Have extra coals and oak wood on the side to add to the fire when needed, enough to keep the fire burning for 3 hours.

To gauge the temperature of the fire pit, hold your hand 18-inches away from the coals. You should be able to hold your hand over the fire for 4 to 5 seconds before pulling it away. If you can hold your hand longer over the fire, it means there is not enough heat; if less, the coals are too hot.

Remove the pig from the marinade. Place the pig, rib cage facing down towards the coals, and cook for about 2 ½ hours. Do not leave the fire unattended. Turn the pig onto its back and cook for another ½ to 1 hour, or until the pig's skin is crisp and the internal temperature reaches a minimum of 160° on a instant-read thermometer. Throughout the cooking time, check the fire temperature constantly and move the coals around to create a uniform temperature to prevent burning the pig. On a large grill, move meat to smoke side. Once the pig is done cooking, serve with fresh salads.

Marinade:

3 c. vegetable oil
4 ½ c. dry white wine
(recommended: Chilean
Sauvignon Blanc)
1 ½ c. chopped onions or
scallions
¾ c. minced fresh Italian
parsley leaves

3 tsp. chopped garlic
6 tsp. dried thyme
6 tsp. dried oregano
3 tsp. black pepper
3 tsp. ground cumin
6 tsp. salt

Mix all ingredients together in a bowl. This marinade can be prepared a day in advance.

† MOLASSES AND BARBECUED SPARERIBS †

William Woodland
Memphis, TN

2 Tbsp. Worcestershire sauce
¼ c. prepared mustard
¼ c. soy sauce
1 tsp. Tabasco sauce

3 lb. ribs
¼ c. light molasses
3 Tbsp. vinegar

Place ribs in shallow pan. Slowly add molasses and mustard. Add remaining ingredients; pour over ribs. Chill 3 hours or longer. Spoon sauce over ribs. Bake at 350° about 1 ½ hours or until tender, basting occasionally. Turn once during baking. Makes 3 to 4 servings. Serve with rice.

* * * * *

Rub a dub dub, thank you for the grub.

† WHITE SAUCE †

Mrs. Malinda's Recipe Collection

(Makes 1 Cup)

Thin:

1 Tbsp. butter flavor Crisco all-vegetable shortening or 1 Tbsp. butter flavor Crisco stick	1 Tbsp. all-purpose flour ½ tsp. salt ⅛ tsp. white or black pepper 1 c. milk

Medium:

2 Tbsp. butter flavor Crisco stick or 2 Tbsp. butter flavor Crisco all-vegetable shortening	2 Tbsp. all-purpose flour ½ tsp. salt ⅛ tsp. white or black pepper 1 c. milk

Thick:

3 Tbsp. butter flavor Crisco all-vegetable shortening or 3 Tbsp. butter flavor Crisco stick	3 Tbsp. all-purpose flour ½ tsp. salt ⅛ tsp. white or black pepper 1 c. milk

In 1-quart saucepan, melt butter flavor Crisco. Remove from heat. Stir in flour, salt and pepper. Slowly blend in milk. Cook over medium heat, stirring constantly, until mixture thickens and bubbles.

Herb Sauce: Follow the recipe above, adding ¼ teaspoon dried herbs (basil, oregano, thyme, dill, summer savory, etc.) with flour, salt and pepper.

Cheese Sauce: Follow the recipe above, adding ½ cup shredded cheese after mixture thickens. Stir until cheese melts.

* * * * *

Weeping may endure for a night..
But joy cometh in the morning.

† HONEY GARLIC BBQ SAUCE †

Mrs. Malinda's Recipe Collection

2 c. ketchup
1 bulb garlic, peeled and
  crushed
1 c. water
2 Tbsp. hot sauce
¼ c. honey
2 Tbsp. molasses
2 Tbsp. brown sugar
1 tsp. Worcestershire sauce
1 tsp. soy sauce

1 tsp. salt
2 Tbsp. Cajun seasoning
1 pinch paprika
1 pinch crushed red pepper
1 pinch ground white pepper
1 pinch ground black pepper
2 Tbsp. cornstarch
1 Tbsp. water
½ c. butter

In a large saucepan over medium-low heat, mix together ketchup, garlic, 1 cup of water, hot sauce, honey, molasses, brown sugar, Worcestershire sauce, soy sauce, salt, Cajun seasoning, paprika, red pepper, white pepper and black pepper. Allow the mixture to simmer approximately 30 minutes.

In a small bowl, dissolve cornstarch in 1 tablespoon of water. Adjust amount of water as needed to fully dissolve cornstarch. Stir into the sauce mixture. Continue simmering approximately 15 more minutes or until butter is melted and the sauce has begun to thicken. Serve over meats prepared as desired.

† FOUR-ALARM BARBECUE SAUCE †

Jeremiah Johnson
Carson, CA

1 Tbsp. red pepper
1 Tbsp. black pepper
1 (6 oz.) can tomato paste
juice of 1 lemon
1 c. vinegar

½ c. sugar
2 Tbsp. salt
2 Tbsp. chili powder
2 Tbsp. ketchup
1 tsp. dry mustard

Combine all ingredients in saucepan and boil 5 minutes or until thick. Makes 2 cups.

† BLACKBERRY BBQ SAUCE †

Mrs. Malinda's Recipe Collection

½ c. blackberry preserves
1 ½ c. ketchup
⅛ c. brown sugar

⅛ tsp. cayenne pepper
¼ tsp. mustard powder
2 Tbsp. red wine vinegar

In a medium bowl, mix together blackberry preserves, ketchup, brown sugar, cayenne pepper, mustard powder and red wine vinegar. Use to baste pork or beef ribs while grilling.

† APPLE BARBECUE SAUCE †

Mrs. Malinda's Recipe Collection

1 c. catsup
¼ c. soy sauce
¼ c. cider vinegar
¼ c. apple juice
2 Tbsp. Worcestershire sauce
¼ medium onion, finely grated

2 tsp. green bell pepper, grated
¾ tsp. granulated garlic
¾ tsp. ground white pepper
sugar to taste
½ Golden Delicious apple, grated

Combine all the ingredients, except the apple, and place in a saucepan and cook over medium heat for 5 to 10 minutes. Add the grated apple and simmer a little more. Add this sauce to your meat the last 10 to 15 minutes of grilling. This can be stored in the refrigerator for a week. This sauce can also be used as a table sauce.

* * * * *

For God so loved the world, that He gave his only begotten son. That whosoever believeth in Him shall have everlasting life.

Meats, Gravies, Rubs & Sauces

† ALL AROUND BBQ SAUCE †

Mrs. Malinda's Recipe Collection

2 c. ketchup
2 c. tomato sauce
1 ¼ c. brown sugar
1 ¼ c. red wine vinegar
½ c. unsulfured molasses
4 tsp. hickory-smoked liquid
  smoke
2 Tbsp. butter
½ tsp. garlic powder

½ tsp. onion powder
¼ tsp. chili powder
1 tsp. paprika
½ tsp. celery seed
¼ tsp. ground cinnamon
½ tsp. cayenne pepper
1 tsp. salt
1 tsp. coarsely ground black
  pepper

In a large saucepan over medium heat, mix together the ketchup, tomato sauce, brown sugar, wine vinegar, molasses, liquid smoke and butter. Season with garlic powder, onion powder, chili powder, paprika, celery seed, cinnamon, cayenne, salt and pepper. Reduce heat to low and simmer for up to 20 minutes.

For thicker sauce, simmer longer and for thinner, less time is needed. Sauce can also be thinned using a bit of water if necessary. Brush sauce onto any kind of meat during the last 10 minutes of cooking.

† DEBORA'S GRAVY FOR TURKEY AND † DRESSING

Debora J. Vanzant
Los Angeles, CA

½ c. flour
1 stick margarine
1 ½ c. onion, bell pepper and
  celery, chopped and
  browned (reserve; trinity mix)

6 c. broth
salt and pepper
2 c. cooked giblet meat,
  chopped

Brown ½ cup of flour in margarine, stirring constantly. Add broth. Mix well to remove lumps. Add trinity mix. Add cooked meat. Cook to desired consistency. Season to taste. Add broth as necessary.

YOUR FAVORITE RECIPES

Recipe   **Page Number**

Salads,
Pickles & Preserves

Salads

Additions and Garnishes

Sliced hard-cooked eggs
Radishes
Chopped green or ripe olives
Nut meats
Pimento
Green pepper
Sardines
Anchovies
Slivered cheeses
Julienned ham
Chicken
Grated carrots
Cubed celery
Onions - pickled, grated or
   pearl onions
Tomatoes, sliced and dipped in
   finely chopped parsley or chives
Capers
Dwarf tomatoes stuffed with
   cottage cheese
Fresh herbs - sprigs or chopped
Mint leaves
Cooked beets, cut into shapes
   or sticks
Lemon slices with pinked edges
   and dipped in chopped parsley
Raw cauliflower

Tips for Tossed Salads

Always handle salad greens
   with care.
Wash well, drain and dry greens
   before storing; chill well
   before using.
To core lettuce, smack head stem
   end down on counter top. Then
   twist the core out.
It is better to tear greens into bite-
   sized pieces to avoid bruising
   with knife.
Don't cut up tomatoes for a tossed
   salad since their juices thin the
   dressing and wilt the greens.
   Use them only for garnishing
   the salad bowl.
Select only firm, hard, green
   cucumbers. The skin should
   have a slight sheen, but if it is
   highly polished, it is probably
   waxed and the skin should be
   removed.
Use wild greens such as dandelion,
   sorrel or water cress for a
   different flavor and texture in
   tossed salads.

About Potato Salad

Potato salad is best made from
potatoes cooked in their jackets
and peeled and marinated while
still warm. Small red waxy
potatoes hold their shape when
sliced or diced and do not absorb
an excessive amount of dressing
or become mushy.

Soup Accompaniments

Clear Soups - crisp crackers,
cheese pastry, cheese-spread
toast strips.
Cream Soups - cheese popcorn,
seeded crackers, pretzels,
pickles and olives.
Chowders and Meat Soups -
Melba toast, sour pickles, oyster
crackers, bread sticks, relishes,
toasted garlic bread.

Salads, Pickles & Preserves

---

† FRUIT SALAD †

Mrs. Malinda's Recipe Collection

(Serves 20)

5 apples
5 oranges
5 bananas (add just before
serving)

1 large can pineapple chunks
plus any other fruit you might
want

Cut up fresh fruit, except bananas.

Sauce for Fruit Salad:

2 eggs
2 Tbsp. flour
$\frac{2}{3}$ c. sugar

1 c. canned pineapple juice
3 Tbsp. lemon juice

Beat eggs until light. Combine well with flour and sugar. Stir in fruit juice and cook, stirring constantly, until thick. Chill dressing.

† FRUIT SALAD II †

Mary Wallace
Memphis, TN

3 or 4 apples
1 can chunk pineapple
1 (12 oz.) tub cottage cheese
½ c. coconut
3 bananas

1 c. mini marshmallows
½ c. walnut chunks
¼ c. salad dressing
raisins

Leave skin on apples. Dice into large bowl. Peel and cut up bananas into bowl. Drain pineapple and add to bowl. Break nuts into bite-size pieces and add. Add remaining ingredients. Mix and chill. This fruit salad is an excellent appetizer. All ingredients are optional.

† MAMA'S QUICK SALAD †

Debora J. Vanzant
Los Angeles, CA

1 green iceberg lettuce
4 medium red tomatoes, sliced
2 yellow onions, thinly sliced

mayo or salad dressing
black pepper

Wash lettuce and other vegetables. Break lettuce into bite sized pieces by hand. Drain onto paper towel or in colander. Spread lettuce on clear crystal plate (Mama style). Top lettuce with tomatoes. Arrange onion slices on top. Put droplets of mayo or dressing on top. Sprinkle with pepper.

* * * * *

If you are willing and obedient,
You shall eat the Good of the Land.

Salads, Pickles & Preserves

✝ BBQ CHICKEN SALAD ✝

Mrs. Malinda's Recipe Collection

2 skinless, boneless chicken
  breast halves
4 stalks celery, chopped
1 large red bell pepper, diced
½ red onion, diced

1 (8.75 oz.) can sweet corn,
  drained
¼ c. barbeque sauce
2 Tbsp. fat-free mayonnaise

Preheat grill for high heat. Lightly oil grate. Grill chicken 10 minutes on each side or until juices run clear. Remove from heat; cool and cube. In a large bowl, toss together the chicken, celery, red bell pepper, onion and corn. In a small bowl, mix together the barbeque sauce and mayonnaise. Pour over the chicken and veggies. Stir and chill until ready to serve.

� ✝ FAVORITE FRUIT SALAD ✝

Pastor Carl McCorkle
Los Angeles, CA

(Low Calorie)

1 (No. 303) can (2 c.) dietetic
  fruit salad
1 envelope unflavored gelatin
juice of 1 lemon

1 banana, diced
1 (8 oz.) can dietetic ginger
  ale
2 oranges, sectioned and cut

Drain juice from canned fruit. Pour gelatin over juice to soften. Stir. Heat until dissolved. Cool. Add ginger ale and refrigerate until thickened. Mix all fruits together. Fold into the gelatin mixture. Refrigerate until firm.

* * * * *

Name it and claim it.
Believe it and receive it.

† FRESH FRUIT AND PASTA SALAD †

Mrs. Malinda's Recipe Collection

Packed with fresh fruit and healthful pasta, this salad is an excellent source of carbohydrates and fruit nutrients.

8 oz./227g dry wagon wheel or mini lasagna (malfalda) pasta
1 (15 oz./425g) can juice-packed pineapple chunks, drained
1 large orange, peeled, seeded and cut into sections
1 c./250 ml seedless green grapes (halved if large)
1 c./250 ml red seedless grapes (halved if too large)

1 large red apple, cored and chopped
1 banana, peeled and sliced
1 (8 oz./227g) container plain nonfat yogurt
¼ to ⅓ c./60 to 8 ml frozen orange juice concentrate, thawed
¾ tsp./4 ml pineapple extract
¾ tsp./4 ml cinnamon

Cook pasta according to package directions; drain and rinse with cold water. Combine pasta and fruit in large bowl. In smaller bowl, combine yogurt, orange juice concentrate, pineapple extract and cinnamon; mix well. Pour over fruit and pasta; toss to coat. Cover and chill thoroughly. Toss gently again before serving. Makes 10 servings.

† MACARONI FRUIT SALAD †

Mrs. Malinda's Recipe Collection

1 c. tiny macaroni, cooked
1 can fruit salad (1 lb.)
¾ c. sugar
pinch of salt

1 can mandarin oranges
2 Tbsp. flour
2 eggs

Drain the fruit with the mandarin oranges before mixing and save. Mix fruit and cooked macaroni. To the saved fruit juice, add the sugar, salt, flour and eggs. Cook until thickened and then pour over the macaroni-fruit mixture. Refrigerate overnight, then mix well with Cool Whip before serving.

† PICNIC POTATO SALAD †

Mrs. Malinda's Recipe Collection

6 white or Yukon Gold
  potatoes (3 lb.)
3 large eggs
½ Vidalia onion, peeled and
  finely chopped
¼ c. chopped pimento

3 Tbsp. sweet pickle relish
½ c. spicy brown mustard
½ c. mayonnaise
salt and freshly ground pepper
1 tsp. paprika

Peel the potatoes and cut them into 1 ½-inch chunks. Put the potatoes in a pot and add water to cover them by about 2-inches. Salt the water generously. Cover the pot and set it over high heat. Bring the water to a boil, then add the eggs. Reduce the heat to a brisk simmer and cook, covered, until the potatoes can just be pierced by a fork, about 15 minutes. With a slotted spoon, remove the eggs from the pot and set them aside. Drain the potatoes and place them in a large bowl. Rinse the eggs under cold running water until cool enough to handle. Peel and chop 2 of the eggs and add them to the potatoes. Add the onion, pimento and relish to the potatoes. In a small bowl, mix together the mayonnaise and mustard. Spoon over the potato salad. Season with salt and pepper and mix gently. Peel the remaining egg and slice it, placing the slices on top of the potato salad. Sprinkle with the paprika. Serve immediately or cover with plastic wrap and refrigerate for up to 4 hours. Serve chilled or at room temperature.

* * * * *

The spirit of the Lord is here. I can feel Him in the atmosphere.

† SEAFOOD PASTA SALAD †

Mrs. Malinda's Recipe Collection

1 Tbsp./15 mL chicken soup base

8 oz./227 g vegetable rotini (mixed green and red corkscrew pasta)

1 (6 oz./170 g) jar marinated artichoke hearts (undrained)

1 lb./454 g surimi (fish and crab blend), shredded or sliced

1 c./250 mL fresh cauliflower florets

1 c. /250 mL broccoli florets

1 c./250 mL shredded reduced-fat Monterey Jack cheese

½ c./125 mL sliced green onions

1 c./250 mL nonfat mayonnaise

½ c./125 mL buttermilk

1 ½ tsp./7.5 mL chicken soup base

1 tsp./5 mL garlic granules

½ tsp./2.5 mL onion granules

½ tsp./2.5 mL black pepper

½ tsp./2.5 mL thyme

lettuce leaves

Cook rotini per package directions, substituting the soup base for salt called for in directions. Drain; rinse with cold water and drain again. Combine rotini and all of the remaining ingredients, except lettuce, in large bowl; toss to mix. (More buttermilk may be added to obtain desired consistency.) Serve on a bed of lettuce. Makes 4 servings.

† WATERMELON SALAD †

Mrs. Malinda's Recipe Collection

1 (6 oz.) pkg. raspberry jello

1 c. miniature marshmallows

1 c. crushed pineapple

1 c. diced cantaloupe

1 c. seedless grapes

1 ½ c. cubed watermelon, seeds removed

Dissolve gelatin in water. Add marshmallows, stirring until dissolved. Chill until slightly thickened. Fold in remaining ingredients. Spoon into an 8-cup mold; chill until firm.

† WATERMELON SALAD FLOAT †

Balinda Moore
Memphis, TN

½ medium watermelon
1 cabasa melon
1 cantaloupe
1 honeydew melon

2 pkg. strawberries
4 bananas
1 c. mayonnaise
3 Tbsp. lemon juice

Cut melons in half and scoop out with small end of melon baller. Put in large bowl. Cut watermelon in half. Scoop out with large end of melon baller; be sure to get seeds out. Scrape watermelon shell out and scallop edges. Mix all melon balls and strawberries together and pour into shell. Mix mayonnaise and lemon juice up; pour over top. Cover and refrigerate overnight. Just before serving, cut bananas and mix in.

† RED AND WHITE WATERMELON SALAD †

Mrs. Malinda's Recipe Collection

6 oz. strawberry gelatin
2 c. hot water
3 c. watermelon balls
8 ¼ oz. can crushed pineapple
  (undrained)
1 ¼ c. chopped pecans,
  divided

4 oz. container refrigerated
  nondairy topping, thawed
½ c. milk
8 oz. cream cheese, softened
  to room temperature

Dissolve gelatin in hot water; let set until slightly firm, 40 to 50 minutes. Add melon balls, pineapple and 1 cup pecans. Pour into a 9 x 13-inch pan. Chill until firm.

Beat cream cheese until fluffy. Gradually add milk and heat until smooth. Fold in nondairy topping and place on chilled fruit mixture. Sprinkle with remaining ¼ cup pecans. Refrigerate until served. Serves 12.

✝ PASTEL RIBBON JELLO MOLD ✝

Mrs. Malinda's Recipe Collection

1 (16 oz.) sour cream
4 pt. vanilla ice cream

4 (3 oz.) pkg. Jell-O (orange, lime, lemon and strawberry)

Start the day before you are planning to serve. Make only 1 layer at a time. Be sure to use Pam or oil on mold.

Mix 1 package of Jell-O with 1 cup hot water. Stir in 1 pint of ice cream. Stir until ice cream is completely dissolved. When first layer is set, spread thin layer of sour cream, then continue with next layer of Jell-O and ice cream mixture and layer of sour cream. You will need a very large mold to make this recipe (using all the flavors of Jell-O). I used an 11-cup mold and 3 flavors.

✝ COLORADO DELIGHT ✝

Sis. Mary Brooks
Memphis, TN

1 (8 oz.) pkg. Philadelphia cream cheese
1 pkg. lime Jell-O, dissolved in 1 c. hot water

15 marshmallows, cut small
1 c. nuts
1 carton cream
1 medium can fruit cocktail

Dice cream cheese and mix with Jell-O/water mixture. Put in the refrigerator to chill. Dice nuts and marshmallows and mix with fruit cocktail. Whip cream and add 1 tablespoon sugar. Mix all ingredients together, but add cream last.

* * * * *

Tis so sweet to trust in Jesus. Just to take Him at his word.

✝ SWEET PEA SALAD ✝

Pamela J. Johnson
Carson, CA

2 cans green peas, drained
¼ c. chopped onions
½ c. sliced celery
½ tsp. salt
¼ tsp. pepper
¼ tsp. dried whole basil
⅔ c. commercial sour cream

2 tsp. sugar
1 ½ c. shredded Cheddar
   cheese
¼ c. real bacon bits
2 boiled eggs, chopped
1 small jar pimentos, drained

Mix ingredients in a 1-quart serving bowl; cover and chill at least 4 hours. Yield: 8 servings.

✝ CORNBREAD SALAD ✝

Sis. Sheryl Scott

1 (9-inch) pan cornbread,
   crumbled and cooked
2 cans pinto beans, drained
2 cans whole kernel corn,
   drained

1 (8 oz.) pkg. shredded
   Cheddar cheese
1 head lettuce, chopped
1 onion, chopped
3 tomatoes, chopped
Dressing (below)

Mix all of these ingredients together except the cornbread. Place the crumbled cornbread over the entire top of the salad and spread Dressing over cornbread.

Dressing:

1 c. mayonnaise
1 c. sour cream
a little milk (to make
   spreadable)

1 envelope Ranch dressing
mix

Mix well and spread over the cornbread. Serves 12 to 16.

✝ BLT SALAD ✝

Mrs. Malinda's Recipe Collection

8 strips bacon, cooked crisp
½ head lettuce, torn into small
  pieces
2 medium tomatoes
mayonnaise

salt and pepper to taste
4 green onions, chopped
  (optional)
1 c. croutons

Combine bacon, lettuce, tomato, salt and pepper and onion with enough mayonnaise to moisten well. Refrigerate until ready to serve and mix in croutons.

✝ BUTTERMILK SALAD ✝

Mrs. Malinda's Recipe Collection

1 large pkg. peach jello
1 large bowl Cool Whip
2 c. buttermilk

1 Tbsp. sugar
1 c. chopped nuts
1 large can crushed pineapple

Mix together jello, sugar and pineapple; cook for 20 minutes and let cool. Pour buttermilk and nuts into cool jello mixture. Mix well. Fold in Cool Whip. Chill until set.

Note: I cooked mine in double boiler and it tastes better if made the night before.

* * * * *

Oh how beautiful it is for brethren to dwell together in unity.

† CHICKEN SALAD †

Mrs. Malinda's Recipe Collection
(Serves 8 to 10)

breast of 6 chickens or 1
  turkey (breast)
1 c. whipped cream
1 medium-sized onion

2 c. seedless grapes
1 c. toasted almonds
½ c. mayonnaise
4 stalks celery

Use only white meat of chicken or turkey. Get the breasts of 6 chickens or 1 turkey to serve 8 to 10 people. Boil breasts the day before. Add salt, celery and onions for seasoning. Let stand overnight in the refrigerator. Remove from cold broth and drain. Cut with scissors in pieces larger than dice. Cut up celery hearts very fine and add to chicken. Add dash of cayenne. Wash 2 heaping cupfuls of seedless green grapes and let drain. Add to chicken and celery. Marinate all in good French dressing. Drain most of French dressing. Next, mix together ½ cup mayonnaise and 1 cup whipped cream. Stir into chicken. Just before serving, stir in 1 cup toasted almonds. This is a very extravagant but delicious salad. You can add more grapes and almonds for bulk to serve more people.

† CORN SALAD †

Mrs. Malinda's Recipe Collection

12 oz. can corn, drained
1 c. chopped celery
1 c. green onions
2 tsp. prepared mustard

1 jar chopped pimentos
3 Tbsp. salad oil
¼ c. vinegar

Combine all ingredients and chill. Great with fried fish.

† CHRISTMAS SALAD †

Mrs. Malinda's Recipe Collection

2 (3 oz.) pkg. cream cheese, softened
⅓ c. mayonnaise
1 c. whipping cream, whipped
1 (16 oz.) can pineapple (crushed), drained

½ c. maraschino cherries (red), drained and chopped
½ c. maraschino cherries (green), drained and chopped
1 ½ c. miniature marshmallows

Blend cheese and mayonnaise together. Whip cream until stiff and fold into mayonnaise mixture along with fruits. Freeze until ready to serve. Cut in squares and serve on lettuce leaves. Serves 10 to 12.

† CRANBERRY SALAD †

Mrs. Malinda's Recipe Collection

2 pkg. red Jell-O
½ c. sugar
1 c. pineapple syrup
grated rind of 1 orange
1 c. crushed pineapple
1 c. chopped apples

1 c. hot water
1 Tbsp. lemon juice
1 c. orange juice
1 lb. cranberries, ground
1 c. chopped celery
½ c. chopped pecans

Dissolve Jell-O in hot water. Add sugar, juices and pineapple syrup. Chill until partially set. Add other ingredients and pour into a lightly greased mold. Top with mayonnaise if desired.

* * * * *

Come on over here, the table is spread. The feast of the Lord is going on.

✝ CRANBERRY SALAD 2 ✝

Mrs. Malinda's Recipe Collection

1 qt. cranberries	3 ½ c. boiling water
2 c. sugar	2 Tbsp. gelatin
½ c. cold water	1 c. chopped nuts
1 c. diced pineapple	1 c. grapes

Cook cranberries in boiling water until the skins burst. Strain and add sugar immediately so it will dissolve. Soften gelatin in cold water and add to hot mixture. Cool. Add nuts, grapes and pineapple. Pour into a lightly greased mold or individual molds. Chill until firm. Unmold on lettuce and top with mayonnaise.

✝ 4 P'S SALAD ✝

Mrs. Malinda's Recipe Collection

1 (No. 3) can peas, drained	⅓ c. salad dressing
½ c. pimiento cheese, diced	¾ tsp. salt
½ c. sweet pickles, diced	2 tsp. sugar
¾ c. chunk pineapple, drained	

Blend the salad dressing with the salt plus sugar and add to the salad ingredients. Refrigerate an hour or more and serve on lettuce leaf.

Equal can be used for sugar.

* * * * *

Up above my head, I hear music. I hear music in the air. There must be a God somewhere.

† FROSTED FRUIT SALAD †

Mrs. Malinda's Recipe Collection

1 (3 oz.) pkg. orange gelatin
1 (3 oz.) pkg. lemon gelatin
2 ½ c. water (hot)
½ c. water (cold)
juice of 1 lemon
2 bananas, mashed

1 c. miniature marshmallows
1 (20 oz.) can pineapple
(crushed), drained
(reserve ½ c. liquid for
sauce)
1 c. fine coconut

Dissolve gelatin in 2 ½ cups hot water. Add ½ cup cold water and juice of lemon. Chill until thick. Add drained pineapple, bananas, ½ cup coconut and marshmallows. Chill until set.

Sauce:

2 Tbsp. all-purpose flour
2 Tbsp. butter
½ c. sugar

1 egg, beaten
1 c. pineapple juice
1 c. nondairy whipped topping

Put in top of double boiler the first 5 ingredients; cook until thick. Cool. Spread on top of salad mixture. Top with whipped topping and sprinkle with test of the coconut. Serves 15 to 18.

† MEXICAN CHEF SALAD †

Mrs. Malinda's Recipe Collection

1 medium onion
4 small tomatoes
1 head lettuce
4 oz. grated Rumiano Cheddar
cheese
1 lb. ground beef
½ tsp. salt

1 can drained red kidney
beans
1 small bag Doritos chips
1 large sliced avocado
1 (8 oz.) bottle Thousand Island
dressing

Chop onion, tomatoes and lettuce; toss with grated cheese. Brown the ground beef with salt. Cool. Add kidney beans. Crush and add Doritos chips and avocado. Toss all ingredients together with Thousand Island dressing. Add hot sauce to taste.

† 7 LAYER SALAD †

Mrs. Malinda's Recipe Collection

1 medium head lettuce, shredded	2 boxes frozen peas
1 c. purple onion, chopped	2 c. mayo
1 c. chopped pepper	1 Tbsp. sugar
1 c. celery	1 c. Longhorn cheese
	bacon crumbs

In a saucepan over medium heat, cook peas for 3 minutes and cool. Fry bacon and crumble. In a pan, layer lettuce, onion, pepper and celery. Add cooled peas. In a separate bowl, mix mayo and sugar and spread on the layers, making sure to spread to the edges of the pan to seal the lettuce. Sprinkle cheese and bacon on top. Cover pan and refrigerate overnight before serving.

† SEVEN LAYER SALAD II †

Mrs. Malinda's Recipe Collection

1 head lettuce, torn in small pieces	3 medium tomatoes, sliced
1 red onion, chopped	1 c. Parmesan cheese, grated
3 to 4 stalks celery, chopped	1 c. Romano cheese, grated
1 can water chestnuts, sliced	4 hard-boiled eggs, sliced
1 pkg. frozen peas (unthawed)	½ lb. bacon, fried crisp and crumbled (artificial bacon
2 c. Hellmann's mayonnaise	bits may be substituted)

Cover the bottom of a 12 x 10 x 3-inch (or larger) pan with shredded lettuce. Now, build layer by layer. Scatter chopped onion and celery next. Cover with sliced water chestnuts. Form the next layer with the unthawed peas, covering the other layers well. With a spatula, spread a thick layer of mayonnaise over this. (It may be necessary to use more than 2 cups.) Sprinkle the grated cheese over the top. Next, layer the hard-boiled eggs, tomatoes and crumbled bacon or substitute. Do not toss. Refrigerate 6 hours before cutting into squares to serve.

✝ TACO SALAD ✝

1 lb. ground beef, cooked and
  crumbled
¼ lb. grated Cheddar cheese
1 small onion, chopped
sliced black olives
2 small tomatoes, chopped

1 small head lettuce
Doritos chips
pinto beans or chili pinto
  beans
taco chips (if you like)

Combine ingredients in a salad bowl. Add dressing. Combine 2 to 4 tablespoons taco sauce with a small amount of Catalina dressing. Mix dressing with other salad ingredients. Use pinto beans or chili pinto beans if you like and use taco chips if you like.

✝ K F C COLE SLAW ✝

8 c. very finely chopped
  cabbage (1 head)
¼ c. shredded carrot (1
  medium carrot)
2 Tbsp. minced onion
⅓ c. granulated sugar
½ tsp. salt

⅛ tsp. pepper
¼ c. milk
½ c. mayonnaise
¼ c. buttermilk
1 ½ Tbsp. white vinegar
2 ½ Tbsp. lemon juice

Be sure the cabbage, carrot and onion are chopped up into very fine pieces about the size of rice kernels. Combine sugar, salt, pepper, milk, mayonnaise, buttermilk, vinegar and lemon juice. Beat until smooth. Add cabbage, carrot and onions. Mix well. Cover and refrigerate at least 2 hours before serving. Serves 8.

Note: The critical part of this cole slaw recipe is the flavor-enhancement period prior to eating. Be absolutely certain the cole slaw sits in the refrigerator for at least a couple of hours prior to serving.

♡ † GUACAMOLE †

Mrs. Malinda's Recipe Collection

2 avocados, mashed
1 Tbsp. lemon juice
2 Tbsp. lime juice
1 Tbsp. onion, grated
1 tsp. salt
1 c. grated cheese

¼ tsp. chili powder
dash of cayenne pepper
⅓ c. mayonnaise
¼ c. ripe olives, chopped
4 slices crisp bacon, crumbled

Blend all ingredients thoroughly. Serve with warmed corn chips or spoon over shredded lettuce as a salad. Cheese is optional.

♡ † SUMMER SALAD †

Mrs. Malinda's Recipe Collection

1 (7 oz.) pkg. (2 c. uncooked)
  elbow macaroni
1 (16 oz.) can Veg-All, drained
1 (7 oz.) can tuna, drained and
  flaked
1 c. Cheddar cheese, diced
½ c. sweet pickles, diced

½ c. onion, diced
½ c. sour cream
½ c. salad dressing
1 ½ Tbsp. lemon juice
1 tsp. seasoned salt
¼ tsp. black pepper

Prepare macaroni according to package directions; drain. Add Veg-All, tuna, cheese, onion and pickles. Mix remaining ingredients and toss with macaroni mixture; chill.

* * * * *

This little light of mine.
I'm going to let it shine.

† SUNSHINE SALAD †

Mrs. Malinda's Recipe Collection

1 small can pineapple
1 small pkg. orange jello
1 small pkg. cream cheese

1 small can evaporated milk
¼ c. nuts
¼ c. celery

Bring to a boil a small can of pineapple. Add the jello and boil about 3 minutes. Grate the cream cheese into above mixture; stir until almost dissolved. Put into the refrigerator until it starts to congeal. Put evaporated milk in freezer to cool it off. Whip the evaporated milk and add it, nuts and celery to the salad.

† MACARONI SALAD †

Mrs. Malinda's Recipe Collection

2 c. macaroni, cooked
1 onion, chopped
1 large green pepper, chopped
1 large carrot, chopped
1 stalk celery, chopped

2 sweet pickles
1 large tomato (fresh or canned)
2 boiled eggs
salt and pepper to taste

Combine macaroni with chopped vegetables and eggs. Mix with enough mayonnaise to moisten. Add seasonings.

* * * * *

I have never seen the righteous forsaken, nor his seed begging bread.

† CREAMY COLE SLAW †

Mrs. Malinda's Recipe Collection
(A Creamy Delight Thanks to the Richness of Pet)

1 small can (²⁄₃ c.) Pet (the cream of evaporated milk)	¼ tsp. celery seeds
¼ c. Musselman's apple cider vinegar	⅛ tsp. pepper
	½ c. mayonnaise
2 Tbsp. sugar	4 c. shredded cabbage
1 tsp. salt	1 carrot, shredded
	1 stalk celery, diced

Stir together Pet, vinegar, sugar, salt, celery seeds, pepper and mayonnaise; chill until ready to serve.

Combine cabbage, carrot and celery; chill.

To Serve: Pour Pet mixture over cabbage mixture. Toss to coat well. Serve immediately. Makes 6 servings, ½ cup each.

♡ † GREEN WONDER SALAD †

Mrs. Malinda's Recipe Collection

1 (No. 303) can French green beans	1 (6 oz.) can water chestnuts
	3 medium onions, sliced
1 (No. 303) can small English peas	1 c. sugar (I use ²⁄₃ c.)
1 ½ c. celery, diced	¾ c. vinegar
	1 tsp. salt
1 (No. 303) can fancy Chinese vegetables (without meat)	pepper to taste

Drain all cans and place in large bowl, also celery and onions. Heat the sugar, vinegar, salt and pepper. Pour over vegetables. Refrigerate 8 hours or more. Good for 3 weeks.

* * * * *

Be blessed!

♡ † RAW BROCCOLI SALAD †

Mrs. Malinda's Recipe Collection

1 bunch broccoli, washed and
  cut
½ c. onion, chopped
½ c. ripe olives, sliced
3 hard-cooked eggs, sliced

1 Tbsp. lemon juice
salt and pepper
1 pkg. "Hidden Valley Ranch"
  buttermilk dressing

Combine all raw vegetables, except eggs. Mix dressing according to package directions and use enough to coat broccoli mixture well. Add sliced eggs last and stir as little as possible.

† ANYTIME FRUIT SALAD †

Mrs. Malinda's Recipe Collection

2 to 3 bananas, sliced
2 to 3 apples, cored and cut
  into ½-inch cubes
lettuce (optional)

1 (15 ½ oz.) can pineapple
  chunks, drained
1 (8 oz.) carton Mandarin
  orange flavored yogurt

Combine fruit and yogurt; mix well. Chill thoroughly. Serve on lettuce, if desired. Yield: 6 to 8 servings.

Note: May also be served for breakfast or as a dessert.

* * * * *

If thou shall confess with thy mouth and believe in the Lord Jesus, thou shall be saved.

Salads, Pickles & Preserves

✝ "CRANBERRY'S FOR THE HOLIDAYS" ✝

Mrs. Dianne Pallay
Pasadena, CA

1 lb. fresh cranberries
1 orange (seedless), chopped
¼ c. raisins
¼ c. currants
1 c. chopped pecans
1 ½ c. raspberry syrup
1 c. sugar

1 c. light brown sugar
2 Tbsp. orange extract
½ tsp. cinnamon
¼ tsp. ground cloves
pinch of white pepper
pinch of salt

Combine all ingredients except pecans in a saucepan over medium heat. Bring to simmer. Cook about 10 minutes or until most of the cranberries pop open. Skim any foam off the top. Stir in pecans. Serve at room temperature.

✝ POTATO SALAD ✝

Mrs. Malinda's Recipe Collection

4 medium Irish potatoes
2 hard-boiled eggs
1 small can pimento
3 medium sweet cucumber
  pickles
salt

2 pieces celery, chopped
½ c. finely chopped onion
salad dressing
vinegar
sugar

Boil potatoes with jackets on until you can prick easily with a fork. Allow to cool until you can dice. Remove jackets; dice and add the chopped eggs, pimentos, pickles, celery and onion. Mix well, adding salt to taste. Add about 3 tablespoons of salad dressing, diluted with 1 tablespoon of vinegar, again mixing thoroughly. After placing in serving bowl, add paprika, if desired. Serves 6.

♡ † PICKLED RED BEETS OR STRING † BEANS

Mrs. Malinda's Recipe Collection

1 scant c. sugar
1 ¼ c. vinegar
1 Tbsp. salt

dash of pepper
2 c. water

Bring sugar, vinegar, salt, pepper and water to boil. Pour over cooked red beets or cooked string beans.

† PURPLE PEA HULL JELLY †

Mrs. Malinda's Recipe Collection

4 c. juice*
1 box Sure-Jell

5 c. sugar

*Made from simmering hulls of purple hull peas until water is purple colored, 30 to 40 minutes; strain.
Bring juice and Sure-Jell to a boil, stirring constantly. Add sugar all at once. Bring back to boil and boil hard for 2 minutes, stirring constantly. Pour into sterilized jars and seal.

† PEPPER JELLY †

Mrs. Malinda's Recipe Collection

1 ½ c. sweet pepper (green
and red)
½ c. hot pepper

1 ½ c. vinegar
6 ½ c. sugar
1 (6 oz.) bottle Certo

In blender, place peppers and vinegar. Blend for a few seconds. In a large saucepan, combine pepper mixture and sugar; cook for 5 minutes. Add Certo; cook 2 minutes longer. Stir while you add Certo. Seal in hot jars. Real good with chicken and dressing and fried fish.

✝ YELLOW SQUASH PICKLES ✝

Mrs. Malinda's Recipe Collection

8 c. thinly sliced yellow squash
2 c. green bell peppers, sliced
   in strips
2 c. thinly sliced onions
2 regular red bell peppers,
   thinly sliced

4 c. sugar
3 c. vinegar
2 Tbsp. celery seed
1 Tbsp. thyme
2 Tbsp. mustard seed

Soak squash in brine water for 1 hour (mix ¾ cup of salt with 3 quarts of water). Bring vinegar to boil. Add thyme, sugar, celery seed and mustard seed. Add squash, pepper and onion. Bring to boil. Remove from heat. Fill 6 pint jars. Seal and store. This is very good with vegetables, meat and on hot dogs.

✝ MRS. MALINDA'S BREAD AND BUTTER ✝ PICKLES

Mrs. Malinda's Recipe Collection

4 qt. cucumbers, sliced
6 medium onions, sliced
2 green peppers, sliced
⅓ c. salt
5 c. sugar

3 c. white distilled vinegar
1 ½ tsp. turmeric
1 ½ tsp. celery seed
2 Tbsp. mustard seed

Pour salt over sliced cucumbers, onions and green peppers. Cover with ice and soak 3 hours. Mix together, then drain. Set aside.

In a large pan, mix sugar, vinegar, turmeric, celery seed and mustard seed together and bring to a boil but DO NOT BOIL. Add to cucumber mixture; then pack into sterilized jars and seal. Yields 3 pints.

† CHA-CHA †

Mrs. Malinda's Recipe Collection

12 tomatoes
½ lb. hot peppers
6 onions
1 medium cabbage

1 c. sugar
3 c. vinegar
1 Tbsp. salt

Use no water for vegetables.

Chop all ingredients up fine. Cook until done. Place your jar into a pan of water and put your Cha-Cha in the jar.

† CHA-CHA 2 †

Mrs. Malinda's Recipe Collection

5 small green tomatoes
¼ head cabbage
¼ head cauliflower
1 green pepper
1 red pepper

1 small onion
1 Tbsp. pickling allspice
1 c. sugar (optional)
4 c. vinegar

Wash tomatoes, cabbage, cauliflower and peppers. Cut up all vegetables and combine in a large cooking pot. Add remaining ingredients to vegetables. Let stand overnight covered. Then let cook over medium heat for 25 to 30 minutes.

Preheat jar and its top while cooking Cha-Cha in a separate pot. Spoon Cha-Cha into jar, top and let cool. Yields 1 quart jar.

* * * * *

Are you saved?

✝ FIG PRESERVES ✝

Mrs. Malinda's Recipe Collection
(Excellent)

2 gal. (32 c.) figs   16 c. water
32 c. sugar   1 lemon

Sprinkle 1 cup baking soda over the figs. Cover with boiling water; let stand 15 minutes. Drain, then rinse in cold water. Cook sugar and water until sugar has dissolved and liquid is boiling. Gradually put in figs and cook until they are tender and transparent, about 1 ½ hours. Lift figs out and cook syrup until consistency of honey. Return figs to syrup; let stand 12 hours before sealing.

✝ PEAR CONSERVE ✝

Mrs. Malinda's Recipe Collection

5 lb. hard pears   5 lb. sugar
rind of 2 oranges   juice of 3 oranges
juice of 2 lemons   1 lb. raisins
½ lb. walnuts or pecans,
   broken

Cut pears in ½-inch cubes. Let stand with sugar overnight. Next day, add remaining ingredients and boil for 2 hours or until thick. Just before taking from the fire, add the chopped nuts. Can in glass canning jars.

✳ ✳ ✳ ✳ ✳

Do you love the Lord?

† WOLF RIVER BOTTOM MUSCADINE †
JELLY

Mrs. Malinda's Recipe Collection

bucket of muscadines
4 c. sugar

4 c. juice from muscadines
water

You will need 4 pint canning jars.

Cross railroad track. Climb up Tucker Hill. Pick muscadines along Wolf River Bottom. Come down from the hill, cross railroad track and go home. Wash the muscadines under the faucet on the side of the house. Go inside and place fruit in pan. Barely cover with water. Bring to a boil and cook approximately 30 minutes. Put in cloth bag (pillow case) and let drip for several hours. Let drip in pan; do not squeeze. Boil juice 10 minutes. Add sugar and boil until drops form sheet from side of spoon. Skim while cooking. Pour into sterile jars and let cool. Makes 4 pint jars.

† CHOW-CHOW †

Mrs. Malinda's Recipe Collection

1 gal. cabbage
1 gal. green tomatoes
1 qt. onions
6 bell peppers
2 bunches celery
1 c. salt (scant)
3 Tbsp. mustard seed
4 Tbsp. mustard

2 Tbsp. ginger
2 Tbsp. cinnamon
1 Tbsp. cloves
1 Tbsp. nutmeg
4 Tbsp. turmeric
2 hot peppers, diced (optional)
3 lb. sugar
2 qt. vinegar

Chop but do not grind vegetables. Reserve and refrigerate celery. Mix all vegetables except celery in large pan. Sprinkle with salt and let stand overnight.

Next day, drain all vegetables, squeezing out surplus juice. Add celery. Put all ingredients into large vessel and allow to come to a fast boil. Spoon into jars, seal and process.

† PEPPER JELLY †

Mrs. Malinda's Recipe Collection

¼ c. hot pepper
¾ c. bell pepper
6 ½ c. sugar

1 ½ c. cider vinegar
6 oz. Sure-Jell
green or red food coloring

Seed and dice peppers (use gloves!). Combine peppers, vinegar and sugar. Cool 10 minutes. Strain. Add Sure-Jell and food coloring to strained liquid. Pour into sterilized jars and seal.

† STRAWBERRY PRESERVES †

Mrs. Malinda's Recipe Collection

2 c. mashed strawberries
4 c. sugar

1 box Sure-Jell
1 c. water

In a bowl, mix strawberries and sugar. Let stand for 20 minutes. In saucepan, cook 1 cup water and Sure-Jell. Stir rapidly while boiling. Mix it well. Pour over berries and stir for 2 minutes. Can and let stand at room temperature for at least 4 hours.

† EQUAL STRAWBERRY PRESERVES †

Mrs. Malinda's Recipe Collection

2 c. coarsely chopped
strawberries (would be 1 qt.
whole)
1 c. water

1 envelope unflavored gelatin
1 tsp. lemon juice
9 pkg. Equal sweetener

Pour water in saucepan. Sprinkle gelatin over it. Let set 5 minutes. Add berries and lemon juice; heat just to boiling. Remove from heat; add Equal and stir well. Pour into containers. Freeze.

✝ SYRUP ✝

In making syrup, add sugar into water and dissolve by cooking and continual stirring. When boiled and the mixture thickens it is ready to use.

To make a light syrup, place 5 cups granulated sugar in 1 gallon of water; a medium syrup is made with 12 cups of sugar to 1 gallon of water and heavy syrup is made with 28 cups of sugar to 1 cup of water. Syrup should be strained and placed in a covered container for future use.

✳ ✳ ✳ ✳ ✳

He's still able and available.

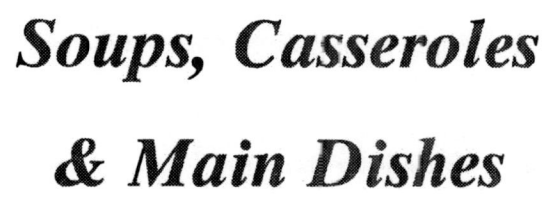

Soups, Casseroles & Main Dishes

Common Kitchen Pans to Use as Casseroles

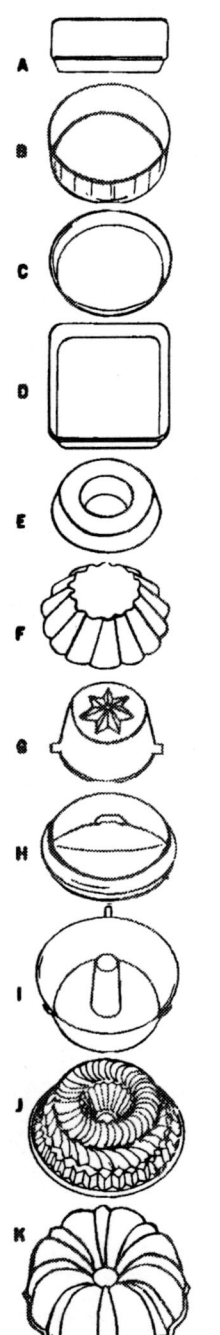

WHEN THE RECIPE CALLS FOR:

4-cup baking dish:
9-inch pie plate
8 x 1-1/4-inch layer-cake pan -**C**
7 3/8 x 3 5/8 x 2 1/4-inch loaf pan -**A**

6-cup baking dish:
8 or 9 x 11 1/2-inch layer-cake pan -**C**
10-inch pie plate
8 1/2 x 3 5/8 x 2 5/8-inch loaf pan -**A**

8-cup baking dish:
8 x 8 x 2-inch square pan -**D**
11 x 7 x 1 1/2-inch baking pan
9 x 5 x 3-inch loaf pan -**A**

10-cup baking dish:
9 x 9 x 2-inch square pan
11 3/4 x 7 1/2 x 1 3/4-inch baking pan
15 x 10 x 1-inch jelly-roll pan

12-cup baking dish or over:

13 1/2 x 8 1/2 x 2-inch glass baking pan	12 cups
13 x 9 x 2-inch metal baking pan	15 cups
14 x 10 1/2 x 2 1/2-inch roasting pan	19 cups

TOTAL VOLUME OF VARIOUS SPECIAL BAKING PANS

Tube Pans

7 1/2 x 3-inch "Bundt" tube -**K**	6 cups
9 x 3 1/2-inch fancy tube or "Bundt" pan -**J** or **K**	9 cups
9 x 3 1/2-inch angel-cake pan -**I**	12 cups
10 x 3 3/4-inch "Bundt" or "Crownburst" pan -**K**	12 cups
9 x 3 1/2-inch fancy tube -**J**	12 cups
10 x 4-inch fancy tube mold (kugelhupf) -**J**	16 cups
10 x 4-inch angel-cake pan -**I**	18 cups

Melon Mold

7 x 5 1/2 x 4-inch mold -**H**	6 cups

Spring-Form Pans:

8 x 3-inch pan -**B**	12 cups
9 x 3-inch pan -**B**	16 cups

Ring Molds

8 1/2 x 2 1/4-inch mold -**E**	4-1/2 cups
9 1/4 x 2 3/4-inch mold -**E**	8 cups

Charlotte Mold:

6 x 4 1/4-inch mold -**G**	7-1/2 cups

Brioche Pan:

9 1/2 x 3 1/4-inch pan -**F**	8 cups

Soup, Casseroles & Main Dishes

† JOE'S MULLIGAN STEW †

Mrs. Malinda's Recipe Collection

1 small onion, chopped
2 Tbsp. fried meat grease

1 can tomatoes or tomato
 juice
2 to 3 slices bread

Brown onion in meat grease. When browned, add tomatoes or tomato juice. Let boil a few minutes. Sweeten to taste. Break in small pieces the bread and add to mixture. Continue cooking until bread is dissolved, about 3 or 4 minutes. You may use a little green pepper, if desired. Brown it along with onion. Add any leftover meat or vegetables in the refrigerator. Season to taste.

† RIPE TOMATO VEGETABLE SOUP †

Mrs. Malinda's Recipe Collection

24 lb. ripe tomatoes
1 lb. snap beans
1 lb. purple hull peas
1 lb. baby lima beans
1 lb. speckled butter beans
1 lb. English peas
1 lb. cream peas

2 lb. cut corn
2 lb. okra, cut
6 carrots, sliced
8 potatoes, cubed
4 bell peppers, chopped
6 onions, chopped
1 tsp. salt (to qt.)

Use fresh or frozen vegetables. Mix in water bath cooker. Peel, core and trim tomatoes. Mix with vegetables. (Thaw frozen vegetables while chopping other ingredients.) Place on slow heat until thawed and comes to boil. Prepare jars; fill and seal. (Add 1 teaspoon salt to quart.) Place in pressure cooker with warm water. Bring pressure cooker up moderately slow. Cook with 10 pounds pressure for 85 minutes. Makes approximately 19 quarts soup.

* * * * *

What a mighty God we serve.

✝ BEAN MIX FOR 12 BEAN SOUP ✝

Mrs. Malinda's Recipe Collection

16 oz. bag lentils
16 oz. bag barley
16 oz. bag pinto beans
16 oz. bag kidney beans
16 oz. bag Great Northern
  beans
16 oz. bag pink beans

16 oz. bag green split peas
16 oz. bag baby lima beans
16 oz. bag black-eyed peas
16 oz. bag red beans
16 oz. bag small white beans
16 oz. bag yellow split peas

Mix and store in large Tupperware bowl.

12 Bean Soup:

16 oz. bean mix
2 qt. water
1 lb. ham hock or chunked
  ham (optional)
1 large onion, chopped
1 (28 oz.) can stewed
  tomatoes

2 bay leaves
4 Tbsp. Worcestershire sauce
1 tsp. Italian seasoning
1 tsp. pepper
2 cloves garlic, chopped
1 tsp. liquid smoke

Wash beans. Place in a large kettle and cover beans with water. Add 2 tablespoons salt. Soak overnight.

In the morning, drain off water and add to beans all remaining ingredients. Bring to a boil, then simmer slowly 4 hours, stirring occasionally.

❉ ❉ ❉ ❉ ❉

There is a brighter day ahead.

† UNCLE JOE'S MULLIGAN STEW #2 †

Louis Burton Johnson
Memphis, TN

2 to 3 lb. beef
2 to 3 lb. pork
5 lb. potatoes, cubed
6 or 7 cans carrots, sliced
2 or 3 cans whole kernel corn,
    drained

2 or 3 cans green beans,
    drained
1 bunch diced celery (leaves
    and all)
1 c. diced onions
1 Tbsp. salt

230

May combine in large kettle and fill half full with water. Cook about 3 hours.

The outdoor method is to cook over a fire in a lard can ½ full of water and stir with a new axe handle. The more it is reheated, the better it is.

* * * * *

According to your faith it shall be done unto you.

† 212 †   Soup, Casseroles & Main Dishes

✝ AUTUMN STEW ✝

Mrs. Malinda's Recipe Collection
(Makes 6 to 8 Servings)

¼ c. all-purpose flour
2 tsp. dried parsley flakes
½ tsp. dried thyme leaves
½ tsp. salt
½ tsp. ground ginger
¼ tsp. ground nutmeg
¼ tsp. pepper
2 lb. pork stew meat, cut into
   1 ½-inch cubes
3 Tbsp. Crisco oil
1 (16 oz.) can pumpkin
1 (15 oz.) can garbanzo
   beans, rinsed and drained

2 c. water
1 medium sweet potato,
   peeled and cut into ¾-inch
   cubes
½ c. chopped green onion
1 Tbsp. packed brown sugar
2 tsp. instant chicken bouillon
   granules
1 bay leaf
1 medium zucchini, cut into
   julienne strips

Mix flour, parsley flakes, thyme, salt, ginger, nutmeg and pepper in large plastic food storage bag. Add pork. Shake to coat. Heat Crisco oil in Dutch oven. Add pork and any remaining flour mixture. Brown over medium-high heat. Stir in remaining ingredients except zucchini. Heat to boiling. Cover. Reduce heat and simmer, stirring occasionally, 1 ½ to 2 hours. Add zucchini; re-cover. Simmer 30 minutes longer or until pork is tender. Remove and discard bay leaf.

Rutabaga Variation: Follow recipe above, substituting 1 ⅓ cups cubed rutabaga (½-inch cubes) for sweet potato.

* * * * *

Oh how I love Jesus because He first loved me.

† BRUNSWICK STEW †

Debora J. Vanzant
Los Angeles, CA

(For 100 or More)

1 small hog's head	3 pt. corn
1 hen	3 pt. butter beans
1 qt. canned tomatoes	3 pt. garden peas
2 cans tomato soup	3 lb. Irish potatoes
2 bottles catsup	2 lb. ground beef

Cook hog's head and hen until very tender. Remove meat from bones and cut fine. To broth, add vegetables and cook until almost done. Add ground beef, tomatoes, soup and catsup and finish cooking. Add hog's head and hen. Season with black pepper, salt and a little sugar to taste. If too juicy, add crackers or oatmeal to thicken.

† GRANT STEW †

Jeremiah Johnson
Carson, CA

45 to 50 lb. chicken	1 gal. can Veg-All vegetables
20 lb. beef	1 gal. field peas
1 large turkey or 2 small	2 to 3 qt. bell pepper and hot peppers
30 lb. potatoes	6 celery
12 to 15 lb. carrots	1 ½ gal. okra
1 to 1 ½ gal. butter beans	25 lb. onions
2 gal. green beans	2 large cans tomato sauce
1 gal. English peas	1 gal. or more tomato juice
3 to 4 gal. canned tomatoes	2 gal. corn (whole kernel and cream-style)
2 bottles syrup	
3 to 5 bottles hot sauce	
1 bottle Worcestershire sauce	

Season according to taste. Cook all meats ahead of time. Toss all ingredients in a black pot. Cook to desired consistency. Makes 30 to 40 gallons.

† 214 †   Soup, Casseroles & Main Dishes

✝ SAUSAGE JAMBALAYA ✝

Mrs. Malinda's Recipe Collection

2 large onions
1 green pepper
1 clove garlic, crushed
2 lb. smoked sausage (½ hot, optional)
2 c. rice
2 Tbsp. Worcestershire sauce

2 (8 oz.) tomato sauce
2 Tbsp. hot sauce
¼ tsp. red pepper
2 c. white wine
1 ¾ c. water
salt and pepper to taste

In Dutch oven, saute onions, green pepper and garlic in olive oil. Add sausage cut into small circle pieces. Add all the rest of the ingredients; bring to a boil. Cover and cook slowly ¾ hour.

* * * * *

Fairest Lord Jesus.

✝ ONION SOUP GRATINEED WITH CHEESE ✝

Mrs. Malinda's Recipe Collection

5 c. thinly sliced yellow onions
3 Tbsp. butter
1 Tbsp. oil
1 tsp. salt
¼ tsp. sugar
3 Tbsp. flour
5 c. canned beef broth
3 c. water

½ c. dry white wine
12 to 16 slices French bread,
  cut ¾-inch thick
2 oz. Swiss cheese
1 Tbsp. grated onion
1 ½ c. grated Swiss cheese
1 Tbsp. melted butter
salt and pepper to taste

Simmer onions in butter and oil in covered, heavy 4-quart pan for 15 minutes. Uncover, raise heat and stir in salt and sugar. Cook another 30 to 40 minutes, stirring often, to evenly golden brown. Add flour, sprinkling and stirring for 3 minutes. In another pan, bring liquid to boil, then stir into onions. Simmer 30 to 40 minutes and salt and pepper to taste.

TO MAKE BREAD: Place bread in pan. Bake at 325° for 30 minutes. After first 15 minutes, rub each slice on both sides with cut end of garlic clove.

To gratinee, bring soup liquid to boil and stir in 2 ounces Swiss cheese. Pour into casserole or soup tureen. Float toast rounds on top. Sprinkle with grated cheese and melted butter. Bake at 325° for 20 minutes. Serve piping hot to 6 to 8.

This one is worth the trouble.

* * * * *

Love thy neighbor as thyself.

Soup, Casseroles & Main Dishes

† PO' MAN'S SOUP †

Mrs. Malinda's Recipe Collection

1 pkg. neck bones
1 small pkg. purple hull peas
1 small pkg. lima beans
1 chopped onion
2 small cans tomato sauce

1 pkg. cut corn
3 large red potatoes
1 ½ c. sliced okra
salt and pepper to taste

Boil neck bones half done. Combine peas, beans, corn and onion. Cook for 45 minutes, then add all other ingredients. Cook until potatoes are done. While this is simmering, prepare bread of choice (hot water bread). Now, sit back and enjoy. Happy eating.

† SOUTHERN CHICKEN AND DUMPLINGS †

Mrs. Malinda's Recipe Collection

1 cut up chicken
½ Tbsp. salt

¼ tsp. pepper
1 c. milk

Dumplings:

2 c. all-purpose flour
1 tsp. baking powder
1 tsp. salt

⅓ c. Crisco
1 egg, beaten
½ c. milk

Combine chicken, salt and pepper in a large pot and cover with water. Cook until chicken is tender. Remove chicken from water. Remove bone and skin. Set chicken aside. (While chicken is cooking, prepare dumplings.)

Dumplings: In a large bowl, mix flour, salt and shortening with a fork. Add ½ cup milk; mix to form dough. Roll dough to ¼-inch thickness on floured surface. Cut into 4-inch strips with sharp knife. Drop dumplings into simmering chicken broth. Simmer until dumplings are done. Add chicken to dumplings and 1 cup milk. Cook slowly for 10 minutes. Yield: 6 to 8 servings.

🕐 † QUICK CHICKEN AND †
DRESSING

Mrs. Malinda's Recipe Collection

1 pkg. Stove Top dressing with
  cornbread
1 (2 ½ to 3 lb.) frying chicken
1 can celery soup

1 can mushroom soup
1 ½ c. chicken broth (in which
  chicken was cooked)
1 c. milk

Stew chicken until tender; cool, skin and debone. Cut chicken into bite-sized pieces. Place in large casserole. Mix soups and milk and pour over chicken. Remove package of herbs and sprinkle small amount on soups. Pour half of cornbread on soups. Alternate herbs with cornbread. Add chicken broth over all. Place in 350° oven for 40 minutes. Serve with jellied cranberry sauce.

† DIFFERENT CORN BREAD DRESSING †

Mrs. Malinda's Recipe Collection

1 recipe corn bread
10 to 12 slices bread
2 (1 ⅜ oz.) pkg. onion soup
  mix
¼ tsp. pepper
1 tsp. salt
1 ¼ tsp. poultry seasoning or
  more to taste

2 eggs, slightly beaten
2 (10 ¾ oz.) cans cream of
  celery soup
2 (10 ¾ oz.) cans cream of
  chicken soup
1 ½ to 2 c. chicken broth

Crumble corn bread and bread. Add soup mix, pepper, salt and poultry seasoning. Stir in eggs, soups and enough broth to make a very moist dressing. Put in casserole and bake at 400° for 30 minutes or until browned. Stir once or twice during first 20 minutes of baking. This dressing freezes well. Serves 12 to 14.

Soup, Casseroles & Main Dishes

✝ CALIFORNIA CHICKEN AND WILD RICE ✝

Mrs. Malinda's Recipe Collection

½ green pepper, chopped
1 ½ c. chopped celery
4 oz. canned mushrooms
1 tsp. pepper
¼ tsp. curry powder
1 pimiento, chopped
1 (12 oz.) pkg. wild rice
1 c. slivered almonds

1 ½ c. chopped onion
fat (for frying)
2 cans mushroom soup
1 tsp. salt
¼ tsp. sage
4 c. cooked diced chicken
2 beaten eggs

Saute green pepper, onion and celery in fat in large skillet until tender. Add mushrooms with liquid, 1 can soup, seasonings and pimiento. Stir in chicken gently. Cook rice according to package directions; combine rice and eggs. Blend into chicken mixture. Stir in almonds. Spoon chicken mixture into greased 3-quart casserole. Bake at 350° for 1 hour. Heat remaining soup and ½ cup water in saucepan until smooth. Serve mushroom sauce with chicken dish. Yield: 12 servings.

✝ MILLION DOLLAR SPAGHETTI ✝

Mrs. Malinda's Recipe Collection

7 oz. spaghetti
1 ½ lb. ground beef
1 Tbsp. butter
salt and pepper
8 oz. tomato sauce

8 oz. cream cheese
¼ c. sour cream
½ lb. cottage cheese
⅓ c. chopped onion
1 Tbsp. minced green pepper

Cook spaghetti. Saute ground beef in butter. Add salt and pepper; remove from heat. Add tomato sauce. Combine cream cheese, sour cream, cottage cheese, onion and green pepper. Butter a 2-quart pan. Spread half the spaghetti. Cover with cheese mixture. Spread remaining spaghetti. Pour 2 tablespoons melted butter over spaghetti. Spread meat mixture on top. Chill. Before cooking, let it warm up for 20 minutes at room temperature. Bake at 350° for 45 minutes until hot and bubbly.

† LASAGNE II †

Mrs. Malinda's Recipe Collection

1 ¼ lb. ground chuck
1 clove garlic, minced
1 Tbsp. basil
1 ½ tsp. salt
1 (16 oz.) can tomatoes
2 (6 oz.) cans tomato paste
1 medium onion, minced
8 lasagne noodles, cooked,
   drained and rinsed
2 eggs

¼ c. Parmesan cheese
3 c. cottage cheese
2 Tbsp. parsley flakes
1 tsp. salt
¼ tsp. pepper
½ lb. Swiss cheese, grated
¾ lb. Mozzarella cheese,
   grated
¼ c. Parmesan cheese

238

Brown meat slowly n oil and drain off fat. Add next 6 ingredients and simmer, uncovered, stirring occasionally, for 30 minutes.

Cook lasagne noodles according to package directions; drain and rinse. Beat eggs and add next 5 ingredients. Mix Swiss and Mozzarella cheeses together. Place 4 noodles in bottom of dish; spread with half the cottage cheese mixture. Add half Swiss and Mozzarella mixture; add half the meat sauce. Repeat layers. Top with Parmesan cheese and a sprinkle of parsley flakes. Bake in 375° oven for approximately 30 minutes. (Can be refrigerated before baking, then bake for 45 minutes.) Let stand 10 minutes before serving. Serves 8.

* * * * *

Do unto others as you would have them do unto you.

✝ CORN BREAD STUFFING ✝

Mrs. Malinda's Recipe Collection

6 c. crumbled corn bread
6 c. toasted bread crumbs or 1
pkg. herb dressing mix
½ c. butter or margarine,
melted
3 c. celery and leaves,
chopped

½ c. onion, chopped
2 tsp. salt
1 ½ tsp. poultry seasoning
2 eggs, well beaten
1 ½ to 2 c. broth from turkey or
chicken broth

Crumble corn bread and toasted bread into large mixing bowl. Sauté onions lightly in butter over low heat. Stir in celery, salt, poultry seasoning, well beaten eggs and broth. Mix and pour over the corn bread mixture. Toss lightly to blend. Pack stuffing lightly into fowl as stuffing expands during baking. Do not mix stuffing until just before it is to go into fowl for roasting. Makes enough stuffing for a 12-pound turkey. Use one-half of recipe to stuff a 4 to 5 pound hen.

✝ SOUTHERN CORNBREAD DRESSING ✝

Mrs. Malinda's Recipe Collection

2 skillets cornbread
2 medium onions, chopped
3 ribs celery, chopped
4 hard-cooked eggs, coarsely
chopped

about 1 Tbsp. sage, crumbled
3 to 4 c. chicken broth
salt and pepper to taste
oleo or oil (about 2 Tbsp.)

Make cornbread the day before, using any nonsweet recipe or mix. Allow to dry somewhat. Crumble cornbread (the next day) into a large bowl. Add chopped eggs, salt, pepper and sage to taste. In a small skillet, melt oleo or oil and saute onion and celery until nearly done, stirring frequently. Add to cornbread. Add chicken broth, stirring lightly to maintain texture until the cornbread is very moist. Bake in an oiled baking pan at 375° until lightly browned, about 30 minutes.

Mrs. Malinda's Recipe Collection

240

Cornbread:

3 c. self-rising cornmeal	1 egg
1 c. flour	2 Tbsp. cooking oil
1 tsp. baking powder	3 c. milk

Dressing Mix:

Cornbread	sage to taste
6 slices mixed breads (wheat, white)	1 stick butter, melted
	salt and pepper to taste
5 eggs	1 c. turkey or chicken broth or
1 large onion, finely chopped	chicken or turkey parts,
1 c. chopped celery	cooked and chopped

Make Cornbread recipe first. Mix all ingredients together. Bake in cast-iron skillet in 425° oven for 20 to 25 minutes.

Crumble cornbread and mixed breads together. Add 5 eggs; blend together with hands. Continue to add onion, celery and seasonings, blending well. Add butter and broth last with spoon; mix well. Pour ingredients into a 9 ½ x 14-inch pan or larger. Bake in 350° oven for 30 to 45 minutes or until golden brown. Serve with chicken or turkey.

* * * * *

You must be born again.

✝ YELLOW SQUASH AND MACARONI ✝ CASSEROLE

Mrs. Malinda's Recipe Collection

1 c. sliced yellow squash
1 c. cooked macaroni
1 c. grated Cheddar cheese
1 egg, beaten

½ c. milk
2 Tbsp. butter, melted
4 saltine crackers, crushed

In medium bowl, combine squash, macaroni and cheese. Combine egg, milk and butter; stir into squash mixture. Place mixture in a 1-quart casserole. Top with crushed crackers. Bake at 350° for 40 minutes or until lightly browned.

✝ PREACHER PIE ✝

Mrs. Malinda's Recipe Collection

1 lb. ground beef, browned
1 can cream of chicken soup
1 can cream of mushroom
  soup

1 jar mild taco sauce
1 large bag Doritos
grated cheese

Brown meat and drain. Heat soups and taco sauce. Crush Doritos. Layer meat, soups and Doritos. Heat oven to 350°. Add grated cheese and melt on top of pie.

* * * * *

He that believeth and is baptized shall be saved.

✝ TUNA NOODLE CASSEROLE ✝

Mrs. Malinda's Recipe Collection

16 oz. egg noodles
7 oz. tuna, drained and flaked
2 (10 ¾ oz.) cans cream of
  mushroom soup
1 c. milk

1 tsp. salt
¼ tsp. pepper
4 slices American cheese
1 (17 oz.) can peas, drained

242

Preheat oven to 350°. Cook noodles. Mix tuna, soup, milk, peas and seasonings. Combine noodles and tuna mixture in baking dish. Top with cheese slices. Bake in moderate 350° oven for 20 to 25 minutes.

✝ WILD RICE CASSEROLE ✝

Mrs. Malinda's Recipe Collection

½ c. margarine
2 Tbsp. chopped green pepper
1 c. pecans, chopped
3 c. chicken broth
2 cans sliced B & B mushrooms

1 clove garlic, minced
1 c. wild rice
salt and pepper
1 onion, chopped

Heat margarine. Add mushrooms, 1 chopped onion, green pepper and garlic; cook about 5 minutes. Add pecans and cook 1 minute. Wash rice well and drain. Mix with first mixture. Add broth and season to taste with salt and pepper. Turn into a greased casserole and cover. Bake at 325° about 1 hour. Serves 8.

* * * * *

There is room at the cross for you.

† SPANISH RICE †

Mrs. Malinda's Recipe Collection

1 c. rice	4 Tbsp. bacon fat
3 onions, chopped	2 c. tomatoes
2 cloves garlic	1 green pepper, chopped
1 can pimento	2 tsp. salt

Place rice in skillet with bacon grease; brown. Add onion, green pepper and the garlic, minced fine. Fry 10 minutes. Add tomatoes, cut up with juice and 1 cup water. Cook slowly about 1 hour. As water evaporates, add more to keep it from sticking. Cook only until rice is tender. Should be served very dry.

† RICE DRESSING †

Mrs. Malinda's Recipe Collection

1 lb. ground meat	1 lb. ground pork
½ to 1 lb. ground calves liver	2 large onions, chopped fine
1 bell pepper, chopped fine	¼ c. parsley, chopped fine
½ c. green onions, chopped fine	2 or 3 c. cooked rice

In skillet, cook ground meat and ground pork. Drain off grease. Saute onions, bell pepper, celery and green onions about 15 minutes. Add liver; cook about 3 minutes. Add ground meat and ground pork, also parsley. Cook together about 10 minutes. Salt and pepper to taste. Add the amount of rice you like. Serves 15 to 20.

* * * * *

Whosoever will, let him come.

† CHICKEN CASSEROLE WITH DRESSING †

Mrs. Malinda's Recipe Collection

1 (16 oz.) pkg. seasoned
  stuffing
1 ¼ c. chicken stock or water
3 c. chicken, cooked and
  diced
4 Tbsp. green onions, sliced
½ tsp. salt
2 eggs

1 (10 ¾ oz.) can cream of
  mushroom soup (undiluted)
1 ½ to 2 c. Cheddar cheese,
  grated
¼ lb. butter or margarine
½ c. mayonnaise
½ c. onion, chopped
½ c. celery, diced
½ c. milk

Melt butter in stock and stir into dressing. Place one-half of stuffing in buttered 9 x 12-inch pan. Mix chicken, vegetables, mayonnaise and salt and spread over the dressing. Place the rest of the dressing over the chicken. Beat eggs and milk together and pour over the dressing. Cover and refrigerate for 24 hours.

Remove from the refrigerator about 1 hour before baking. Spread mushroom soup over top and bake in pre-heated oven at 325° for 45 minutes. May cover lightly with foil during baking. Remove from oven; sprinkle generously with grated cheese and return to oven, cooking until golden brown. Serves 12.

* * * * *

They shall know we are Christians by our love.

Soup, Casseroles & Main Dishes

✝ QUICK, GOOD AND EASY ✝ LIMA AND BEEF BALL CASSEROLE

Mrs. Malinda's Recipe Collection

10 oz. pkg. frozen lima beans
2 to 3 slices bread
¼ c. milk
1 ½ tsp. salt
½ tsp. pepper
1 egg

1 clove garlic
1 lb. ground beef
4 Tbsp. butter
½ c. water
1 c. sour cream

Start oven to 350°. Cook lima beans until tender according to directions on the package. Drain. While beans are cooking, soak slices of bread in milk in a little bowl. In another bowl, mix 1 teaspoon salt, ¼ teaspoon pepper, egg and mashed garlic. After bread has soaked a few minutes, squeeze out any excess milk and mix bread, ground beef and egg mixture together with a fork. Shape meat mixture into little balls. Handle them lightly. Fry in 1 tablespoon butter until brown; then transfer to bottom of casserole. Pour water into skillet in which meat was fried; stir and pour over meatballs. Season lima beans with remaining salt, pepper and butter. Add to meat in casserole. Bake 30 minutes. Spoon sour cream over the top and bake another 5 minutes. Sprinkle paprika on top. Serves 4.

* * * * *

Oh taste and see that the Lord is good.

† SPINACH LASAGNA †

Mrs. Malinda's Recipe Collection

1 (1 ½ oz.) pkg. spaghetti
  sauce mix (I use only
  about ¼ to ⅓ of this pkg.)
1 (6 oz.) can tomato paste
1 (8 oz.) can tomato sauce
1 ¾ c. water
2 eggs
1 (16 oz.) carton Ricotta or
  cottage cheese

½ tsp. salt
1 (10 oz.) pkg. frozen chopped
  spinach, thawed and
  drained
½ c. grated Parmesan cheese
1 (8 oz.) pkg. uncooked
  lasagna noodles
1 (8 oz.) pkg. Mozzarella
  cheese

Combine spaghetti sauce mix, tomato paste, tomato sauce and water in medium saucepan; bring to a boil over low heat. Remove from heat. Combine eggs, Ricotta cheese, salt, spinach and ¼ cup Parmesan cheese, mixing well. Set aside. Spread ½ cup tomato sauce in greased 13 x 9-inch baking dish. Place ½ the lasagna noodles over sauce. Spread with ½ spinach mixture, ½ Mozzarella cheese and ½ tomato sauce. Repeat layers using remaining ingredients. Sprinkle with remaining Parmesan cheese. Cover dish, securing with aluminum foil and bake at 350° for 1 hour. Let stand 10 minutes before serving. Serves 8 to 10. Can be frozen.

* * * * *

Come let us reason together.

† BROCCOLI SPAGHETTI BAKE †

Mrs. Malinda's Recipe Collection

3 bunches green onions (tops
  and bottoms), chopped
1 stick butter (¼ lb.)
3 small pkg. broccoli pieces or
  1 large bag

salt and red pepper to taste
1 (7 oz.) pkg. angel hair pasta
1 c. cream or half and half
3 c. grated American cheese

Preheat oven to 375°. Cook onions in butter for 5 minutes. Add broccoli; cover and cook until just barely tender. Season with salt and pepper. Grease oblong shallow dish. Place cooked spaghetti on bottom and sprinkle with half of the cheese. Pour broccoli on top and pour cream over all. Top with rest of cheese. This may be made a day ahead, but do not put cheese on top until you bake. Can add shrimp or crawfish when cooking broccoli and onions for a great casserole. Serves 10.

† ROTEL CHICKEN-GETTI †

Debora J. Vanzant
Los Angeles, CA

12 oz. pkg. spaghetti
1 can Ro-Tel (hot or mild)
½ c. chopped onion
½ c. chopped mushrooms
  (optional)

1 ½ c. grated Cheddar cheese
  (reserve 1 c.)
½ c. chopped bell pepper
1 can cream of chicken soup
2 c. chopped cooked chicken

You will need 1 ovenproof dish.

Cook spaghetti according to package instructions. Mix Ro-Tel, cream of chicken soup, onions and bell pepper together well. Add spaghetti to mixture; mix well. Add other ingredients, 1 cup cheese and mushrooms; mix well. Toss chicken into mix. Top with reserved cheese. Cook at 375° for 35 minutes or until bubbly.

This recipe was given and supervised by Mama (Mrs. Malinda).

✝ BASIC FRIED RICE ✝

Mrs. Malinda's Recipe Collection

2 to 3 Tbsp. soybean oil
¾ tsp. salt
1 egg, well beaten
1 c. bean sprouts (optional)
½ c. onions, cubed

½ tsp. Accent
4 to 5 c. cooked cold rice
2 to 3 green onions, diced
2 tsp. soy sauce
dash of black pepper

Heat oil in deep cast-iron skillet. When hot, add salt. Scramble egg in oil quickly and leave in skillet. Add bean sprouts, onions and Accent and stir 1 minute. Turn heat down to avoid burning rice. Add rice and continue stirring and mixing for 3 to 4 minutes. Add green onions, pepper and soy sauce, stirring constantly to mix. Serves 3 to 4.

CHICKEN FRIED RICE: Use Basic Fried Rice recipe and add 1 cup raw or cooked chicken meat when adding onions. Chicken may be diced or sliced thinly across grain.

SHRIMP FRIED RICE Use 6 ounces raw or cooked shrimp which has been thoroughly defrosted and drained. Dice or slice, if large.

HAM FRIED RICE: Use 1 cup diced or sliced ham.

PORK FRIED RICE: Use 1 cup pork steak or pork chop, diced or sliced.

COMBINATION FRIED RICE: Using lesser amounts of each type meat desired, mix for a total 1 cup meat.

* * * * *

We will sit at the welcome table.

† ORANGE RICE †

Mrs. Malinda's Recipe Collection

2 c. diced celery and leaves
6 Tbsp. chopped onion
½ c. melted butter
2 c. uncooked rice

1 tsp. salt
2 ½ c. boiling water
1 ½ c. orange juice
¼ c. grated orange rind

Sauté celery and onion in butter until tender. Set aside. Stir rice and salt into boiling water; cover and simmer 15 to 17 minutes. Add orange juice, rind and sautéed vegetables. Cover; cook 5 minutes or until tender. Serves 6.

† CAJUN COUNTRY RICE DRESSING †

Mrs. Malinda's Recipe Collection

1 lb. ground beef
1 lb. ground pork
1 large eggplant
1 large onion
1 medium bell pepper
1 clove garlic

1 Tbsp. Tony Chachere seasoning
1 can cream of mushroom soup
½ c. water
4 c. cooked rice

Brown ground meat well, then drain off most of the fat. Finely chop onions, bell peppers, eggplant and garlic. Add the chopped vegetables to meat and cook until all are tender, about 20 minutes. Then add soup and water. Cook under low heat for another 20 minutes, uncovered; stir often. Add additional hot sauce and salt to taste. Mix with 4 cups cooked rice.

* * * * *

Bread of heaven feed me until I want no more.

† LAYERED GRECIAN BAKE †

Pastor Balinda Moore
Memphis, TN

1 ½ lb. ground chuck
½ c. onion, chopped
1 egg, slightly beaten
½ c. fine dry bread crumbs
1 tsp. basil
¼ tsp. Cavender's Greek
  seasoning
¼ tsp. pepper

2 (8 oz.) cans tomato sauce
  with cheese
1 small eggplant, pared and
  sliced
½ c. sour cream
1 c. grated Cheddar cheese
½ red and ½ yellow bell
  pepper
1 large onion, sliced

Sauté ½ red and ½ yellow bell pepper, cut into strips. Saute 1 large onion; reserve. Reserve ⅓ cup grated Cheddar cheese. Combine first 7 ingredients with 1 can tomato sauce with cheese. Pack half the meat mixture into an 8 x 8-inch square or round baking dish. Place eggplant slices on top. Combine sour cream and shredded cheese; spread over eggplant slices. Top with remaining meat mixture. Bake at 350° for 1 hour. Drain off excess fat. Top with remaining can of tomato sauce. Add sautéed vegetables reserved. Finish with ⅓ cup reserved cheese. Bake an additional 15 minutes. Serves 6.

* * * * *

Joy to the world the Lord is come.

✝ CHICKEN ROTEL ✝

Mrs. Malinda's Recipe Collection

1 medium hen
2 large bell peppers, chopped
2 large onions, chopped
1 ½ sticks butter
1 (7 oz.) pkg. vermicelli

1 (10 oz.) can Ro-Tel tomatoes
2 Tbsp. Worcestershire
2 lb. Velveeta cheese
1 (17 oz.) can tiny English peas

Season and cook hen in enough water to have at least 1 ½ quarts broth. Sauté pepper and onion in butter. Cook vermicelli in 1 ½ quarts broth and leave it in the broth. Add tomatoes and ½ the juice; add Worcestershire and cook until thick. Cut up cheese. Add to vermicelli mixture and stir until melted. Add drained peas and the onion mixture. Remove chicken from bone, cut into pieces and add to vermicelli mixture. Salt and pepper well. Place in 2 or 3-quart casserole. Bake at 350° about 30 to 40 minutes.

✝ CURRIED RICE ✝

Mrs. Malinda's Recipe Collection

2 Tbsp. butter
½ c. chopped onion
2 c. chicken broth
⅛ tsp. pepper
1 tsp. salt

1 tsp. curry powder
juice of 1 lemon
2 Tbsp. parsley flakes
dash of paprika
1 c. uncooked rice

Melt butter in 2-quart saucepan; add onion, cooking slowly until tender. Combine broth, salt, pepper, curry powder, lemon juice and parsley. Add to onion and bring to a boil. Add rice; cover and cook over low heat for 20 minutes. Remove from heat; set aside for 10 minutes. Garnish with paprika.

✝ BOILED RICE ✝

Mrs. Malinda's Recipe Collection

2 c. long-grain rice

Rinse the rice in a 2 to 3-quart pot with a thick bottom. Pour off milky water. When clear, add fresh water to measure 1-inch above rice. Bring rice to vigorous boil with pot covered. (If desired, you may leave uncovered.) When water has evaporated, reduce heat to simmer and steam with pot covered for about 20 minutes. Fluff with fork before serving. Serves 4 to 6.

✝ OLD FASHION BAKED MACARONI AND ✝ CHEESE

Maurice Brown
Inglewood, CA

12 oz. long macaroni
¾ to 1 lb. block Cheddar cheese, shredded
½ Tbsp. butter
⅛ c. milk

Preheat oven to 325°. Boil noodles as indicated on package. Set aside. Place half of the noodles in 9 x 13-inch baking pan. Dot ¼ teaspoon butter on top of macaroni. Pour half of the milk on top of the noodles, then sprinkle half of the cheese over top. Repeat another layer of noodles, butter, milk and cheese. Bake until golden brown. Serves 8.

* * * * *

He is Lord.

† NOODLE PUDDING RING †

Mother Irene Kess
Baltimore, MD

1 doz. eggs
½ c. sugar
½ tsp. cinnamon
1 tsp. vanilla
1 pkg. egg noodles (wide)

1 c. whole milk
1 c. raisins
½ tsp. nutmeg
1 stick butter

You will need 1 tube cake pan.

Boil noodles until tender; drain and reserve. Beat eggs in bowl. Add next 6 ingredients. Mix well. Grease tube pan with butter. Arrange noodles in tube pan. Pour egg mixture in pan over noodles. Bake at 350° for 15 to 20 minutes until firm and golden brown. Invert onto glass plate and serve.

† HOT GRILLED GRITS †

Mrs. Malinda's Recipe Collection

10 ½ oz. chicken broth
8 oz. processed cheese
  spread
½ c. water
¼ c. butter

1 Tbsp. pickled jalapenos,
  minced
½ tsp. salt
1 c. quick-cooking grits
1 Tbsp. olive oil

Bring the first 6 ingredients to a boil in a large saucepan over medium heat. Stir in grits; cover, reduce heat and cook, stirring often, 6 to 8 minutes. (Note: They cook faster than this.) Pour into a lightly greased 9-inch pie plate. Cool. Unmold grits and cut into 6 wedges. Lightly brush each side with oil. Coat food rack with cooking spray. Place on grill over medium heat (300° to 350°). Place wedges on rack and grill, covered with lid, 4 minutes on each side or until golden. Serve with salsa.

Note: Also does well in cast-iron skillet.

Recipe   **Page Number**

254

Appetizers,
Party Foods
& Beverages

Appetizers

Appetizers are those treats that can be served either at the start of a meal or at a reception or open house. Listed below are quick appetizers that can be served anytime with crackers, thin sliced toasted bread or potato chips:

1. Caviar flavored with onion juice.

2. Cream cheese with chopped chutney and dash of curry powder.

3. Lobster tail moistened with lemon juice.

4. Almonds or pecans roasted and chopped, then mixed with anchovy paste.

5. Cream cheese with chopped pickle.

6. Chicken livers minced and moistened with mayonnaise.

7. Cheese squares with olive attached by toothpick.

8. Liverwurst with pistachio nuts.

9. Sardines with caviar paste.

10. Minced eggs with anchovies.

11. Cream cheese and horseradish.

12. Cream cheese and anchovy paste with grated onion.

13. Herring squares mashed in its own juice with dash of vinegar and Tabasco sauce.

14. Peanut butter and bacon toasted on dark bread.

15. Deviled ham with chopped onions and Spanish olives.

16. Stilton cheese moistened with Port wine.

17. Shrimp flavored with French dressing.

18. Caviar mixed with cream cheese with dash of Worcestershire sauce.

19. Peanuts roasted, crushed and mixed with anchovy paste.

20. Sardine slices topped with chopped olives.

21. Pimento cheese mixed with a dash of horseradish.

22. Minced shrimp with onion juice.

23. Cream cheese with dash of Worcestershire sauce and chives.

Appetizers, Party Foods & Beverages

---

† BEST EVER POPCORN BALLS †

Mrs. Malinda's Recipe Collection

1 c. sugar
⅓ c. water
⅓ c. white corn syrup
¼ c. butter

¾ tsp. salt
¾ tsp. vanilla
3 qt. popped corn

Pop the corn and place in large bowl or kettle. Set aside.

Syrup: Mix sugar, water, corn syrup, butter and salt in pan large enough to avoid boiling over. Stir over medium heat until sugar dissolves. Cook until syrup reaches the soft-crack stage on candy thermometer. Watch carefully not to burn syrup. Add vanilla. (If children are helping with cooking, an adult should make syrup.) Coloring can be added at this point. Let syrup cool slightly and let mom or an adult pour syrup over popped corn. Form balls.

† JEREMIAH'S MOLASSES-HONEY † POPCORN

Jeremiah Johnson
Carson, CA

¾ c. butter
¾ c. dark molasses
⅓ c. honey
½ c. water
½ tsp. soda

1 c. salted peanuts (optional)
⅔ c. ribbon coconut
3 or 4 qt. popped popcorn
(approximately ½ to ¾ c.
unpopped)

Use at least a 2-quart pan. Melt butter. Add molasses and honey. Heat to boiling. Add water carefully, it may splatter. Heat to soft-ball stage. Test with candy thermometer or by dropping small bit into water. Add soda (it will foam) and mix well. Use a large (greased) roasting pan or something similar to toss molasses mixture into popped corn. Add peanuts and coconut while tossing. Coat well. Allow to cool a few minutes, then stir through and bake in low 250° oven for 20 to 25 minutes, tossing frequently. Remove from oven. Stir to break up. Corn will crisp as it cools. Store in airtight container after completely cooled.

* * * * *

Peace on earth, good will toward men.

✝ CRISP CHICKEN ROLLS ✝

Mrs. Malinda's Recipe Collection

3 chicken breasts, halved,
  boned and skinned
1 ¼ c. chopped cooked
  shrimp
¾ c. softened butter
¼ c. chopped green onion

1 ½ tsp. salt
oil
1 c. flour
1 ¼ tsp. baking powder
1 tsp. salt
¾ c. water

About 2 ½ hours before serving, pound chicken to ¼-inch thickness. Combine shrimp, butter, onion and salt. Spoon into center of breast, leaving ½-inch edge all around. Roll from narrow end; fasten with toothpicks. Cover and refrigerate 15 minutes.

In Dutch oven, over medium-high heat, heat 1-inch oil to 370°. Mix flour, baking powder, salt and water until blended. Dip 3 chicken rolls, one at a time, into flour mixture, then into oil. Fry until golden for 10 to 15 minutes, turning occasionally. Drain and repeat with other 3 breasts. Remove toothpick. Keep warm on heated platter.

✝ BUFFALO WINGS ✝

Mrs. Malinda's Recipe Collection

2 ½ lb. chicken wings (12 to 15
  wings)

¼ c. red hot sauce
½ c. butter, melted

Split each wing at joint and discard tips. Deep-fry at 400° for 12 minutes; drain. Mix red hot sauce and butter. Dip wings in sauce to coat completely. Serve with celery sticks and Bleu cheese dressing.

* * * * *

Let there be peace, let it begin with me.

† SALMON LOG †

Mrs. Malinda's Recipe Collection

6 oz. can pink salmon, drained
and flaked
8 oz. softened cream cheese
1 Tbsp. lemon juice

2 tsp. horseradish sauce
¼ tsp. salt
¼ tsp. liquid smoke
parsley

258

Combine all ingredients except parsley and chill for approximately 90 minutes. When firm, shape in the form of a log and roll in parsley.

† SAUSAGE BALLS †

Mrs. Malinda's Recipe Collection

1 lb. sausage
1 lb. sharp Cheddar cheese,
grated

3 c. Bisquick

Let sausage and grated cheese stand for 1 hour. Add Bisquick. Mix with hands. Remove rings before beginning for easier cleanup. Roll into balls. Bake at 350° for 7 to 10 minutes, turning once. Can be served warm or cold.

* * * * *

Ain't going to study war no more.

† LAYERED BEAN DIP †

Mrs. Malinda's Recipe Collection

1 or 2 cans refried beans
½ bottle Mexican hot sauce
2 avocados, peeled and
   mashed
1 carton sour cream (16 oz.)

½ block Cheddar cheese,
   grated
1 or 2 tomatoes, chopped
2 cans sliced olives
6 green onions, chopped

Mix refried beans and hot sauce. Spread in the bottom of a bowl or 9 x 13-inch dish to form bottom layer. Mash avocados and spread over top. Spread sour cream to form third layer. Combine cheese, olives, tomatoes and onions. Layer on top for fourth layer. Serve with corn or tortilla chips.

† PARTY MIX †

Mrs. Malinda's Recipe Collection

1 ½ sticks margarine
8 tsp. Worcestershire sauce
¾ tsp. garlic powder
¼ tsp. salt
½ box Wheat Chex

½ box Rice Chex
½ box Corn Chex
½ box thin pretzels
1 can mixed nuts (assorted)

Melt margarine in saucepan. Add Worcestershire sauce, garlic powder and salt. Combine cereals, pretzels and nuts in baking pan. Drizzle liquid mixture over this and stir. Heat oven to 250°. Bake for 45 minutes, stirring every 15 minutes.

* * * * *

The Lord will provide.

† CORN DOGS †

Late Mrs. Onelia Corley
President of Missionary Society
Memphis, TN

1 c. self-rising meal
1 c. self-rising flour
1 tsp. salt
3 Tbsp. prepared mustard

2 eggs
1 ½ c. milk
2 lb. wieners

Mix the batter with all ingredients, then put wooden skewer in each wiener. Heat oil to 370°. Cook until golden brown. Drain and serve with mustard and ketchup.

* * * * *

Good bread, good meat, good God, let's eat.

✝ FROSTED SANDWICH LOAF ✝

Mrs. Malinda's Recipe Collection

unsliced sandwich loaf bread
3 (3 oz.) pkg. cream cheese

5 Tbsp. light cream
toasted slivered almonds

Egg-Salad Filling:

4 chopped hard-cooked eggs
2 Tbsp. mayonnaise

2 Tbsp. pickle relish
¼ tsp. salt and pepper

Ham Filling:

1 c. ground cooked ham
⅓ c. mayonnaise

1 tsp. horseradish

Chicken Salad Filling:

½ c. boned chicken (5 oz. can)

2 Tbsp. mayonnaise
¼ c. chopped stuffed olives

It is best to use bread which is 2 days old as it slices more readily. Remove crust from bread and slice loaf lengthwise in 4 slices. Spread one side of each of the long slices with butter or margarine. Spread first slice, butter side up, with Egg Salad Filling, second slice with Ham Filling and third with Chicken Salad Filling Top with the fourth slice of bread. Combine the cream cheese and cream; beat until fluffy and smooth. Spread mixture generously on top and sides of loaf. Sprinkle with toasted slivered almonds. Chill loaf several hours so it will be easy to slice. Serve on platter garnished with parsley and pickled peaches. If desired, the top may be decorated with a daisy, using half slices of hard-cooked egg for the petals and green pepper strips for the stem and leaves.

✻ ✻ ✻ ✻ ✻

Rise, Peter, slay and eat.

† POPCORN BALLS †

Mrs. Malinda's Recipe Collection

2 c. white sugar
1 c. light corn syrup

1 c. water
3 Tbsp. butter

Cook to soft-crack stage. Mix in with 3 quarts popcorn. Butter hands and make into balls. Let cool and eat.

† FLAVORFUL POPCORN BALLS †

Mrs. Malinda's Recipe Collection

3 qt. popped corn
3 c. tiny marshmallows

6 Tbsp. butter
3 Tbsp. flavored gelatin

Pop corn without adding butter or salt. In a big pan over medium heat, melt butter. Add marshmallows. Stir in dry jello of your choice. Pour over popcorn, stirring corn to mix well. With buttered hands, form into balls on popsicle sticks and put in Styrofoam cup or just make into balls.

† CHEESY CHICKEN WINGS †

Mrs. Malinda's Recipe Collection

16 chicken wings
2 Tbsp. butter or margarine
¾ c. crumbled crackers
¾ c. Parmesan cheese
1 tsp. dried basil leaves

½ tsp. dried oregano leaves
½ tsp. garlic salt
fresh basil or parsley (for
  garnish)

Preheat oven to 375°. Wash chicken wings; pat dry. In a bowl, combine the crumbled crackers, herbs and Parmesan cheese. Add seasonings; mix well to blend. Melt butter. Dip chicken wings first in melted butter, then into crumb coating. Arrange chicken wings in lightly oiled baking dish. Bake chicken wings or until lightly brown/done. Chicken wings should be tender.

† SUPER NACHOS †

Mrs. Malinda's Recipe Collection

1 can bean dip
Monterey Jack cheese
Cheddar cheese
1 lb. hamburger
taco chips

onions, sliced
1 can pinto beans
1 pkg. taco seasoning
salt and pepper

Spread bean dip in 9 x 13-inch pan. Sprinkle with grated cheese. Brown hamburger; drain. Add onions, pinto beans with juice, taco seasoning mix, salt and pepper to hamburger and cook until onions soften. Sprinkle hamburger mixture over the beans and cheeses. Bake at 350° until cheeses melt. Serve as a dip with taco chips.

† TURKEY SALAD STUFFED EGGS †

Mrs. Malinda's Recipe Collection

8 eggs
3 Tbsp. mayonnaise
2 celery stalks
2 Tbsp. Dijon mustard
2 green onions

1 Tbsp. cider vinegar
½ sweet red pepper
1 tsp. sugar
¾ lb. leftover cooked turkey
¼ tsp. salt

Place eggs with enough water to cover in medium-sized saucepan. Bring to a boil; reduce heat to simmer for 10 minutes. Drain; hold under cold running water to cool. Peel. Halve crosswise. Remove yolks and reserve for another use. Cut celery, green onions, red pepper and turkey into 1-inch cubes. Place in food processor. Whirl with on-off pulses until finely chopped; do not overprocess. Scrape into medium-size bowl. Stir in mayonnaise, mustard, vinegar, sugar and salt. Spoon 1 rounded tablespoonful into hollow of each egg half. Serve or refrigerate up to 12 hours.

Michael Vanzant
Los Angeles, CA

2 (8 oz.) cream cheese
1 (8 oz.) can chopped black olives
1 (16 oz.) red salsa (medium)

1 lb. grated Cheddar cheese
2 bunches green onions, chopped
1 pkg. round tortilla chips

264

You will need an 8-inch glass plate.

Soften cream cheese at room temperature. Fluff cream cheese with a fork until soft and fluffy. Smooth over with a knife onto glass plate. Spread salsa on top of cream cheese. Top salsa with grated Cheddar cheese. Next, top with green onions. Add olives. Lastly, arrange chips on side and top of dish.

Much loved by Mama (Mrs. Malinda).

* * * * *

Rub a dub dub, thank you for the grub.

† CANDIED APPLES †

Mrs. Malinda's Recipe Collection

8 medium sized red apples
2 c. sugar
1 c. light corn syrup
½ c. water

¼ c. (1 ¾ oz. bottle) red
   cinnamon candy
10 drops red food coloring

You will need 8 flat wooden sticks.

Wash and dry apples. Remove stems and insert sticks into stem ends. Mix sugar, corn syrup and water in heavy 2-quart saucepan. Cook over medium heat, stirring constantly, until mixture boils and sugar is dissolved. Then cook, without stirring, until temperature reaches 250° or until small amount of syrup dropped into very cold water forms a ball which is hard enough to hold its shape, yet plastic. Add cinnamon candies and continue cooking to 285° or until small amount of syrup dropped in very cold water separates into threads which are hard but not brittle. Remove from heat. Stir in red food coloring, if desired.

Hold each apple by its stick and quickly twirl in syrup, tilting pan to cover apple with syrup. Remove apple from syrup; allow excess to drip off, then twirl to spread syrup smoothly over apple. Place on lightly greased baking sheet to cool. Store in cool place. If mixture cools too quickly, reheat over low heat.

* * * * *

For God so loved the world, that He gave his only begotten son. That whosoever believeth in Him shall have everlasting life.

† EDIBLE CENTERPIECE †

Mrs. Malinda's Recipe Collection

1 bunch curly leaf lettuce
1 pkg. baby carrots
4 stalks celery, cut in 1-inch
   pieces
2 summer squashes

1 zucchini squash
1 lb. purple grapes
cubes of cheese
1 cucumber, sliced
1 pkg. cherry tomatoes

266

Special Equipment: You will need one 8-inch tall Styrofoam cone, 1 large plate, floral tape or clay, 1 package floral pins and toothpicks (round).

In a large plate, secure the Styrofoam cone to center with floral tape or floral clay. Beginning at the top and working down the cone, tear and attach the curly lettuce to the cone with floral pins, finishing with the bottom and a tray lined with lettuce leaves. With toothpicks, secure the veggies randomly around the cone. Place grapes and cheese over lettuce on tray. Serve with your favorite vegetable dip.

Can substitute spinach for lettuce and fruit for vegetables.

* * * * *

Weeping may endure for a night..
But joy cometh in the morning.

✝ OVERNIGHT BREAKFAST PIE ✝

Mrs. Malinda's Recipe Collection

1 c. milk
4 eggs, slightly beaten
8 slices white bread, cut in half diagonally
1 (10 oz.) pkg. frozen chopped broccoli or spinach, thawed and drained
1 c. chopped fully cooked ham

1 recipe thick white sauce
1 tsp. dried parsley flakes
½ tsp. dried basil leaves
⅛ tsp. garlic powder
1 c. shredded Swiss or Cheddar cheese
¼ c. grated Parmesan cheese

Spray a 9 or 10-inch deep-dish pie plate with Crisco no-stick spray; set aside.

In shallow dish, blend milk and eggs. Dip 8 halves of bread in egg mixture, coating both sides. Arrange to cover bottom of prepared pie plate. Set aside remaining bread halves and egg mixture

Spread broccoli over bread layer. Top with ham. Prepare white sauce as directed. Stir in parsley flakes, basil and garlic powder. Pour over broccoli and ham. Top with Swiss cheese. Dip both sides of remaining bread halves in remaining egg mixture.

Arrange to cover top of pie. Pour remaining egg mixture over the bread. Cover with plastic wrap. Refrigerate overnight.

Preheat oven to 350°. Sprinkle top of pie with Parmesan cheese. Bake at 350° for 45 to 50 minutes or until puffed and golden brown. Let stand 10 minutes before cutting. Prep time: 25 minutes. Chilling time: Overnight. Cook time: 45 to 50 minutes. Makes 6 to 8 servings.

* * * * *

If you are willing and obedient,
You shall eat the Good of the Land.

✝ LAYERED SHRIMP PARTY PLATE ✝

Pastor Balinda Moore
Memphis, TN

Bottom Layer:

2 (8 oz.) pkg. cream cheese,
  softened
2 Tbsp. Worcestershire sauce

2 to 4 Tbsp. Tabasco sauce
2 to 4 pods garlic, minced

Blend together all ingredients.

Second Layer:

1 medium size bottle Kraft cocktail sauce

Third Layer:

1 lb. shrimp, boiled and chopped

Fourth Layer:

½ to 1 lb. grated Mozzarella cheese

Fifth Layer:

6 to 8 green onions, chopped
1 green pepper, chopped

2 to 3 tomatoes, peeled and
  chopped

Mix all ingredients together.
On 10 or 12-inch serving plate, begin with cream cheese mixture and spread flat. Add layers in order. Cover layers evenly and well. Decorate rim of plate with fresh parsley and boiled shrimp. Need Melba rounds or party crackers and spreading knife. Serves 8 to 10.

* * * * *

Name it and claim it.
Believe it and receive it.

♡ † ORANGE JULIUS †

Jeremy Johnson
Carson, CA

½ (6 oz.) can frozen orange
  juice concentrate
½ c. milk

½ c. water
½ Tbsp. vanilla
5 to 6 ice cubes

Combine all ingredients in blender for 30 seconds. Serve immediately. If you have some leftover in blender, blend a few seconds before serving again.

† RECIPE FOR LIFE †

Dorothy Johnson
Memphis, TN

1 cup of good thoughts
1 cup of kind deeds
1 cup of consideration

3 cups of forgiveness
2 cups of well beaten thoughts

Mix thoroughly. Add tears of joy, sorrow and sympathy for others. Fold in 4 cups of prayer and faith to lighten other ingredients and raise the texture to great heights of Christian life. After pouring all this into your family life, bake well with heat of human kindness. Serve with a smile.

* * * * *

The spirit of the Lord is here. I can feel Him in the atmosphere.

✝ HOLY ROLLER PARTY PUNCH ✝

Mrs. Malinda's Recipe Collection

1 small bottle lemon juice
3 large cans frozen orange juice
1 large can pineapple juice
1 can Hawaiian Punch
1 large can apple juice
1 qt. cranberry juice
1 gal. apple cider
2 qt. Canada Dry ginger ale
½ box or more whole cloves to taste
2 c. water

Boil cloves in 2 cups of water; cool. Make orange juice according to directions on can. Add all other juices except ginger ale. Add sugar, if desired. Just before serving, add ginger ale.

For decoration, instead of ice cubes, make ice rings in your salad ring mold to float in punch. Slice 2 lemons thin and allow to float on top.

✝ MOTHER'S DAY PARTY PUNCH ✝

Sheryl Scott
Memphis, TN

1 (32 oz.) can pineapple juice
1 (32 oz.) can orange juice
1 c. sugar
1 c. fruit cocktail
juice of 24 fresh lemons
juice of 24 fresh oranges
1 large bottle cherries
4 bottles ginger ale (cold)

Mix all of the above ingredients except the ginger ale. Freeze them into a solid block. Take out of the freezer an hour before serving and place in a large punch bowl. Pour the cold ginger ale over the ice block and serve. Serves 30.

* * * * *

Tis so sweet to trust in Jesus. Just to take Him at his word.

Appetizers, Party Foods & Beverages

✝ PRETTY PARTY PUNCH ✝

Mrs. Malinda's Recipe Collection

2 pkg. cherry powdered drink
  mix
1 (48 oz.) can pineapple juice

2 c. sugar
2 qt. water
1 qt. ginger ale

Mix all ingredients in a gallon plastic jug except ginger ale. Place in freezer and stir every 2 or 3 hours to keep from freezing solid. When mixture has attained desired slush stage, place in the refrigerator until ready to serve. Add chilled ginger ale at serving time. (No ice needed.)

✝ HONEY'S AID (KOOL-AID) ✝

Barbara Johnson-Simons
Los Angeles, CA

2 c. sugar
2 to 3 packs Kool-Aid
1 (12 oz.) frozen lemonade

1 Honey (find your own Honey)
water (to fill container)

You will need a 1-gallon container.
Pour all ingredients into container. Stir briskly and kiss your Honey. Fill glass. Garnish with fresh lemon and ice.

✝ HOT APPLE CIDER ✝

Sean Boston
Carson, CA

1 gal. apple cider
3 to 4 cinnamon sticks
5 to 6 white cloves

dash of nutmeg
butter (optional; see directions)

Combine all ingredients in a slow cooker. Heat on high until hot. Turn cooker to medium or low to maintain temperature and allow flavors to reach peak. Do not boil. May be heated as much as 4 hours in advance of serving. The number served depends on size of servings. Top with pat of butter in cup (optional).

✝ AVOCADO MALT ✝

Rev. Barbara Johnson
Las Vegas, NV

4 avocados
1 c. milk

2 handfuls ice
2 Tbsp. condensed milk

Peel and remove seeds from avocados. Blend all ingredients in blender 1 minute.

✝ WATERMELON PUNCH ✝

Mrs. Malinda's Recipe Collection

1 watermelon (about 14 lb.,
  that yields approximately 10
  c. juice)

2 pt. strawberries
3 (6 oz.) cans lemonade
ginger ale (optional)

Scoop out melon and remove seeds. Blend melon. Add other ingredients, then blend again and chill. Add ginger ale right before serving. Use watermelon rind as a punch bowl.

✝ VANILLA-CINNAMON MILKSHAKE ✝

Mrs. Malinda's Recipe Collection

1 c. cold milk
½ tsp. vanilla (double-strength)
2 c. vanilla ice cream (low-fat
  or regular)

¼ tsp. cinnamon
¼ tsp. nutmeg

Place all ingredients, except nutmeg, into blender container; process until smooth. Pour into chilled glasses and sprinkle with nutmeg.

✝ MINT TEA ✝

1 qt. boiling water
5 to 7 small tea bags
2 ½ c. sugar
1 (12 oz.) can frozen orange
  juice

1 (12 oz.) can frozen
  lemonade
fresh mint leaves
1 qt. ginger ale

Mix tea bags with boiling water. Dissolve sugar in hot tea. Add mint leaves, rinsed and broken into pieces. Add orange juice and lemonade according to directions on can. Combine. Add 1 quart ginger ale. Yield: 1 gallon.

✝ ICED TEA SWEET ✝

Barbara Johnson-Simons
Los Angeles, CA

10 bags Lipton tea
12 oz. frozen lemonade
2 c. sugar

fresh lemon (to garnish)
1 gal. boiled water

You will need a 1-gallon container.
Boil water. Add tea with sugar and brew at least 20 minutes. Add remaining ingredients, except lemon.
Note: If using glass container, put a stainless steel spoon inside the container to prevent cracking. Serve with ice and garnish with fresh lemon.

* * * * *

Oh how beautiful it is for brethren to dwell together in unity.

274

Seafood

Helpful Cooking Hints

Frozen gravies or sauces may be a little thicker after thawing than when they were freshly made. Adding a little appropriate liquid - milk, broth, bouillon or wine - will thin them to the desired consistency.

For extra juicy, extra nutritious hamburgers, add 1/4 cup evaporated milk per pound of meat before shaping.

To ripen green pears, just place 2 or 3 in a brown bag, loosely closed, and store at room temperature out of direct sunlight.

In making pickles, use white vinegar to make clear pickles and coarse salt which comes in 5 pound bags. This is not rock salt. Avoid using iodized salt for pickle making. Most pickles are better if allowed to stand six weeks before using.

Lemon gelatin dissolved in 2 cups of hot apricot nectar with 1 teaspoon of grated lemon added for zip makes a perfect base for jellied fruit salad.

Put a tablespoon of butter in the water when cooking rice, dried beans, macaroni, to keep it from boiling over. Always run cold water over it when done to get the starch out. Reheat over hot water, if necessary.

A pair of scissors (not the fowl kind - they are heavy and awkward to handle) are fine for slivering celery, onion, meats, and cheese.

Never put a cover on anything that is cooked in milk unless you want to spend hours cleaning up the stove when it boils over.

Anything that grows under the ground, start off in cold water - potatoes, beets, carrots, etc. Anything that grows above ground, start off in boiling water - English peas, greens, beans, etc.

To clean aluminum pots when they are stained dark, merely boil with a little cream of tartar, vinegar or acid foods.

Baking powder will remove tea or coffee stains from china pots or cups.

Learn where your fuse box and master cut-off switch is. If you know where the lever is to pull you can always cut the current off until a service man can come.

Canned cream soups make excellent sauces for vegetables, fish, etc. Celery with lobster, black bean or onion with cauliflower, tomato with lamb chops.

Slip your hand inside a waxed sandwich bag and you have a perfect mitt for greasing your baking pans and casserole dishes.

To reheat roast, wrap in aluminum foil and heat in a slow oven.

Hard boiled eggs will peel easily when cracked and placed in cold water immediately after taking out of the hot water.

You can cut a meringue pie cleanly by coating both sides of the knife lightly with butter.

When recipe calls for adding raw eggs to hot mixture, always begin by adding a small amount of hot mixture to the beaten eggs slowly to avoid curdling.

To remove fish odor from hands, utensils and dish cloths, use one teaspoon baking soda to quart of water.

To keep icings moist and to prevent cracking, add a pinch of baking soda to the icing.

If soup tastes very salty, a raw piece of potato placed in the pot will absorb the salt.

Pour water into mold and then drain before pouring in mixture to be chilled. Will come out of mold easier.

When rolling cookie dough, sprinkle board with powdered sugar instead of flour. Too much flour makes the dough heavy. When freezing cookies with a frosting, place them in freezer unwrapped for about 2 hours - then wrap without worrying about them sticking together.

Seafood

† RABBIT LOUISIANA CREOLE †

Mrs. Malinda's Recipe Collection

1 cleaned rabbit (3 lb.)
1 tsp. salt
1 tsp. black pepper
½ tsp. cayenne pepper
¼ c. onion, chopped
3 garlic cloves, minced
2 Tbsp. white vinegar
1 tsp. browning sauce

8 oz. can mushrooms, drained
1 Tbsp. butter or margarine, melted
1 Tbsp. parsley, minced
2 Tbsp. green bell pepper, minced
2 Tbsp. green onions, chopped
⅔ c. white wine (dry)

Dry rabbit and place in bowl. Combine salt, black pepper, cayenne pepper, onion, garlic and vinegar. Pour over rabbit, turning pieces to coat. Cover bowl and marinate overnight in the refrigerator. Transfer rabbit and marinade to well-greased baking dish. Bake in preheated 450° oven 1 hour. Combine remaining ingredients and pour over rabbit. Bake 30 to 45 minutes longer until rabbit is fork-tender.

✝ SHRIMP AND RICE ✝

Mrs. Malinda's Recipe Collection

1 ½ lb. shrimp
1 ½ sticks oleo
1 can Ro-Tel tomatoes
1 can cream of mushroom
   soup
1 bell pepper, chopped
3 tsp. salt

½ c. parsley
2 c. raw rice
1 ½ sticks oleo
1 can onion soup
1 onion, chopped
2 sticks celery, chopped
½ c. green onion

Saute onion, bell pepper, green onion, parsley and celery in oleo. Add soups, Ro-Tel tomatoes and seasoned shrimp. Add raw shrimp and put in casserole dish. Bake 1 hour at 350°, stirring every 30 minutes. Bake, covered.

✝ OGEECHEE RIVER FRIED FISH ✝

Mrs. Malinda's Recipe Collection

2 ½ to 3 lb. catfish fillets
1 tsp. salt
2 c. buttermilk

2 c. self-rising cornmeal
1 c. self-rising flour
lemon quarters (optional)

Place fish in a shallow pan; sprinkle with salt. Pour buttermilk over top; refrigerate 30 minutes. Combine cornmeal and flour; mix well. Remove fish from buttermilk; dredge fish in cornmeal mixture. Carefully drop fish into deep hot oil (370°). Fry until fish floats to the top and are golden brown; drain well. Serve hot. Garnish with lemon quarters, if desired.

* * * * *

Come on over here, the table is spread. The feast of the Lord is going on.

♡ † BAKED FISH †

Mrs. Malinda's Recipe Collection

1 (8 lb.) redfish	1 green pepper
1 onion	2 lb. crabmeat
1 c. melted butter	3 c. Creole Sauce

Split fish in half through the center and bone. Place one-half on a baking dish, cut side up. Mince green pepper and onion; combine with crabmeat. Spread on fish. Pour butter over this. Place the second half of the fish on top of stuffing, cut side down. Tie together with heavy cord. Salt and pepper well. Pour Creole Sauce over all. Bake at 350° for 45 minutes, basting frequently.

Creole Sauce:

1 Tbsp. minced shallot	1 green pepper, chopped
1 Tbsp. butter	cayenne
1 c. tomato juice	salt
½ c. white wine	1 tsp. Kitchen Bouquet
1 sprig parsley	juice of 1 lemon
1 small carrot, minced	1 stalk celery, minced
1 Tbsp. flour	1 can chopped mushrooms
1 clove garlic, bruised	

Brown flour in butter. Gradually add liquids, then other ingredients. Cook for 30 minutes over a low flame until vegetables are soft.

* * * * *

Up above my head, I hear music. I hear music in the air. There must be a God somewhere.

† OVEN-FRIED FISH †

Mrs. Malinda's Recipe Collection

1 (6 oz.) pkg. Aunt Jemima white cornbread mix
1 tsp. paprika
½ tsp. salt
¼ tsp. pepper

⅛ tsp. ground red pepper (optional)
⅔ c. milk
1 egg
1 lb. fresh fish fillets
⅓ c. margarine

Heat oven to 400°. Combine dry ingredients. Combine milk and eggs. Coat fish with meal mixture. Dip in egg mixture and coat again with meal mixture. Place fish in 15 x 10-inch jelly roll pan. Bake about 20 minutes. Makes 4 servings.

† DEEP-FRIED FISH BATTER †

Mrs. Malinda's Recipe Collection

1 egg
8 oz. 7-Up

1 c. pancake mix
additional pancake mix

Mix egg, 7-Up and pancake mix together well. Dip thin fish fillets which have been coated with pancake mix (shake both in plastic bag) and chill about 20 minutes in mixture. Remove, one at a time, and deep-fry 4 to 6 minutes at about 400°. Remove onto paper towels to drain.

⏰ † QUICK SEAFOOD DIP †

Mrs. Malinda's Recipe Collection

1 c. mayonnaise
½ tsp. curry powder

2 tsp. chili sauce

Combine ingredients and chill. Serve with cooked, chilled lobster chunks, shrimp or fried fish bites. Yields 1 cup.

Seafood

† SALMON CROQUETTE †

Mrs. Malinda's Recipe Collection

1 (15 ½ oz.) can red sock-eye
   salmon
1 medium onion, chopped fine
½ green bell pepper, chopped
   fine

1 egg
1 tsp. black pepper
¼ tsp. salt
1 ½ c. cracker crumbs
½ c. Crisco oil

Take bone out of the salmon. Mix salmon, onion, bell pepper, egg, pepper and salt. Add ½ cup cracker crumbs; mix well. Make 6 (1-inch) patties and roll into the balance of the cracker crumbs. Fry in oil over medium heat until golden brown.

* * * * *

This little light of mine.
I'm going to let it shine.

† SEAFOOD OKRA GUMBO †

Dorothy May
Palmdale, CA

1 lb. shrimp
½ lb. crab
1 pt. oysters (with liquid)
1 lb. okra
4 Tbsp. bacon drippings
2 Tbsp. browned flour
1 large onion, chopped fine
3 green onions (with tops), cut
  fine
⅓ c. celery, chopped fine
¼ c. bell pepper, chopped
  fine

1 (6 oz.) can tomatoes,
  chopped fine
1 Tbsp. parsley, chopped fine
1 large bay leaf
½ tsp. thyme
1 clove garlic, minced
salt, pepper and cayenne
  pepper or Tabasco sauce
1 ½ qt. water
2 lb. chicken wings (precook)

Fry okra in 2 tablespoons bacon fat until it quits roping. In another pot, stir flour and remaining fat. Add onions, celery and green pepper, stirring until well blended. Add fried okra. Stir in tomatoes, parsley, bay leaf, thyme, garlic, salt, pepper and cayenne or Tabasco sauce. Add slowly 1 ½ quarts hot water. Add chicken wings. Simmer for 30 minutes. Add crabs, shrimp and liquid from oysters. Simmer 30 minutes more. About 15 minutes before serving, add oysters and correct for seasoning. Serve in soup bowls with a mound of cooked rice and garlic bread. Serves 8.

* * * * *

I have never seen the righteous forsaken, nor his seed begging bread.

✝ MACARONI AND SHRIMP ✝

Mrs. Malinda's Recipe Collection
(Serves 10)

1 ½ c. cooked macaroni
1 Tbsp. minced onion
3 Tbsp. butter
1 ½ Tbsp. flour
1 ½ c. milk
¾ c. grated cheese

1 tsp. Worcestershire sauce
½ tsp. lemon juice
1 tsp. salt
½ tsp. Beau Monde seasoning
2 c. cleaned shrimp

Saute minced onion in butter. Stir in flour until blended. Stir in milk, cheese, Worcestershire sauce, lemon juice, salt, paprika and seasoning until smooth. Place macaroni and shrimp in Pyrex baking dish. Pour sauce over it. Cover top with bread crumbs and grated cheese. Bake in a moderate oven, 325°, for about 45 minutes.

✝ FISH A LA DISH (WASHER) ✝

Mrs. Malinda's Recipe Collection

1 whole cleaned fish
lemon pepper

garlic powder
Season-All

You will need heavy-duty aluminum foil.

Clean fish and season to taste. Double wrap tightly in foil. Place in top tray of dishwasher. Run it through a full regular cycle. (DO NOT ADD SOAP.) The fish will be perfectly cooked with no hot kitchen. You can add separately wrapped foil packages of seasoned and buttered carrots, peas and broccoli for side dishes.

* * * * *

If thou shall confess with thy mouth and believe in the Lord Jesus, thou shall be saved.

✝ BACON WRAPPED BARBEQUE SHRIMP ✝

Jeremiah Johnson
Carson, CA

16 large headless shrimp   **barbeque seasoning to taste**
8 slices bacon

Clean and devein the shrimp, leaving the last section of the tail. Wrap with ½ slice of bacon, securing with a toothpick. Be sure and use the large shrimp; the cooking time for the shrimp and the bacon is similar. If you do use medium, you might want to precook the bacon a little; overcooked shrimp are tough and rubbery and a real sin!

Line a jellyroll pan (15 x 18 x 1-inch baking pan) with aluminum foil and place baking rack in pan. Place the shrimp on the rack and sprinkle with barbeque seasoning to taste; turn and sprinkle second side. Set aside for 15 to 20 minutes while the oven preheats. The bacon will turn from creamy white to a little opaque and the seasoning will soak in.

Preheat oven to 450°F (230°C). Bake wrapped shrimp in preheated oven for 10 to 15 minutes. The bacon should be crisp and the shrimp pink and tender. The rack keeps the shrimp from sitting in the draining bacon fat.

* * * * *

Be blessed!

† SIZZLIN CRAB CAKES †

Mother Irene Dunn
Baltimore, MD

2 lb. lump crab meat,
  squeezed
1 ½ c. seasoned bread crumbs
dash of kosher salt
dash of black pepper
½ c. celery, diced fine

½ c. onion, minced fine
1 tsp. curry powder
1 fresh lemon (juice only)
½ tsp. Worcestershire sauce
½ tsp. Howlin Hollar Hot Sauce

Mix the crab meat with the bread crumbs, salt, pepper, celery, onion, curry powder, eggs, lemon juice, Worcestershire sauce and Howlin Hollar Hot Sauce. Divide mixture into 3 ounce portions; form into ½-inch thick patties. Place 3 tablespoons oil and 3 tablespoons butter into a saute pan. Heat pan, then add crab cakes and cook until brown; turn and cook the other side. Serve on a pool of Mango Curry Sauce.

Mango Curry Sauce:

1 ½ Tbsp. olive oil
½ Tbsp. fresh garlic, minced
1 tsp. curry powder
½ c. mayonnaise
½ c. sour cream

1 Tbsp. frozen orange juice
  concentrate
1 Tbsp. sugar
1 fresh lemon (juice only)
1 Tbsp. mango puree

Saute garlic in olive oil. Do Not Burn! Add 1 teaspoon curry powder. Put garlic, oil and curry powder into food processor and puree. Blend until smooth. Add rest of the ingredients and blend until smooth.

* * * * *

Are you saved?

† BAKED FISH †

Mrs. Malinda's Recipe Collection

1 (8 lb.) redfish	1 green pepper
1 onion	2 lb. crabmeat
1 c. melted butter	3 c. Creole Sauce

Split fish in half through the center and bone. Place one-half on a baking dish, cut side up. Mince green pepper and onion; combine with crabmeat. Spread on fish. Pour butter over this. Place the second half of the fish on top of stuffing, cut side down; tie together with heavy cord. Salt and pepper well. Pour Creole Sauce over all. Bake at 350° for 45 minutes, basting frequently.

Creole Sauce:

1 Tbsp. minced shallot	1 green pepper, chopped
1 Tbsp. butter	cayenne
1 c. tomato juice	salt
½ c. white wine	1 tsp. Kitchen Bouquet
1 sprig parsley	juice of 1 lemon
1 small carrot, minced	1 stalk celery, minced
1 Tbsp. flour	1 can chopped mushrooms
1 clove garlic, bruised	

Brown flour in butter Gradually add liquids, then other ingredients. Cook for 30 minutes over a low flame until vegetables are soft.

† CHARLIE'S FRIED FISH †

Mrs. Malinda's Recipe Collection

2 c. flour	1 tsp. onion salt
1 Tbsp. Lawry's seasoning salt	3 to 4 shakes garlic powder
1 Tbsp. black pepper	3 Tbsp. margarine

Roll fish fillets in flour mixture. Fry and enjoy.

Seafood

† MUSTARD FRIED FISH †

Mrs. Malinda's Recipe Collection

1 fish, cut into boneless filets
1 c. flour
1 c. cornmeal
2 Tbsp. onion salt

1 tsp. black pepper
1 ½ Tbsp. red pepper
1 Tbsp. Accent
prepared mustard

Cover each filet liberally with prepared mustard. Refrigerate for 2 hours. In paper bag, mix the other ingredients and shake filets in bag. Fry a few at a time in hot fat.
Tip: Put match in oil. When it ignites, the oil is hot.

† SPICY LOUISIANA BAYOU FRIED FISH †

Mrs. Malinda's Recipe Collection

3 lb. fresh fish fillets
8 oz. Cajun King Cajun Fry® or
  8 oz. cornmeal

¼ c. flour
1 (12 oz.) bottle "Original"
  Louisiana Hot Sauce®

Place fish fillets in large bowl. Pour sufficient "Original" Louisiana Hot Sauce® over fillets and marinate for 1 hour. Pour Cajun King Cajun Fry® or cornmeal and flour into a paper bag. Remove fish from marinade; drop in bag. Shake. Fry fish in hot vegetable oil until golden. Drain on absorbent paper. Serve immediately.

CAJUN FRYING TIPS: Chill foods to be fried as cold as possible (in ice water or chilled marinades and batters) prior to breading. The colder the food when immersed in properly heated oil, the better the seal, holding natural juices in and oil out.

Never bread foods until the last possible moment. Shake off excess breading; never overcrowd the fryer. When oil darkens, strain prior to further use.

† **CAJUN KING'S® SEAFOOD** † **BOIL**

Mrs. Malinda's Recipe Collection

5 lb. shrimp, crabs or crawfish
1 (6 oz.) Cajun King Seafood
  Boil Blend®
1 c. salt

new potatoes,
  corn-on-the-cob, onions,
  celery, garlic and halved
  lemons (as desired)

In a container other than boiling pot, place seafood, adding chilled water. Measure water, placing in boiling pot. Heat to a simmer, then add seafood boil mix, stirring until dissolved using the ratio of 1 bottle mix per gallon of water. As desired, add small potatoes, corn-on-the-cob, onions, celery, garlic and halved lemons to mixture. Return to a boil, then simmer for 10 minutes. Drain chilled water from seafood; add seafood to simmering solution. Return solution to a rolling boil. Time for 3 minutes. Remove or turn off heat, adding 1 cup salt per gallon of liquid. Stir to dissolve salt, then add several trays of ice to stop the cooking. Start timing soak. Correct soak times are as follows:

Shrimp: 5 to 10 minutes.
Crabs: 20 to 30 minutes.
Crawfish: 20 to 30 minutes.

As a dipping sauce with the boiled seafood, dry out Louisiana Gold's "Louisiana Seafood Cocktail Sauce®."

* * * * *

Do you love the Lord?

✝ SHRIMP JAMBALAYA ✝

Mrs. Malinda's Recipe Collection

1 c. ham, cooked and diced
1 c. onions, diced
¾ c. green pepper, diced
¼ c. butter
1 ½ c. water (boiling)
½ tsp. thyme
3 ⅓ c. canned tomatoes
2 c. (about 19) oysters and
 liquid
1 ½ lb. fresh shrimp, shelled
 and deveined

2 ⅔ c. packaged precooked
 rice
1 clove garlic, minced
2 cubes chicken bouillon
¼ c. parsley, chopped
1 ½ tsp. salt
dash of cayenne
dash of cloves
dash of nutmeg

Sauté onions, garlic, green pepper and ham in butter in deep saucepan. Cook until vegetables are just tender. Dissolve bouillon cubes in hot water. Add seasonings, parsley and tomatoes. Bring to a boil, then simmer 10 minutes. Add oysters and liquid and shrimp. Simmer 3 minutes, then bring to a slow boil. Stir in rice. Cover; remove from heat and let stand for 5 minutes.

* * * * *

He's still able and available.

† PECAN-CRUSTED CATFISH WITH WHITE † CHEDDAR GRITS

Mrs. Malinda's Recipe Collection

Fish:

1 c. flour	1 bunch fresh thyme, chopped
1 Tbsp. onion powder	2 c. finely ground pecans
salt to taste	pepper
3 eggs	4 (6 oz.) catfish fillets
2 c. milk	3 c. Crisco pure canola oil

Grits:

4 c. chicken broth	½ c. shredded white Cheddar
2 c. stone-ground grits or	cheese
instant grits	salt and pepper
¼ c. heavy cream	4 green onions, thinly sliced

For the Catfish: Mix together the dry ingredients in a shallow dish. In another shallow dish, whisk together the eggs and milk. In a third shallow dish, mix the thyme, pecans and salt and pepper to taste. Coat each catfish fillet in the flour mixture, then egg, then nuts, coating completely.

Prepare the Grits: Bring broth to a boil in a 2-quart saucepan. Reduce heat to simmer. Whisk in grits and cook until grits are soft but not mushy, about 12 to 15 minutes. Stir in heavy cream, Cheddar cheese, salt and pepper.

In a large, heavy skillet, heat the Crisco pure canola oil to 350°. Carefully place the catfish fillets into the hot oil; cook about 8 minutes, turning occasionally, until both sides are golden brown. Divide grits between 4 large bowls. Top each with a catfish fillet. Garnish with sliced green onions and serve.

† TARTAR SAUCE OR COLESLAW BASE †

Mrs. Malinda's Recipe Collection

½ pt. salad dressing
½ c. milk
½ c. sugar
1 tsp. vinegar

1 tsp. lemon juice
½ c. chopped green onions
½ c. pickles

Mix dressing, milk, sugar, vinegar and lemon juice. This makes a good coleslaw base. Add onions and pickles for tartar sauce.

⏲ † QUICK TARTAR SAUCE †

Jamal Leach
Memphis, TN

½ c. mayonnaise
¼ c. sweet pickle relish, well
  drained
1 tsp. instant minced onion

¼ tsp. Worcestershire sauce
4 drops liquid hot pepper
  seasoning
½ tsp. lemon juice

Mix well and use in pike and shrimp casserole or any other dish requiring tartar sauce.

* * * * *

What a mighty God we serve.

YOUR FAVORITE RECIPES

INDEX OF RECIPES

✝ A ✝

Breads & Vegetables

Meats, Gravies, Rubs & Sauces

Soup, Casseroles & Main Dishes

LIST OF CONTRIBUTORS

† G †

– R –

– S –

– T –

– V –

– W –

Making The Right Food Choices

A guide to healthy cooking and eating

People are more concerned than ever about making the right choices when it comes to eating. Once primarily concerned with weight and calories, now consumers want to know more about what they are putting into their bodies. Their concerns include a number of diet related topics such as cholesterol, fat, fiber, sodium, as well as calorie intake.

Fundcraft Publishing has gathered important nutritional information to help consumers eat smart. The following pages include topics such as nutrient content claims, health claims and the new food label and how this information can play a role in your family's diet and overall good health.

The role of fat in your diet

Fat consumption has been linked to heart disease, obesity, some types of cancer and gallbladder disease. Many public and private health authorities now recommend that Americans strive to reduce their intake of dietary fat.

The problem that confronts so many people now is how to translate these recommendations for a reduced-fat diet to their every-day menu. Basically, this means selecting foods which are low in fat or fat free *more often*. Choosing vegetables and fruits, cereals and grain products, fish, lean meats and low-fat dairy products will help reduce your daily intake of fat.

Not all fats are created equal and not all fats are bad. Cholesterol and saturated fats are the hardest on your heart, while monounsaturated and polyunsaturated fats are the easiest. Here's how to recognize all four in your diet:

CHOLESTEROL is a fatty substance found in animal foods including meat, poultry, fish, egg yolks, milk, cream, cheese, butter and other dairy products. Foods derived from plants such as fruits, vegetables, grains and nuts contain no cholesterol at all.

SATURATED FATS are primarily contained in animal foods including red meat and whole milk dairy products. Saturated fats can also be found in certain types of oils, notably coconut and palm and palm kernel oils, which are used in commercially baked goods. It's a good idea to cut down on foods high in saturated fats and to make substitutions whenever possible.

MONOUNSATURATED FATS are not considered harmful to your heart, and new research suggests they may actually reduce your blood cholesterol level and, thus, your risk of cardiovascular disease. This type of fat is found in olive oil, and in certain plant foods including avocados.

POLYUNSATURATED FATS also tend to reduce blood cholesterol levels. It's the kind of fat you find most typically in sunflower, corn, soybean and safflower oils.

Decreasing Your Fat Intake

You can lower your cholesterol level and decrease your risk of heart disease by cutting down on your fat consumption. Here are some ways:

- Avoid fried foods; bake or broil.
- Choose lean meats; cut off the fat before cooking.
- Avoid luncheon meats (hot dogs, bologna).
- Eat sparingly of sausage and bacon.
- Remove skin from poultry (before cooking, if possible).
- Steam vegetables.
- Use half the fat (oil, margarine, butter, lard, shortening, mayonnaise) called for in recipes.
- Use less than 1 teaspoon margarine or butter on bread, hot cereals, vegetables.
- Use low-fat salad dressings; limit other salad dressings to 1 tablespoon.
- Season with herbs, lemon, vinegar, onion, garlic, tomato products.
- Thicken sauces, soups with a mixture of corn starch (or flour) and cold water.
- For snacks, choose fruit, vegetables, whole grain bread/cereals/crackers.
- Choose low-fat milk products such as buttermilk, 2% fat milk, non-fat dry milk powder and skim milk.
- Use lean pieces of meat instead of fatback as seasoning for beans, peas, greens.

How to Pick What's Good for Your Diet
Formula % of calories from fat:
(Grams of Fat) x 9/(Calories per serving)=
(Percent of calories from fat)

TABLE FOR COOKING VEGETABLES

Vegetable	Ways To Prepare	Cooking	Time
CELERY	Scrub thoroughly. Cut off leaves and trim roots. Slice into desired lengths.	Cook covered in small amount of boiling water or in consommé.	10-15 mins.
CORN	Remove husks and silks from fresh corn. Rinse and cook whole.	Cook covered in small amount of boiling water; or cook uncovered in enough boiling salted water to cover ears.	6-8 mins.
EGGPLANT	Wash; if skin is tough, pare. Cut in 1/2 inch slices.	Dip in beaten egg, then in fine dry bread crumbs. Brown slowly on both sides in hot oil. Season.	Approx. 4 mins.
MUSHROOMS	Wash; cut off tips of stems. Leave whole or slice.	Add to melted margarine in skillet; sprinkle with flour and mix. Cover and cook slowly, turning occasionally.	8-10 mins.
OKRA	Wash pods; cut off stems. Slice or leave whole.	Cook covered in small amount of boiling salted water.	8-15 mins.
PARSNIPS	Wash thoroughly; pare or scrape. Slice lengthwise or crosswise.	Cook covered in small amount of boiling salted water.	15-20 mins.
PEAS, Green	Shell and wash.	Cook covered in small amount of boiling water.	8-15 mins.
SPINACH	Cut off roots and wash several times in lukewarm water, lifting out of water as you wash.	Cook covered without adding water. Reduce heat when steam forms. Turn often while cooking.	3-5 mins.
TOMATOES	Wash ripened tomatoes.	Cook slowly, covered, without adding water.	10-15 mins.
ZUCCHINI	Wash; do not pare. Slice thin.	Season and cook covered in margarine for 5 mins. Uncover and cook till tender, turning slices.	10 mins. Total

A "*QUICK*" Summary Of

DILL
Both leaves and seeds of dill are used. Leaves may be used as a garnish or to cook with fish. Leaves or the whole plant may be used to flavor dill pickles.

FENNEL
Has a sweet, hot flavor. Both seeds and leaves are used. Seeds may be used as a spice in very small quantity in pies and baked goods. Leaves may be boiled with fish.

MARJORAM
May be used both green and dry for flavoring soups and ragouts; and in stuffing for all meats and fish.

TARRAGON
Leaves have a hot, pungent taste. Valuable to use in all salads and sauces. Excellent in tartar sauce. Leaves are pickled with gherkins. Used to flavor vinegar.

CURRY POWDER
A number of spices combined to proper proportions to give a distinct flavor to such dishes as vegetables, meat, poultry and fish.

CHIVES
Leaves are used in many ways. May be used in salads, cream cheese, sandwiches, omelets, soups and fish dishes. Mild flavor of onion.

SAGE
Used fresh and dried. May be used in poultry and meat stuffings; in sausage and practically all meat combinations; in cheese and vegetable combinations, as in vegetable loaf, or curry. The flowers are sometimes used in salads.

continued

continued...

CARAWAY   Seeds have a spicy smell and aromatic taste. Used in baked goods, cakes, breads, soups, cheese and sauerkraut.

PAPRIKA   A Hungarian red pepper. Bright red in color. May be used in all meat and vegetable salads, in soups, both cream and stock. As a garnish for potatoes, cream cheese, salads or eggs.

BASIL   Aromatic odor, warm, sweet flavor, used whole or ground. Used with lamb, fish and vegetable dishes.

OREGANO   Whole or ground, strong aromatic odor, used with tomato sauces, pizza and veal dishes.

BAY LEAF   A pungent flavor. Available as whole leaf. Good in vegetable and fish soups tomato sauces and juice. Remove before serving.

GINGER   An aromatic, pungent root, sold fresh, dried or ground. May be used in pickles, preserves, cakes, cookies, puddings, soups, pot roasts.

CHERVIL   Aromatic herb of carrot family, like parsley but more delicate. Used fresh or dry in salads, soups, egg and cheese dishes.

SHALLOTS   Small type onion producing large clusters of small bulbs. Used like garlic to flavor meats, poultry, sausage, head cheese.

VINEGAR   Low percentage natural acid, generally acetic acid. Used as a preservative for all pickling of vegetables and fruit. To give zest or tangy flavor to salad dressings; for meat, fish and vegetable sauces. Different kinds are wine vinegar, white vinegar, cider vinegar, tarragon vinegar.

6

CALORIE COUNTER
CANDIES, SNACKS AND NUTS

Calories

Almonds	12 to 15	93
Cashews	6 to 8	88
Chocolate Bar (nut)	2 ounce bar	340
Coconut (Shredded)	1 cup	344
English Toffee	1 piece	25
Fudge	1 ounce	115
Mints	5 very small	50
Peanuts (salted)	1 ounce	190
Peanuts (roasted)	1 cup	800
Pecans	6	104
Popcorn (plain)	1 cup	54
Potato Chips	10 medium chips	115
Pretzels	10 small sticks	35
Walnuts	8 to 10	100

DAIRY PRODUCTS

American Cheese	1 cube, 1⅛ inch	100
Butter or Oleomargarine	1 level Tbsp.	100
Cheese (blue, cheddar, cream, Swiss)	1 ounce	105
Cottage Cheese (uncreamed)	1 ounce	25
Cream, light	1 Tbsp.	30
Cream, whipped	1 Tbsp.	25
Egg White	1	15
Egg Yolk	1	61
Eggs (boiled or poached)	2	160
Eggs (scrambled)	2	220
Egg (fried)	1 medium	110
Yogurt (flavored)	4 ounces	60

DESSERTS

Cakes:

Angel Food Cake	2" piece	110
Cheesecake	2" piece	200
Chocolate Cake, iced	2" piece	445
Fruit Cake	2" piece	115
Pound Cake	1 ounce piece	140
Sponge Cake	2" piece	120
Shortcake with fruit	1 avg. slice	300
Cupcake, iced	1	185
Cupcake, plain	1	145

Pudding:

Bread Pudding	½ cup	150
Flavored Puddings	½ cup	140

Pies:

Apple	1 piece	331
Blueberry	1 piece	290
Cherry	1 piece	355
Custard	1 piece	280
Lemon Meringue	1 piece	305
Peach	1 piece	280

CALORIE COUNTER
DESSERTS (Cont.)

Calories

Pumpkin	1 piece	265
Rhubarb	1 piece	265

Ice Cream:

Chocolate Ice Cream	½ cup	200
Vanilla Ice Cream	½ cup	150

Miscellaneous:

Chocolate Eclair, custard	1 small	250
Cookies, assorted	1, 3-inch dia.	120
Cream Puff	1	296
Jello, all fla·ors	½ cup	78

BEVERAGES AND JUICES

Chocolate Malted	8 ounces	450
Cocoa (all milk)	8 ounces	235
Cocoa (milk & water)	8 ounces	140
Coffee (black/unsweetened)		0

BREADS AND FLOUR FOODS

Baking Powder Biscuits	1 large or 2 small	129
Bran Muffin	1 medium	106
Cornbread	1 small square	130
Dumplings	1 medium	70
Enriched White Bread	1 slice	60
French Bread	1 small slice	54
French Toast	1 slice	135
Macaroni and Cheese	1 cup	475
Melba Toast	1 slice	25
Noodles cooked	1 cup	200
Pancakes (wheat)	1, 4-inch	60
Raisin Bread	1 slice	80
Rye Bread	1 slice	71
Saltines	1	17
Soda Crackers	1	23
Waffles	1	216
Whole Wheat Bread	1 slice	55

BREAKFAST CEREALS

Corn Flakes	1 cup	96
Cream of Wheat	1 cup	120
Oatmeal	1 cup	148
Rice Flakes	1 cup	105
Shredded Wheat	1 biscuit	100
Sugar Krisps	¾ cup	110

FISH AND FOWL

Bass	4 ounces	105
Brook Trout	4 ounces	130
Crabmeat (canned)	3 ounces	85
Fish Sticks	5 sticks or 4 oz.	200
Haddock (baked)	1 fillet	158
Haddock (broiled)	4 ounces (steak)	207

8

CALORIE COUNTER
FRUITS

Apple (raw)	1 small	70
Banana	1 medium	85
Blueberries (frozen/unsweetened)	½ cup	45
Cantaloupe Melon	½ melon large	60
Cherries, fresh/whole	½ cup	40
Cranberries (sauce)	1 cup	54
Grapes	1 cup	65
Dates	3 or 4	95
Grapefruit (unsweetened)	½	55
Orange	1 medium	70
Peach (fresh)	1	35
Plums	2	50
Tangerine (fresh)	1	40
Watermelon	1" slice	60

MEATS

Bacon (crisp)	2 slices	95
Frankfurter	1	155
Hamburger (a g. fat/broiled)	3 ounces	245
Hamburger (lean/broiled)	3 ounces	185
Ham (broiled/lean)	3 ounces	200
Ham (baked)	1 slice	100
Lamb Leg Roast	3 ounces	235
Lamb Chop (rib)	3 ounces	300
Liver (fried)	3½ ounces	210
Meat Loaf	1 slice	100
Pork Chop (med.)	3 ounces	340
Pork Roast	3 ounces	310
Pork Sausage	3 ounces	405
Roasts (Beef)		
Loin Roast	3½ ounces	340
Pot Roast (round)	3½ ounces	200
Rib Roast	3½ ounces	260
Rump Roast	3½ ounces	340
Spareribs	1 piece, 3 ribs	123
Swiss Steak	3½ ounces	300
Veal Chop (med.)	3 ounces	185
Veal Roast	3 ounces	230

SALADS AND DRESSINGS

Apple and carrot (no dressing)	½ cup	100
Chef Salad/reg. oil	1 Tbsp.	160
Chef Salad/mayonnaise	1 Tbsp.	125
Chef Salad/ French, Roquefort	1 Tbsp.	105
Cole Slaw (no dressing)	½ cup	102
Fruit Gelatin	1 square	139
Potato Salad (no dressing)	½ cup	184
Waldorf (no dressing)	½ cup	140
Boiled Dressing	1 Tbsp.	28
French Dressing	1 Tbsp.	60
Mayonnaise	1 Tbsp.	110

Cooking Hints

Food Guide Pyramid
A Guide to Daily Food Choices

Grains
6 ounces

Vegetables
2 1/2 cups

Fruits
2 cups

Fats, Oils & Sweets
USE SPARINGLY

Milk
3 cups

Meat & Beans
5 1/2 ounces

GRAINS   VEGETABLES   FRUITS   MILK   MEAT & BEANS

How to Use The Daily Food Guide
What counts as one serving?

Grains
Make half your grains whole
Eat at least 3 ounces of whole-grain cereals, breads, crackers, rice, or pasta

1 ounce is about 1 slice of bread, about 1 cup of breakfast cereal, or 1/2 cup of cooked rice, cereal, or pasta

Milk
Get your calcium-rich foods
Go low-fat or fat-free when you choose milk, yogurt, and other milk products

If you don't or can't consume milk, choose lactose-free products or other calcium sources such as fortified foods and beverages

Vegetables
Vary your veggies
Eat more dark-green veggies like broccoli, spinach, and other dark leafy greens

Eat more orange vegetables like carrots and sweet potatoes

Eat more dry beans and peas like pinto beans, kidney beans, and lentils

Meat & Beans
Go lean with protein
Choose low-fat or lean meats and poultry

Bake it, broil it, or grill it

Vary your protein routine – choose more fish, beans, peas, nuts, and seeds

Fruits
Focus on fruits
Eat a variety of fruit

Choose fresh, frozen, canned, or dried fruit

Go easy on fruit juices

> The amount you eat may be more than one serving. For example, a dinner portion of spaghetti would count as two or three servings of pasta.

10

How many servings do you need each day?

Calorie Level*	about 1,600	about 2,200	about 2,800
Bread Group	6	9	11
Vegetable Group	3	4	5
Fruit Group	2	3	4
Milk Group	**2 - 3	**2 - 3	**2 - 3
Meat Group	2, for a total of 5 ounces	2, for a total of 6 ounces	3, for a total of 7 ounces

* These are calorie levels if you choose low-fat, lean foods from the 5 major food groups and use foods from the fats, oils, and sweets group sparingly.

** Women who are pregnant or breastfeeding, teenagers, and young adults to age 24 need 3 servings.

A Closer Look at Fat and Added Sugars

The small tip of the pyramid shows fats, oils, and sweets. These are foods such as salad dressings, cream, butter, margarine, sugars, soft drinks, candies and sweet desserts. These foods provide calories, but few vitamins and minerals. Most people should go easy on foods from this group.

Some fat or sugar symbols are shown in the other food groups. That's to remind you that some foods in these groups can also be high in fat and added sugars, such as cheese or ice cream from the milk group. When choosing foods for a diet, consider the fat and added sugars in your choices from all the food groups, not just fats, oils and sweets from the Pyramid tip.

Nutrition Facts: Helping Consumers Eat Smart

Shopping and planning has never been easy. And now, with so many people concerned about the nutrient contents of foods, the choices are even tougher to make.

But now, new government regulations require food manufacturers and processors to provide dietary information on their food products. There is information on saturated fat, dietary cholesterol, fiber and other nutrients...items that relate to today's health concerns about heart disease, cancer and other diseases linked, at least in part, to diet.

One of the recent changes involves new requirements for food labels. The *new food label* will have a new name. Now it will be called Nutrition Facts. That title will signal to consumers that the product is correctly labeled according to the new Food and Drug Administration guidelines.

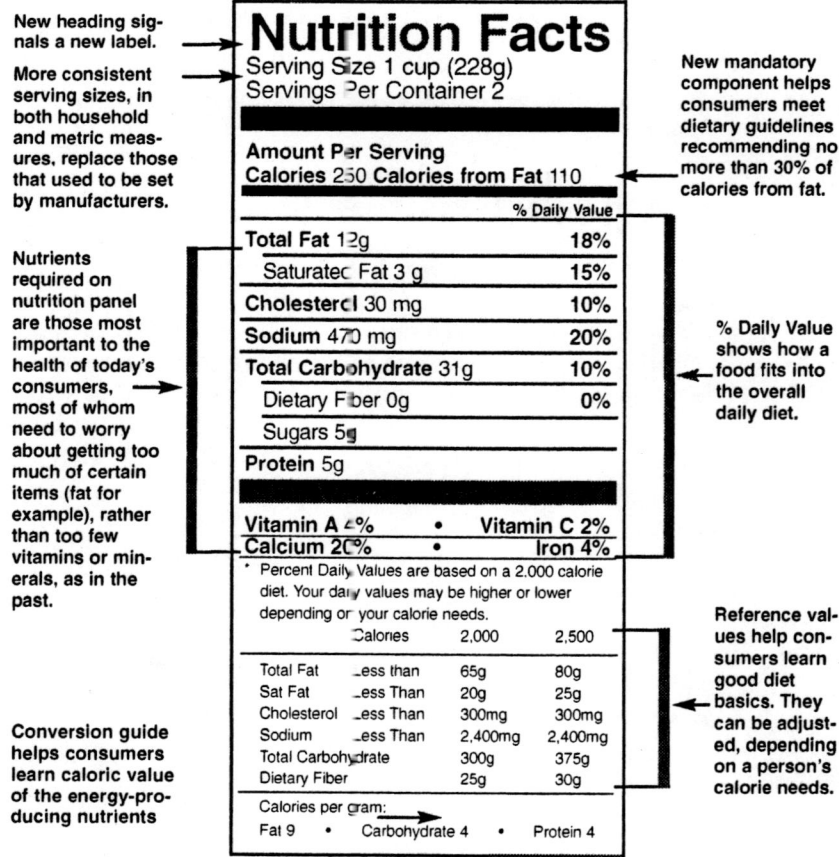

New heading signals a new label.

More consistent serving sizes, in both household and metric measures, replace those that used to be set by manufacturers.

Nutrients required on nutrition panel are those most important to the health of today's consumers, most of whom need to worry about getting too much of certain items (fat for example), rather than too few vitamins or minerals, as in the past.

Conversion guide helps consumers learn caloric value of the energy-producing nutrients

New mandatory component helps consumers meet dietary guidelines recommending no more than 30% of calories from fat.

% Daily Value shows how a food fits into the overall daily diet.

Reference values help consumers learn good diet basics. They can be adjusted, depending on a person's calorie needs.

Nutrition Facts
Serving Size 1 cup (228g)
Servings Per Container 2

Amount Per Serving
Calories 250 Calories from Fat 110

% Daily Value

	% Daily Value
Total Fat 12g	18%
Saturated Fat 3 g	15%
Cholesterol 30 mg	10%
Sodium 470 mg	20%
Total Carbohydrate 31g	10%
Dietary Fiber 0g	0%
Sugars 5g	
Protein 5g	

Vitamin A 4%	•	Vitamin C 2%	
Calcium 20%	•	Iron 4%	

* Percent Daily Values are based on a 2,000 calorie diet. Your daily values may be higher or lower depending on your calorie needs.

	Calories	2,000	2,500
Total Fat	Less than	65g	80g
Sat Fat	Less Than	20g	25g
Cholesterol	Less Than	300mg	300mg
Sodium	Less Than	2,400mg	2,400mg
Total Carbohydrate		300g	375g
Dietary Fiber		25g	30g

Calories per gram:
Fat 9 • Carbohydrate 4 • Protein 4

The New Food Label - What to Look For

The new food label can serve as an important guide to better nutrition, but only if you use it.

What should you look for?

First of all, nutrient content claims, such as "low calorie," may appear on the front label. These claims will signal - truthfully - if a food is high in a nutrient that most of us need to consume less of. This may be good if you're trying to reduce your intake of calories, fat or cholesterol...or if you're trying to eat more fiber or potassium.

Likewise, health claims on some labels will point out a food's nutritional qualities that help reduce the risk of certain long-term diseases, such as heart disease or cancer.

The "Nutrition Facts" will give more in-depth information to help you choose foods that fit in with a more healthful diet. Now it's easier than ever to eat healthy - just read the label.

Nutrition Facts

Serving Size 1 cup (228g)
Servings Per Container 2

Amount Per Serving

Calories 250 Calories from Fat 110

	% Daily Value
Total Fat 12g	18%
Saturated Fat 3 g	15%
Cholesterol 30 mg	10%
Sodium 470 mg	20%
Total Carbohydrate 31g	10%
Dietary Fiber 0g	0%
Sugars 5g	
Protein 5g	

Vitamin A 4%	•		Vitamin C 2%
Calcium 20%	•		Iron 4%

* Percent Daily Values are based on a 2,000 calorie diet. Your daily values may be higher or lower depending on your calorie needs.

	Calories	2,000	2,500
Total Fat	Less than	65g	80g
Sat Fat	Less Than	20g	25g
Cholesterol	Less Than	300mg	300mg
Sodium	Less Than	2,400mg	2,400mg
Total Carbohydrate		300g	375g
Dietary Fiber		25g	30g

Calories per gram:
Fat 9 • Carbohydrate 4 • Protein 4

Getting Specific

Here are examples of the meanings of some descriptive words used in food labeling.

SUGAR

Sugar Free	Less than 0.5 grams per serving. No sugar added	No added sugar Without added sugar	Processing does not increase content above the amount found naturally.
Reduced Sugar	At least 25% less sugar per serving than reference food.		

CALORIES

Calorie Free	Fewer than 5 calories per serving.		
Low Calorie	40 calories or less per serving... or if the serving is 30 grams or less... per 50 grams of the food.		
Reduced Calorie	At least 25% fewer calories per serving than reference food.	Fewer Calories	

CHOLESTEROL

Cholesterol Free	Less than 2 milligrams (mg) of cholesterol and 2 g of saturated fat per serving.
Low Cholesterol	20 mg or less cholesterol and 2 g or less of saturated fat per serving or per 50 g of food than reference food.
Reduced or Less Cholesterol	At least 25% less cholesterol and 2 g or less saturated fat per serving than reference food.

FAT

Fat Free
: Less than 0.5 g of fat per serving.

Saturated Fat Free
: Less than 0.5 g per serving and the level of saturated fatty acids does not exceed 1% of total fat.

Low Fat
: 3 g less per serving...or per 50 g of the food if serving is 30 g or less, or less than 2 tablespoons.

Low Saturated Fat
: 1 g or less per serving and not more than 15% of calories from saturated fatty acids.

Reduced Fat
Less Fat
: At least 25% less per serving than reference food.

Reduced or Less
Saturated Fat
: At least 25% less per serving than reference food.

SODIUM

Sodium Free
: Less than 5 mg per serving.

Low Sodium
: 140 mg or less per serving or per 50 g of food.

Very Low Sodium
: 35 mg or less.

Reduced or Less
Sodium
: At least 25% less per serving than reference food.

FIBER

High Fiber
: 5 g or more per serving. Foods making this claim must meet the definition for low fat or the level of fat must appear next to the high fiber claim.

Good Source of Fiber
: 2.5 g to 4.9 g of fiber per serving.

More or Added Fiber
: At least 25% more fiber than reference food.

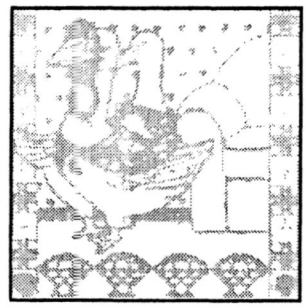

316

FAVORITE RECIPES

Recipe Name	*Page No.*

_____

_____

_____

_____

_____

_____

_____

_____

_____

_____

_____

_____

_____

_____

_____

Notes

Printed in the United States
40352LVS00005B/38

9 780977 372003